CW00733098

THE
Official
SPLATTER
MOVIE®
GUIDE

Other Books by John McCarty

*You're on Open Line: Inside the Wacky World
    of Late-Night Talk Radio*
*The Amazing Herschell Gordon Lewis and His World
    of Exploitation Films* (with Daniel Krogh)
Splatter Movies: Breaking the Last Taboo of the Screen
Alfred Hitchcock Presents (with Brian Kelleher)
*Psychos: Eighty Years of Mad Movies, Maniacs,
    and Murderous Deeds*
The Films of John Huston
The Little Shop of Horrors Book (with Mark Thomas McGee)

THE
Official

SPLATTER
MOVIE®
GUIDE

John McCarty

ST. MARTIN'S PRESS
NEW YORK

Design by H. Roberts

Splatter Movie® is a registered trademark of FantaCo Enterprises, Inc. and is used with their permission.

Library of Congress Cataloging-in-Publication Data

McCarty, John.
    The official splatter movie guide.

        p.   cm.
    ISBN 0-312-02958-6
    1. Horror films—History and criticism.   I. Title.
PN1995.9.H6M326   1989 791.43′09′0916—dc19 89-30150

First Edition
10 9 8 7 6 5 4 3 2 1

For Christopher and Jonathan—a book of their own;
though it's a strange one, I'll admit.

ACKNOWLEDGMENTS

I'd like to thank the following individuals for their help in putting
together this comprehensive peek into the cinematic world of no-holds-
barred blood and gore: my agent, Dominick Abel, for steering the book
to publication; my editor, Stuart Moore, for steering the book *through*
publication; my wife, Cheryl, for putting up with all that screaming that
emanated over so many months from the VCR downstairs; Eric Caidin,
for locating photos and filling me in on the background of some of the
films; Gordon Van Gelder at St. Martin's Press; and last, but far from
least, John Brent, Ken Hanke, and Dan Krogh for tracking down,
screening, and reviewing some new and obscure titles—thanks, guys,
my sanity is in your debt.

INTRODUCTION

A number of years ago, I published a book called *Splatter Movies: Breaking the Last Taboo of the Screen.* One of my purposes in writing the book was to give what I saw to be a clearly evolving genre an appropriate and definitive *name* that I and other critics could use so that we (and our readers) would all recognize what we were talking about—similar to *film noir*. Prior to the book's appearance, no one (save George Romero, on *one* occasion) used the term. Today, everyone does—from the *New York Times*'s Vincent Canby to Siskel and Ebert to *Fangoria* magazine, the splatter buff's bible. Congratulations, John. Mission accomplished.

My larger aim, however, was to go beyond naming the genre and to actually define it—what it was, where it came from, what its appeal was (and to whom it appealed)—to place it within the context of film history at large, and to weigh the controversy surrounding it with a level head and an even hand. All of these things, but the last especially, no one else, again, had done.

My final aim was to paint a picture of what I felt the future held in store for the genre. Would audiences finally become surfeited by the endless array of bloody "film tricks" and tire of "splatter"? Would critical, parent group, and legislative crackdowns result in stricter censorship laws, posing a threat to "splatter's" existence? Or would "splatter" expand beyond the horror film (a genre it had all but consumed) into other genres—the musical, the war film, the police thriller, etc.—to ensure its survival, at least for a time? My guess was the latter, which, in the years that have followed the book's publication, is precisely what happened.

I wish I could say I was prescient, or that I had a crystal ball, but neither is the case. Based on some of the new directions "splatter" had already taken at the time I was writing the book, it simply seemed clear to me that the genre would continue regenerating itself by absorbing additional genres into its collective cinematic bloodstream—similar to what *film noir* did in the forties. I was right—today, without question, "splatter" continues to zoom ahead with a vengeance. It has become one of the most pervasive and popular—not to mention influential—genres in the history of the movies.

All of which suggested to me the need for another book on the subject. But *not* one that would be a mere repetition of, or expansion upon, the book that had preceded it. As a result, you will find no definitions here, no historical perspectives, no in-depth interviews, no heady discussions; for them, I refer you to *Splatter Movies: Breaking the Last Taboo of the Screen*.

The Official Splatter Movie Guide is just what its name implies: not a study of the genre, but a comprehensive and critical *look* at the films themselves. The word *official* is used because it relates back to the themes and ideas set forth in my first book on the subject. The word *comprehensive* is also significant. After getting into the project, I quickly came to realize that no matter how hard I tried, reviewing every splatter movie ever made would prove impossible. In addition to time constraints (one has to do something besides watch movies all day—such as make a living), many films—particularly those made in other countries—were unavailable for screening and appraisal. So, what I decided to do instead was opt for comprehensiveness: to cover as many different *types* of splatter movies as possible; to give readers a broad view of the many different routes the genre has taken since its debut in 1963 with Herschell Gordon Lewis's *Blood Feast*. Perhaps in some future second volume, I'll go back and pick up some of the odds and ends not included here and combine them with reviews of the hundreds of new splatter movies yet to come our way. Then again, perhaps not. For reviewing the 400-plus films that are included in this volume has been a daunting task.

What has made it easier, though, is the invention of the VCR, the release of literally thousands upon thousands of movies (of all kinds) over the past few years, and ready access to them courtesy of video-rental stores—which now proliferate throughout our society the way fast-food joints once did. In my small town alone, there are seven such stores.

This book is not a video guide per se, however. But the fact is, most of the films reviewed herein are available on videocassette (those that aren't soon will be, I'm sure) and were screened for firsthand appraisal via that format. For film critics and historians in general, the videocassette has indeed become a valuable resource. For this film critic and historian in particular, though, it has proven invaluable if for no other reason than that video companies have seen fit over the years to release splatter movies on tape more quickly and in greater numbers than almost any other type of film. Not unexpectedly, however, this phenemenon has given rise to a second round of the controversy that greeted the arrival of splatter movies in the first place. This time, though, the controversy doesn't center on the existence of the films but on their easy accessibility to anyone old enough to peek over the top of a counter and thrust out their mom and dad's video-rental card. I'm speaking, of course, about kids—whose impressionable young minds, some parents and critics say, are in perilous danger of being permanently warped by these R or unrated films, which parents have termed "video nasties" or "violent videos."

The debate has become so heated that groups such as Tipper Gore's Parents Music Resource Center, and others, have begun to fight for legislation curbing the release of splatter movies on videocassette—or, at the very least, coercing the video industry into adopting special ratings such as MMM ("extremely mature") and special content labels such as EV ("extreme violence") for parents to use as guidelines. The merits or demerits of this legislation, which is pending, do not fall within the province of this book. I will say, though, that I tend to agree with my friend Tony Timpone (editor of *Fangoria* magazine) that what parents protesting "violent videos" really seem to want is someone else to do their parenting for them. Agreed, no parent who's not a film buff can know the content of every film well enough to make a decision as to its suitability for viewing by little Johnny or Janie. But the boxes of most theatrical films released on home video do carry the theatrical film's MPAA rating. Even the least aware of parents should realize that those boxes rated R (or which carry no rating)—and which boast such buzzwords as *Blood*, *Cannibal*, *Massacre*, and so on in their titles— might not be proper fare (in their adult view, anyway) for the kiddies.

As I said before, *The Official Splatter Movie Guide* is not a video source book; but most of the films reviewed in it are available on home video, or soon will be. Therefore, for parents who are indeed concerned about what a given "video nasty" may or may not include, I would suggest tucking a copy of this book under their arm the next time they and their kids stop off at the local video emporium to pick up a flick or ten for the weekend. Because, in addition to offering critical appraisals of hundreds of available "nasties," the book pulls no punches in describing precisely what to expect in the form of grisly content. There, I've done my bit!

One final note: To add a bit of variety to the book, and the opinions expressed herein, I've called upon three well-qualified connoisseurs of the genre to contribute some entries in support of my own. The names of these helpful gents are: John Brent, Ken Hanke, and Dan Krogh. Let me tell you a bit about each of them.

John Brent (J. B.) is a film buff who publishes a neat little fanzine called *Phantasma*. An ex-theater manager, John knows all about splatter movies, as the chain he once worked for, in his words, ". . . seemed to book every one of them that came out." His magazine, however, is not devoted to splatter movies—a field that he feels is covered sufficiently by *Fangoria* and other magazines. *Phantasma*, instead, concentrates on less-well-known horror, SF, and fantasy films that are seldom written about (such as Lon Chaney's *The Unknown*, for example). I heartily recommend the magazine, suggest that readers of *The Official Splatter Movie Guide* look out for it—as it will give them an opportunity to expand upon their knowledge of genre filmmaking— and I wish John well with it.

In addition to sharing an interest in the splatter movie genre, Ken Hanke (K. H.) and I harbor an absolute passion for the films of Ken Russell. Ken Hanke has extended his passion far beyond my own, however, by publishing a book about *the great man's* work—*Ken Russell's Films* (Scarecrow Press), which, until Ken updates the current edition and *the great man* himself completes his autobiography,

remains, in my view, the definitive, most insightful (and vastly readable) exploration of the Russell oeuvre to date.

And finally, Dan Krogh (D. K.). Dan is an award-winning filmmaker and author of *The Amazing Herschell Gordon Lewis and His World of Exploitation Films* (a book to which I contributed some editorial assistance). Dan was able to write that book because he knows Lewis and worked with him on several of the Godfather of Gore's most celebrated splatter epics, such as *The Wizard of Gore* and *The Gore Gore Girls*. As a result, Dan brings a real insider's knowledge to *The Official Splatter Movie Guide*. He knows whereof he writes because, unlike the rest of us couch potatoes, Dan has actually made some of the damn things.

Reviews range from the pithy to the lengthy. Regardless of length, all, I hope, are insightful—and, above all, amusing. Unlike mainstream observers of the splatter movie phenomenon, my goal is not simply to trash these films. That would be too easy—and, in the case of not a few splatter movies, completely unwarranted. Still, I don't hesitate to call a spade a piece of junk; nor do my reviewer colleagues.

Beyond this, I've tried to have fun. Critics of splatter movies don't seem to understand that neither the makers of these films nor the fans who enjoy them take the films' graphic excesses seriously. Most, if not all, splatter movies, particularly those made since the mid-eighties, are intended exercises in outrageousness and absurdity. (For serious absurdity, one need look no further than the nightly news.) The worst of these films, one simply laughs *at*; the best of them, one can laugh *with*. Either way, laughter is a key common denominator in appreciating these films—even if, on some occasions, that laughter is of the nervous kind.

THE
Official
SPLATTER
MOVIE®
GUIDE

Alien

Twentieth Century-Fox, 1979; Color;
124 minutes
Director: Ridley Scott
Producers: Gordon Carroll, David
Giler, Walter Hill
Writer: Dan O'Bannon
With: Sigourney Weaver, Tom
Skerritt, John Hurt, Veronica
Cartwright, Ian Holm, Yaphet
Kotto, Harry Dean Stanton

O'Bannon (who wrote the story with Ronald Schusett) lifts the wildest elements from a whole range of B movies, from *It! The Terror from Beyond Space* (1958) to Cronenberg's *They Came from Within* (1979), to tell this tale of an acid-bleeding creature that is taken on board a space-age scavenger vessel, the *Nostromo*. Immediately, the creature starts slaughtering the crew. Atmospheric and genuinely shocking, with a fine score by Jerry Goldsmith and a nice performance by Weaver as the put-upon but resourceful heroine. A scene in which Weaver comes upon the still-alive Skerritt, who has been coccooned by the alien for periodic snacks and other, nastier reasons, was cut prior to release. The scene appears in European-release prints and videocassettes, however. Followed in 1986 by a sequel, *Aliens.*

Alien Contamination

Cannon Films, 1981; Color; 85
minutes
Director: Luigi Cozzi
Producer: Claudio Mancini
Writer: Luigi Cozzi
With: Ian McCulloch, Louise Monroe,
Martin Mase, Lisa Hahn, Siegfried
Rauch

Alien eggs are brought back to earth by a team of astronauts. The eggs hatch and the gore begins. Uninspired, Italian-made rip-off of *Alien* in which the eggs spew a deadly juice (rather than tentacles) that cause victims to explode. Atrociously acted (the English dubbing is even worse), but good special effects and a strong, pounding rock score by Dario Argento's favorite band, The Goblins.

Aliens

Twentieth Century-Fox, 1986; Color;
137 minutes
Director: James Cameron
Producer: Gale Ann Hurd

Writer: James Cameron
With: Sigourney Weaver, Carrie Henn, Michael Biehn, Paul Reiser, Lance Henriksen

This sequel to *Alien* (1979) takes up right where the original left off, as lone survivor Ripley (Weaver) finds her way back to earth. Learning that colonists have since settled the demon planet during her space sleep, she returns—along with a company of space-age marines—to warn them of the danger. Instead of one acid-bleeding alien, this time Ripley and her foulmouthed cohorts encounter dozens. Most found this splattery exercise in alien-blasting to be a thrilling roller-coaster ride. But after the third screeching alien had been obliterated across the wide screen, I frankly began looking at my watch. Too much of a good thing, I guess. The Oscar-winning effects are excellent, though.

Alone in the Dark

New Line Cinema, 1982; Color; 93 minutes
Director: Jack Sholder
Producer: Bob Shaye
Writer: Jack Sholder
With: Jack Palance, Martin Landau, Dwight Schultz, Donald Pleasence, Erland Van Lidth

This variation on Poe's "Dr. Tarr and Professor Fether" has the inmates not only taking over the asylum but much of the surrounding town when a power blackout throws the area into darkness. The gonzos hole up at the house of new therapist Schultz, who, they are convinced, murdered their former therapist. In *Straw Dogs* fashion, Schultz must take up arms to protect his life, his family, and his home. The bloody siege climaxes as the power comes on. When he sees his former therapist talking live on TV, surviving flake Palance realizes his mistake and heads for the nearest punk bar, where, to the music of the "Sick Fucks" and in the company of a girl who enjoys having him press his .45 Magnum against her forehead, he decides the world is just as crazy—perhaps even crazier—as he is. Palance, Landau, and Van Lidth have the times of their lives chewing up the scenery. Deranged, satiric fun.

Alucarda

See Sisters of Satan

American Gothic

Brent Walker PLC/Pinetalk Ltd., 1988; Color; 90 minutes
Director: John Hough
Producers: John Quested, Christopher Harrop
Writers: Burt Wetanson, Michael Vines
With: Rod Steiger, Yvonne DeCarlo, Michael J. Pollard, Fiona Hutchison, Sara Torgov, Mark Lindsay Chapman

Bland, uninspired psycho thriller about some none-too-bright young folks who get stranded on a remote island when their plane breaks down. They stumble on a cabin in the woods, where elderly Pa (Steiger) and Ma (DeCarlo) live in a perpetual time warp with three middle-aged offspring who haven't been allowed to grow up. Seems Ma and Pa are religious fanatics who rejected the world and its sinful ways fifty years ago. They don't have a phone, a radio, or even a TV. The interlopers could easily die of boredom, but they're variously stabbed, hurled off cliffs, and bludgeoned by a bathtub instead. One of the group turns out to be sicker than Ma and Pa and the clan, kills them, and takes up where they left off. Generally speaking, splatter movies don't try to be credible, but this one includes one groaner of a scene where one of the stranded young folks finds an old dress and says, "It's just like the one Mary Pickford wore in *Little Annie Rooney*." Come on, folks, this bubblehead isn't likely to recognize a picture of JFK, let alone Mary Pickford—let alone the dress she wore in a 1925 silent. An insult to film buffs everywhere!

An American Werewolf in London

Universal, 1981; Color; 97 minutes
Director: John Landis
Producer: George Folsey, Jr.
Writer: John Landis
With: David Naughton, Jenny
    Agutter, Griffin Dunne

Despite some marvelous werewolf transformation effects by Rick Baker (for which he received an Oscar), this schizoid mixture of humor, splatter, and rock 'n' roll is little more than a grade-B exploitation film dressed up in a $10 million budget. Some of the scares work; some of the jokes work—especially those involving Dunne, who is killed by a werewolf at the beginning of the film but resurfaces throughout in various states of decomposition to offer advice and counsel to Naughton (the werewolf of the title). The "moonstruck" score featuring the talents of Cat Stevens, Creedence Clearwater Revival, and others certainly works. Overall, though, the film is hollow, pointless, and sleazy.

The Amityville Horror

American-International, 1979; Color;
   117 minutes
Director: Stuart Rosenberg
Producers: Ronald Saland, Elliot
   Geisinger
Writer: Sandor Stern
With: James Brolin, Margot Kidder,
   Rod Steiger

A young couple, the Lutzes (Brolin and Kidder), move into an expensive Long Island home—where six people had been murdered six years earlier—and come face-to-face with something even more monstrous than their first mortgage payment. The house, you see, is "possessed." After months of enduring attacks by flies, slime, and phantom pigs, the couple decide this is no place like home and split, leaving all their "possessions" behind. Spawned by *The Exorcist*, but based on a supposedly true story—as recounted by Jay Anson in his best-selling nonfiction book of the same title. Followed by two equally slime-ridden sequels: *Amityville II: The Possession* (1982) and *Amityville 3-D* (1983).

Amityville II: The Possession

Orion Pictures, 1982; Color; 105
   minutes
Director: Damiano Damiani
Producers: Ira N. Smith, Stephen R.
   Greenwald
Writer: Tommy Lee Wallace
With: James Olson, Rutanya Alda,
   Burt Young, Jack Magner

Instead of taking up where *The Amityville Horror* left off, this film returns to the story's roots to tell how the house became demon-(or ghost-) ridden in the first place. We know from the first film that a man went on a rampage, killed his family and then himself. What was not explained was the man's motivation. This film doesn't explain it either, except to say that, as with Jack Nicholson in *The Shining*, the inherent evil of the place simply drove him (Young)—and everyone else—crazy. There are no phantom pigs this time around, but there is incest (of the brother and sister type) as well as a lot more blood as the family members start whittling each other down. Olson plays a priest who tries to exorcise the family's demons, only to wind up getting possessed himself.

Amityville 3-D

Orion Pictures, 1983; Color; 93 minutes
Director: Richard Fleischer
Producer: Stephen R. Kesten
Writer: William Wales
With: Tony Roberts, Tess Harper, Robert Joy, Candy Clark, Leora Dana, John Beal

Investigative reporter Roberts moves into Long Island's most famous haunted house (the purchase price by now must be practically nil judging by the speed with which Roberts closes the deal) to debunk the place's reputation for paranormal goings-on. Clark is his photographer's assistant, who signs on to capture snapshots of whatever is or is not present in the house. Not as gory as the second film, or as slimy as the first, but full of effects nonetheless—mostly of hideous demons leaping out of the screen, courtesy of 3-D. Without the 3-D, however, this last entry in the Amityville saga (thus far anyway) is a must-miss.

Andy Warhol's Bad

New World Pictures, 1971; Color; 100 minutes
Director: Jed Johnson
Producer: Jeff Tornberg
Writers: Pat Hackett, George Abagnola
With: Carroll Baker, Perry King, Susan Tyrell, Stefania Cassini

Outrageous, absurdist splatter/satire that gives John Waters a run for his money in the bad taste department. Baker plays an enterprising housewife who runs a combination hair-removal business and murder-for-hire racket that specializes in unwanted children and pets. She's a sadistic, hard-nosed exec who countenances little from her layabout husband (she throws lit cigarettes at him) or her female assassins, whom she upbraids for letting their nose hair get too long and for not being quick enough on the job. (One frustrated and impatient customer hurls her tot out a multistory window when the gals fail to show, thus costing Baker money.) Eventually the walls of Baker's empire start to crumble. Testy, she insults a cop who's been on the take; he decides he's had enough and drowns her in the kitchen sink. Full of "bad movie" in-jokes, including a thumb-cutting scene that recalls H. G. Lewis's *Blood Feast*. Not for everyone, but in its own deranged way, frequently quite funny.

Andy Warhol's Frankenstein

Bryanston Pictures, 1974; Color (3-D); 94 minutes
Director: Paul Morrissey
Producer: Andrew Braunsberg
Writer: Paul Morrissey
With: Joe Dallesandro, Udo Kier, Monique Van Vooren, Arno Juerning, Srdjan Zelenovic

Paul Morrissey makes films that are not everyone's cup of tea, but if your tastes happen to run to outrageous gore effects (some very realistic, others on the Monty Python level and below), campy humor, overt sexuality (usually of a depraved nature), inapt and non-sequitur-ridden dialogue (in a mishmash of accents ranging from Brooklynese to Mittel-European), and a strange fairy tale ambience, then his work is fresh and vital. Here, the Warhol student is working from a script (which he claims to have written daily on his ride to the studio!) for the first time, and the results are a demented delight. In Morrissey's version, the Baron (Kier) is a deranged dilettante with delusions of Wagner (every time he waxes rhapsodic about breeding a master race of zombies, we hear the "Pilgrims' Chorus" from *Tann-häuser*!), who is married to his own sister (Van Vooren), and gets his kicks deflowering his semicomatose female zombie in the gall bladder ("Remember, Otto," he tells his sex-crazed sidekick [Juerning], "to know death, you must fuck life in the gall bladder!"). Unfortunately, he has also appropriated the head of a would-be monk (Zelenovic) for his male zombie, making for a singularly unprepossessing stud. Strange and quite special in its own way, the film's companion piece, *Blood for Dracula* is even better. It is aka *Flesh for Frankenstein*.—K. H.

Angel Heart

Carolco, 1987; Color; 110 minutes
Director: Alan Parker
Producers: Alan Marshall, Elliott
    Kastner
Writer: Alan Parker
With: Mickey Rourke, Lisa Bonet,
    Charlotte Rampling, Robert De
    Niro

Despite a somewhat transparent plot and a couple of unnecessary cheap-shot contact-lens effects, this is probably the best film ever made about Satanism, and is almost certainly the masterpiece of quirkily brilliant filmmaker Alan Parker. Adapted from a slightly silly and sophomoric novel, the film follows the basic plot of seedy private detective Harry Angel (Mickey Rourke) trying to locate mysterious crooner Johnny Favorite at the request of creepily enigmatic Louis Cyphre (Robert De Niro). While no prizes are to be awarded to audience members arriving at the truth before Harry Angel does, the thrust of the film is an atmosphere so intense it seeps into your bones, a literate, intelligent script (quite unlike the novel), brilliant performances from Rourke

and De Niro, moody photography, and one of the most creative sound tracks of recent vintage. Extremely bloody and graphic, the film succeeds primarily due to Parker's trademarks—conviction, editing, mood, and symbolism—which come together here as never before. Cleverly, the film raises as many questions (what *is* the connection between Cyphre and fundamentalist religion, etc.?) as it answers, leaving the unsettled viewer much to chew on after the fact in a way ordinary splatter films don't. The bloody lovemaking scene (slightly cut for theatrical release, but intact on video) is one of the strangest and most effective moments in living memory.—K. H.

Angel of Vengeance

See Ms. 45

Anguish

SpectraFilm, 1987; Color; 85 minutes
Director: Bigas Luna
Producer: Pepon Coromina
Writer: Bigas Luna
With: Zelda Rubinstein, Michael
    Lerner, Talia Paul, Angela Jove,
    Clara Pastor

A *Demons*-inspired splatter movie within a splatter movie. Mom-dominated Lerner, who works for an eye doctor, revenges himself on a testy customer whose contacts don't fit by gouging her eyes out. Then mom sends him out on an eye-gouging spree, which he carries out in a theater showing the 1925 *Lost World* of all things. Turns out Lerner's escapades are really a movie being watched by two tremulous teens surrounded by an audience of suspicious-looking characters—one of whom, a mom-dominated psycho like Lerner, starts duplicating the on-screen slaughter. There are some interesting mirror-image shots of the carnage in the "reel theater" paralleling what's happening in the "real theater," and vice versa—plus an obvious nod to Bogdanovich's *Targets*, when the villain in the "real theater" takes a shot at Lerner's gigantic big-screen image. There's also an amusing scene where the two teens recite the splatter buff's credo. One says nervously, "This is going to be too much"; to which the other replies, "Good. That's what we're here for."

The Annihilators

New World Pictures, 1986; Color; 87 minutes
Director: Charles E. Sellier, Jr.
Producers: Allan C. Pedersen, Thomas C. Chapman
Writer: Brian Russell
With: Christopher Stone, Andy Wood, Paul Koslo, Gerrit Graham

The title promises a lot more excitement and suspense than this leaden potboiler delivers—though there's one inventive sequence that gives new meaning to the term *pencil-necked geek*. Stone and his buddies (all Vietnam vets) come to the aid of a murdered comrade's dad who lives in a run-down Atlanta neighborhood preyed on by drug-dealing youth gangs. Similar to Kurosawa's seven samurai (reduced to four) crossed with "The A-Team," the combative vets train the intimidated neighbors to defend themselves and take on the punks, who are led by wild-eyed Roy Boy (Paul Koslo, who overacts shamelessly). Hammers, knives, meat cleavers, and mucho firepower provide the means. Roy Boy tries to neutralize the townies by hijacking a busload of school kids (he must have seen *Dirty Harry*), but the ploy doesn't work and all ends well for the kids and the neighborhood—though not for Roy Boy.

April Fool's Day

Paramount Pictures, 1986; Color; 90 minutes
Director: Fred Walton
Producer: Frank Mancuso, Jr.
Writer: Danilo Bach
With: Jay Baker, Deborah Foreman, Deborah Goodrich, Ken Olandt, Griffin O'Neal, Amy Steel

This one's what you might call a splattery shaggy dog tale. Foreman invites a disparate group of college chums to her island home for a weekend of partying. The unnerving tone of the weekend is set on the ferryboat ride over, when a couple of her male guests pull an April Fool's joke that results in one of the crew members getting his face crushed. More April Fool's pranks ensue as the weekend wears on, then things turn serious as, one by one, the college chums get knocked off in typical *Friday the 13th* fashion: throat slashings, decapitations, castration, etc. Seems Foreman has a demented twin who escaped from a looney bin to take her place for the weekend. Or did she? Perhaps everything's just an elaborate April Fool's joke. Or is it? I won't tell. Cleverly directed and well (and amusingly) acted by its youthful ensemble cast, *April Fool's Day* definitely isn't great, but it does have its moments.

Assault on Precinct 13

Turtle Releasing Corporation, 1976; Color; 91 minutes
Director: John Carpenter
Producer: J. S. Kaplan
Writer: John Carpenter
With: Austin Stoker, Darwin Joston, Laurie Zimmer

Howard Hawks's *Rio Bravo* (1959) meets George Romero's *Night of the Living Dead* (1968) in this tense tale about a group of punks who lay seige to a soon-to-be-closed-down police station in the slums of Los Angeles. The acting ranges from mediocre to horrible, and the character motivation is negligible, but the film works! Suspenseful, unpredictable, and sometimes shocking—such as the scene where a little girl with an ice cream cone is mercilessly shot down by one of the punks. Not as high-tech as some of Carpenter's more recent efforts in the splatter arena —but in many ways it's still his best film.

Autopsy

Joseph Brenner, 1978; Color; 90
  minutes
Director: Armando Crispini
Producer: Leonardo Pescarolo
Writers: Armando Crispini, Lucio
  Battisrada
With: Mimsy Farmer, Barry Primus,
  Ray Lovelock, Angela Goodwin

Murder mystery about a sexually alluring but sexually repressed young woman (Farmer) who has a bad effect on all the men attracted to her—they wind up dead. Not just dead, of course, but horribly mutilated. Could the victims all have committed suicide after being spurned? Did she do it? Or is there some kind of moon madness at work? Who cares! The film's major exploitative ingredient is a much touted hospital autopsy scene, which is often cut from theatrical prints but appears in the video version. Overlong. Good score by Ennio Morricone.

The Awakening

Warner Brothers, 1979; Color; 101
  minutes
Director: Mike Newell
Producers: Robert Solo, Andrew
  Scheinman, Martin Shafer
Writers: Allan Scott, Chris Bryant,
  Clive Exton
With: Charlton Heston, Susannah
  York, Stephanie Zimbalist, Jill
  Townsend

You know you're in trouble when one director is pitted against three producers and three writers. How's this for an original concept? An Egyptologist (Heston) defies a fearful curse and releases the imprisoned spirit of a monstrous Queen of the Nile (no, not *the* Queen of the Nile) to walk again among the living. Includes some diverting "creative deaths" in the tradition of *The Omen* (1976)—most notably York's demise in a shower of broken glass. Despite its title, a real "sleeper"— in the worst sense of the word. Based on Bram (*Dracula*) Stoker's novel *Jewel of the Seven Stars*—filmed once before (and better) by England's Hammer Films as *Blood from the Mummy's Tomb* (1972).

The Axe

Distributor unknown, 1977; Color; 65
  minutes
Director: Frederick Freidel
Producer: J. G. Patterson, Jr.
Writer: Frederick Freidel
With: Leslie Lee, Ray Green,
  Frederick Freidel, Jack Canon

Three murderous thugs hide out in a farmhouse owned by Lee and her infirm grandfather to wait out a police dragnet. They quickly find themselves up to their old tricks, however, terrorizing grandpa and raping the girl. The old man's too sick to strike back, but the girl uses her experience slaughtering chickens and other livestock on the farm and rises to the occasion—slicing up one thug with a razor and beheading the other with an axe. The third is shot down by police. Appropriately nasty *Last House on the Left* clone. It is aka *The Axe Murders*.

The Axe Murders

See The Axe

The Baby

Scotia International, 1974; Color; 86
 minutes
Director: Ted Post
Producers: Milton Polsky, Abe Polsky
Writer: Abe Polsky
With: Anjanette Comer, Ruth Roman,
 Marianna Hill, Suzanne Zenor,
 David Manzy, Michael Pataki

This is a great sick film about the malevolent side of the maternal instinct. Ruth Roman plays the ultimate castrating mother figure who has, with the help of her two nasty bitch daughters, kept her full-grown son in a state of perpetual infancy. They torture "Baby" with an electric cattle prod and beat up a female babysitter who encourages his sexuality. Then Anjanette Comer comes along as a strong-willed child-welfare worker who is bound and determined to save "Baby" from the clutches of mama and the girls. When official methods fail, Comer takes matters into her own hands, and the situation escalates into a murderous conflict in which the female is, indeed, deadlier than the male. Comer's character, aided by her mother-in-law, kills the daughters by slitting their throats and then engages Roman in a battle to the death with an axe, fireplace poker, and knife as weapons. If you want to find out who wins "Baby," why they want him, and is he better off, see this chilling film. You won't regret it.—D. K.

Bad Dreams

Twentieth Century-Fox, 1988; Color;
 84 minutes
Director: Andrew Fleming
Producer: Gale Anne Hurd
Writers: Andrew Fleming, Steven De
 Souza
With: Jennifer Rubin, Bruce Abbott,
 Richard Lynch, Susan Ruttan

Some decent performances. Some offbeat humor. Some startling gore effects. In spite of these good points, *Bad Dreams* just doesn't work. The film lacks a strong central character with whom the viewer can identify. The unfortunate young girl (Rubin) who is the focus of the story just doesn't have it together enough to elicit much sympathy. One minute she seems normal, but a short time later she's going to pieces and, more importantly, has lost the will to fight. (We later learn an unscrupulous doctor has been giving her drugs, but this knowledge doesn't make her a stronger character.) The young psychiatrist (Abbott) who falls in love with her is also weakly written. It isn't very believable that he would fall in love with the girl so quickly. Aside from professional ethics, she's just too uninteresting. If bad dreams are your preference, keep your nightmares on Elm Street.—J. B.

Barn of the Naked Dead

Distributor unknown, 1973; Color; 86
 minutes
Director: Alan Rudolph
Producer: Gerald Cormier
Writer: Roman Valenti
With: Andrew Prine, Manuella Thiess,
 Sherry Alberoni, Gil Lamb

Prine's mom abandoned the family when he was very young, thus driving him over the edge. To get even for the desertion, he kidnaps young women, strips them and chains them up in his barn, where he proceeds to starve them and beat them into submission. His goal: to turn them into performing "beasts" for a bizarre circus act he plans to take on the road. As if all this wasn't enough evening's dementia, Prine's dad, who has always stuck by his boy, has gone crazy from spending too much time in the desert, where he's overdosed on radiation poisoning from the local H-bomb tests. He still helps out, though. When torture and other incentives fail to work on his "performers," Prine trots out mad dad, whom he keeps locked in an outhouse. Dad finally breaks loose on his own, though, to help generate most of the film's gore. It is aka *Terror Circus*. Rudolph worked as an assistant to Robert Altman on *Nashville* and other films and has since eschewed the splatter genre to become the director of such popular, offbeat cult films as *Choose Me*, starring Keith Carradine.

Baron Blood

American-International, 1972; Color; 90 minutes
Director: Mario Bava
Producer: Alfred Leone
Writers: Mario Bava, Vincent Forte, William A. Bairn
With: Joseph Cotten, Elke Sommer, Massimo Girotti

Typical Bava shock movie with gothic overtones and a haphazard plot coupled with a propensity for zooming the camera that rivals the zoom-happy Jesus Franco for annoying overindulgence. Cotten plays a centuries-dead but now revivified devil worshiper (nicknamed Baron Blood on account of his sadistic Gilles de Rais-style love of torturing and butchering people) who buys back his sixteenth-century château, now a hotel, reopens the torture chamber therein, and gets back up to his old tricks—subjecting innocents to the rack and the spike. This time he doesn't get away with it, though—his victims, no less able to return from the dead than he, rise up and destroy him. Easily one of Bava's worst films. Poor Joe Cotten—what a comedown from *Citizen Kane*!

Basket Case

Analysis Films, 1982; Color; 89 minutes
Director: Frank Henenlotter
Producer: Edgar Levins
Writer: Frank Henenlotter
With: Kevin Van Hentenryck, Terri Susan Smith, Beverly Bonner, Diana Browne

Van Hentenryck moves into an apartment in Times Square with his deformed and telepathic Siamese brother (they were surgically separated) whom he carries around in a basket. He and his bro (named "Belial") are determined to kill their father, who sanctioned the operation and then consigned "Belial" to the garbage can, as well as the doctors who performed it. "Belial" is a nasty little tyke, so the revenge murders he spurs on are appropriately gruesome and disgusting. First-time director Henenlotter's canny eye for the absurdities inherent in the splatter genre transforms this low-budget gore-fest into a nice surprise. It's as funny as it is gross, and vice versa. The film is dedicated to Herschell Gordon Lewis.

The Beast Within

United Artists, 1982; Color; 90 minutes
Director: Philippe Mora
Producers: Harvey Bernhard, Gabriel Katzka
Writer: Tom Holland
With: Ronny Cox, Bibi Besch, Paul Clemens, Don Gordon, L. Q. Jones

Raped by a swamp monster (nope, not kidding, folks!), Besch gives birth to Clemens, who grows up to be a screwed-up teenager slowly metamorphosing into a murderous, blood-drinking insect. Tom Burman created the wild transformation effects and the numerous "creative deaths," which coproducer Bernhard (of *The Omen* fame) apparently feels none of his films can do without.

Berserker

Paradise Filmworks, 1987; Color; 85 minutes
Director: Jef Richard
Producer: Jules Rivera
Writer: Jef Richard
With: Joseph Alan Johnson, Valerie Sheldon, Greg Dawson, Rodney Montague, Beth Toussaint

Some vacationing teens install themselves at the Rainbow Valley campgrounds and fall prey to the possessed descendant of an ancient race of Viking were-bear warriors called The Berserkers—humans with claws and flesh-rending bear snouts. It's not hard to figure out who the possessed descendant is, however, because there's only one suspect! The FX consist mostly of bear paws groping victims' faces and smearing them with red jelly. To pad out the running time, there's also a ponderous fight between the were-bear and a real bear. The scenery is nice, though, and the opening scene, an amusing parody of *On Golden Pond* in which the Fonda/Hepburn-styled characters get lost in the woods and are offed by the were-bear, is moderately clever. Otherwise, this is just another pitifully made dead teenager movie.

The Beyond

Distributor unknown, 1981; Color; 90 minutes
Director: Lucio Fulci
Producer: Fabrizio de Angelis
Writers: Giorgio Mariuzzo, Dardano Sacchetti
With: David Warbeck, Katherine MacColl, Sarah Keller

Warm-up for *Gates of Hell* by the prolific, though far from original, director of *Zombie* and many another cannibal/walking dead movie. Here, a decaying southern hotel (the film takes place in America) serves as a gateway to hell—a portal through which the vicious undead can return to the land of the living and raise a little hell of their own. MacColl is the hotel's new owner, who must fend off the flesh-craving creatures and send them back where they belong before they destroy her not exactly thriving business. Cowriter Dardano Sacchetti, whose American screen credits often read "Danny" Sacchetti, is apparently the Italian cinema's reigning expert on cannibals and zombies. His name appears as writer or cowriter on almost every film made in the genre throughout the eighties by Lucio Fulci and other maestros of spaghetti splatter.

Beyond the Door

Film Ventures, 1975; Color, 109 minutes
Director: Oliver Hellman (Sonia Assonitis)
Producer: Edward L. Montoro
Writer: Richard Barrett (R. D'E Piazzoli)
With: Juliet Mills, Richard Johnson, David Colin, Jr.

Italian-made entry in the post-*Exorcist* sweepstakes involving attractive, pregnant wife Mills, who is suddenly possessed by the devil and turns into a revolting, puke-spewing slob. Do we detect an anti-feminist message here? Or a plea for planned parenthood?

Beyond the Door II

Distributor unknown, 1979; Color; 95 minutes
Director: Mario Bava

Producer: Turi Vasile
Writers: Lamberto Bava, Francesco Barbieri, Paolo Briganti, Dardano Sacchetti
With: Dario Nicolodi, David Colin, Jr., John Steiner, Ivan Rassimov

Promoted as a sequel to Oliver Hellman's successful *Exorcist* rip-off, Bava's last theatrical feature has very little to do with the earlier film—except for the presence of Colin, Jr., here playing the possessed son of Nicolodi (in Hellman's film, it was mom [Juliette Mills] who was possessed). Nicolodi has remarried and devilish junior wants no part of his new stepdad. He's got an unresolved Oedipus complex to beat the band and wants mom all to himself even if he has to kill her to get his way. So, he proceeds to terrorize his parents to death. Bava doles out the gore—especially at the bloody climax, where junior finally dispatches mom and stepdad—but he also strives for some nerve-rattling shocks, and delivers them. Though far superior to *Beyond the Door,* the film was not as successful at the box office and, at least in America, was quickly consigned to distribution oblivion. It's worth seeing, though—if you can find it. It is aka *Shock*—a far more appropriate title.

Beyond the Valley of the Dolls

Twentieth Century-Fox, 1970; Color; 109 minutes
Director: Russ Meyer
Producer: Russ Meyer
Writers: Russ Meyer, Roger Ebert
With: Dolly Read, Cynthia Myers, Marcia McBroom, Michael Blodgett, Edy Williams, Erica Gavin

Sex and drugs and rock 'n' roll rule the day as an all-girl rock combo struggles to attain stardom in Tinseltown. What makes it a horror movie—or, more precisely, a splatter movie—is the gruesome and graphic orgy of violence that climaxes the film in true Meyer fashion. Written by film critic and antisplatter crusader Roger Ebert, who has publicly expressed much dismay over gory exploitation films such as this one—but *not* this one. Wonder why? Blodgett, who loses his head in the movie—literally—eventually gave up acting and turned to writing gory, exploitative novels.

The Bird with the Crystal Plumage

U.M. Distributors, 1969; Color; 98 minutes
Director: Dario Argento
Producer: Salvatore Argento
Writer: Dario Argento
With: Tony Musante, Suzy Kendall, Eva Renzi, Mario Adorf

Violent psychodrama about an American writer (Musante) living in Rome who witnesses an attempted murder and is subsequently pursued by the would-be assassin himself. This was cult splatter director Argento's feature-film debut. Visually quite stylish (in the Argento tradition) but full of narrative lapses (again in the Argento tradition).

The Blade in the Body

See The Murder Clinic

A Blade in the Dark

Distributor unknown, 1983; Color; 110 minutes
Director: Lamberto Bava
Producer: Lamberto Bava

Writers: Elisa Briganti, Dardano
 Sacchetti
With: Andrea Occhipinti, Lara
 Naszinski, Fabiola Toledo

Searching for the proper seclusion and ambience in which to churn out a score for a high-octane Italian horror film, a composer moves into one of those sinister old dark houses to which only people in movies seem to be drawn. The composer's concentration is interrupted when a girl is brutally murdered on the property by a phantom mad slasher—and then her body vanishes. The knife blade flashes again and again, the gore murders somewhat paralleling events in the film being scored. As illusion and reality blur, the composer thinks he's going mad. Typical Italian psycho-shocker film (in Italy, the genre is termed *gialli*)—short on sense and long on style.

Blade Runner

Warner Brothers, 1982; Color; 114
 minutes
Director: Ridley Scott
Producer: Michael Deeley
Writers: Hampton Fancher, David
 Peoples
With: Harrison Ford, Rutger Hauer,
 Sean Young, Darryl Hannah

Futuristic hard-boiled detective yarn with Ford miscast as the world-weary *film noir* hero whose job is to smoke out replicants (androids) that have infiltrated the world of humans. Director Scott creates a powerful vision of Los Angeles circa 2019, but fails to provide much of a story to go along with it. Visually compelling but disappointing nonetheless. Nine minutes of splattery footage excised from the theatrical release were reinserted into the videocassette version. They don't help. Based on the novel *Do Androids Dream of Electric Sheep?* by Philip K. Dick.

The Blob

Tri-Star Pictures, 1988; Color; 95
 minutes
Director: Chuck Russell
Producers: Jack H. Harris, Elliott
 Kastner
Writers: Chuck Russell, Frank
 Darabont
With: Kevin Dillon, Shawnee Smith,
 Donovan Leitch, Jeffrey DeMunn,
 Candy Clark

Thoroughly entertaining, ultrasplattery —and ultraslimy—remake of the Jack H. Harris/Steve McQueen chestnut that retains quite a bit of the earlier film's 1950s feel. The FX (by Lyle Conway and many, many others) are high-tech and mostly top-notch; some of the stop-motion and back-projection work does look like early Harryhausen, but that only adds to the charm. As in the original, a meteor lands and oozes forth a gelatinous creature that gobbles up its victims and grows to the size of a house. This time, though, the meteor isn't from outer space; it's a U.S. space capsule containing an experimental germ to be used for biological warfare. Dillon plays the McQueen part, a rebellious teen who's always in trouble with the law, but who, with plucky girlfriend Smith, finally saves the day by freezing the creature into immobility. Fans of *Aliens* and Carpenter's *The Thing* will especially like it as this *Blob* is cut from the same mold.

Blood

Bryanston Pictures, 1974; Color; 74
 minutes
Director: Andy Milligan
Producer: Walter Kent
Writer: Andy Milligan
With: Allen Berendt, Hope Stansbury,
 Eve Crosby, Pamela Adams

Low camp, lowbrow and, for the most part, low gore "epic" from the fertile mind of prolific Staten Island movie mogul Andy Milligan. It's an epic because it's Milligan's most expensive film to date—an apparent shot at mainstream distribution, which most of Milligan's films have not received. This one didn't get much either, and so it marked Milligan's swan song in the horror/splatter genre. The plot has Larry Talbot, Jr. (the son of the wolfman for you nonaficionados) marrying Dracula's daughter so that they can settle down to a life of connubial bliss (on scenic Staten Island, of course) raising man-eating, blood-craving plants.

Blood and Black Lace

Allied Artists, 1964; Color; 84 minutes
Director: Mario Bava
Producers: Masimo Patrizi, Alfred Mirabel
Writers: Mario Bava, Marcello Fondato, Giuseppe Barilla
With: Eva Bartok, Cameron Mitchell, Thomas Reiner, Harriet White

Looking like a fugitive from the silent versions of *The Cat and the Canary* or *The Bat,* a masked killer in a floppy hat and flowing dark coat carves up a model from Bartok and Mitchell's fancy fashion salon. When it turns out the victim had written a diary containing clues to her killer's identity and the diary falls into the hands of the other models, the killer strikes again, and again. The police think the killings are the work of a sex maniac, but we know better, don't we? First of the Italian-made *gialli*/horror films and Bava's splatter debut, though the gore is relatively low key—except for one scene where a model has her face fried on a hot-water heater. Like most *gialli*, it's stylish and colorful—and about as involving as a party at which you're the only guest.

Blood and Lace

American-International, 1971; Color; 87 minutes
Director: Philip Gilbert
Producers: Gil Lasky, Ed Carlin
Writer: Gil Lasky
With: Gloria Grahame, Melody Patterson, Vic Tayback, Dennis Christopher

Grahame runs an orphanage that, by comparison, makes the one in *Oliver Twist* look like a summer camp. New arrival Patterson is quick to experience the wrath of Grahame's iron hand and becomes determined to flee the awful woman's clutches and/or convince the cops that there's something amiss about the demented place. What's amiss is a hooded, punishing figure who prowls about the halls with a hammer and sometimes a cleaver, chopping off orphan limbs and stuffing orphan bodies in the institution's food freezer for God only knows what purpose. Needless to say, this movie is not recommended viewing for orphans. A graphically bloody mess if you see it uncut—with the gore murders eliminated, it comes across as a rather slow-moving but just as sick little potboiler. On its original release, the film somehow got past the MPAA rating board with a GP (now PG) rating!

Blood Beach

The Jerry Gross Organization, 1981; Color; 92 minutes
Director: Jeffrey Bloom
Producer: Steven Nalevansky
Writer: Jeffrey Bloom
With: John Saxon, Marianna Hill, David Huffman, Burt Young

A malevolent creature lurking beneath the sands of a crowded Southern California beach pulls unsuspecting bathers to their bloody doom in this half-serious, half-absurd parody of *Jaws* (1975). My favorite line: "Just when you thought it was safe to go back into the water . . . you can't get to it."

Blood Cult of Shangri-La

See The Thirsty Dead

Blood Diner

Lightning Pictures, 1987; Color; 88 minutes
Director: Jackie Kong
Producer: Jimmy Maslon
Writer: Michael Sonye
With: Rick Burks, Carl Crew, Roger Dauer, Lanette La France, Lisa Guggenheim

Uneven but frequently hilarious parody of splatter movies in general and H. G. Lewis's *Blood Feast* in particular. Mass murderer Uncle Anwar, demented perpetrator of the Happy Times All-Girl Glee-Club Massacre, is shot down by police before he can collect enough body parts for the ritual blood buffet he hopes will bring long-dead Egyptian princess Shitar back to life. He's trained his dim-witted nephews well, however, and when they grow up, they take up where he left off, opening up a successful health-food diner that specializes in things such as "fish fingers," which are actually the severed digits of a snoopy IRS man. The film is filled with outrageous splatter sight gags (like the beheading of a prostitute with the end of a broom) and equally outrageous dialogue, though the latter is sometimes a bit difficult to understand. If its cult reputation grows, *Blood Diner* could become *The Little Shop of Horrors* of splatter movies. Highly recommended.

Bloodeaters

Parker National, 1980; Color; 84 minutes
Director: Chuck McCrann
Producer: Chuck McCrann
Writer: Chuck McCrann
With: Charles Austin, John Amplas, Beverly Shapiro, Dennis Helfend

McCrann's attempt to follow in the footsteps of fellow Pennsylvania filmmaker George Romero is a Romero-ish zombie film (shot on Romero's home turf of Pittsburgh) that features Romero stock-company veteran Amplas as one of several victims of a government experiment gone awry. He and some other potheads get sprayed with an experimental herbicide being tested in the nearby woods, and the chemicals turn them into blood-craving, flesh-ripping monsters. FX technician Craig Harris successfully orchestrates the Savini-like blood and gore, which are both convincing and considerable despite the film's extremely low budget; it was shot in 16mm and blown up to 35mm for theatrical release.

Blood Feast

Box Office Spectaculars, 1963; Color; 75 minutes
Director: Herschell Gordon Lewis
Producer: David F. Friedman
Writer: Allison Louise Downe
With: Connie Mason, Thomas Wood, Mal Arnold, Lyn Bolton, Scott H. Hall

A weirdo by the name of Fuad Ramses (Arnold), who thinks he's sort of a modern Dr. Frankenstein, attempts to revive the corpse of a long-dead Egyptian princess by replacing her moldy old body parts with new ones—which he rips off and out of young girls (literally) while they're still alive and kicking. First of the gore films: a crude, exploitative howler. Writer Downe, by the way, was once a parole officer.

Blood for Dracula

Bryanston Pictures, 1974; Color; 103 minutes
Director: Paul Morrissey
Producer: Andrew Braunsberg
Writer: Paul Morrissey
With: Joe Dallesandro, Udo Kier, Arno Juerning, Maxime McKendry, Vittorio de Sica

It's the 1920s (Elinor Glyn's *Three Weeks* has just been published) and nary a "wirgin" is to be found in Transylvania these days, so Dracula (Kier), who needs the blood of a "wirgin" in the worst way, sets out (coffin tied to the luggage rack of his car) for Italy, where his servant (Juerning) assures him there are "wirgins" aplenty, due to the influence of the Catholic Church. Alas, the locals direct him to the De Fiore family ("Oh, I'm sure they are religious, they have a very nice house!") and their four unmarried daughters, two of whom have been sullied by a randy, Brooklyn-accented, Marxist-spouting handyman (Dallesandro), who sums it up neatly by posing the immortal question, "If he's looking for a virgin, what's he doin' with you two whores?" Such impure blood has a nasty side effect on the Count—he vomits it back up, crying, at one point, "The blood of these whores is killing me!" Lots of skin, blood, sex, and bizarre Paul Morrissey humor, but the film's final impression is that of a somber and sad fairy story about the passing of an age. There's more here than mere camp and it's all beautifully shot by Luigi Kuveiller and moodily scored by Claudio Gizzi (with aptly titled pieces like "From Bohemia's Meadows and Crypts" and "The Blood of These Whores Is Killing Me"). Look for Roman Polanski in an uncredited cameo.—K. H.

Blood from the Mummy's Tomb

American-International, 1972; Color; 94 minutes
Directors: Seth Holt, (uncredited) Michael Carreras
Producer: Howard Brandy
Writer: Christopher Wicking
With: Andrew Keir, James Villiers, Valerie Leon, Rosalie Crutchley

Archaeologist Keir desecrates the tomb of murderous Egyptian queen Tera, who takes her revenge by possessing the body of Keir's daughter (Leon). Excellent Hammer horror liberally laced with splatter. Holt died of a heart attack before filming was finished and Hammer executive producer Carreras took over. Most of the film is Holt's, however. Based on Bram Stoker's *Jewel of the Seven Stars* and remade (far less well but with a lot more splatter) as *The Awakening.*

Blood Legacy

Universal Entertainment, 1971; Color; 89 minutes
Director: Carl Monson
Producer: Carl Monson
Writer: Eric Norden
With: Faith Domergue, John Russell, Merry Anders, Rodolfo Acosta, John Carradine

An elderly millionaire (Carradine) fakes his own death in order to observe the family squabbling he knows (probably from seeing *The Cat and the Canary* [1927] and scores of other "will read at midnight" movies) will ensue among his heirs. The squabbling quickly turns to murder, however, as the heirs start killing each other off in all sorts of creatively grisly ways. (Obviously they saw *The Cat and the Canary,* too). An early example of the "creative death" form of splatter filmmaking—though in terms of gory effects it rates fairly low on the Splat-O-Meter. It is aka *Legacy of Blood*, but not to be confused with Andy Milligan's 1978 *Legacy of Blood*—which rates fairly high.

Blood Mania

Crown International Pictures, 1970;
    Color; 90 minutes
Director: Robert O'Neil
Producers: Peter Carpenter, Chris
    Marconi
Writers: Toby Sacher, Tony Crechales
With: Peter Carpenter, Maria De
    Aragon

Low budgeter (naturally) in which the daughter of a retired surgeon (I'm being polite; he actually specializes in abortions), who hates her father dearly, decides to do him in in order to (1) collect the family inheritance and (2) take over the family business.

Blood Orgy of the She-Devils

Gemini, 1972; Color; 73 minutes
Director: Ted V. Mikels
Producer: Ted V. Mikels
Writer: Ted V. Mikels
With: Lila Zaborin, Tom Pace, Leslie
    McRae, Victor Izay

West Coast filmmaker Mikels's work is a cross between that of Russ Meyer and Herschell Gordon Lewis. His films incorporate the over-the-top gore of Lewis, often perpetrated by buxom, hot-blooded, violent females of the kind found in Meyer's splatter fantasies. Mikels says he draws his female stock company from among the women with whom he lives—often ten at a time, or so he claims. The title of this film implies more than it actually delivers either in the gore or sex department, though there is some of both. It's

about a beautiful witch (Zaborin) and a bevy of beautiful followers who torture and torch men as ritual sacrifices to their cult. Tame.

Blood Simple

Circle Films, 1984; Color; 96 minutes
Director: Joel Coen
Producer: Ethan Coen
Writers: Joel and Ethan Coen
With: John Getz, Frances
    McDormand, Dan Hedaya,
    Samm-Art Williams, M. Emmet
    Walsh

Smashing debut feature by the Coen Brothers that blends splatter with *film noir*. The title is taken from Dashiell Hammett. McDormand is married to Hedaya but is having an affair with Getz. Hedaya hires sleazy private eye Walsh to kill them. But Walsh turns the tables and kills Hedaya instead. Getz thinks McDormand did it and tries to cover up the murder. McDormand thinks Getz is going crazy. Hedaya comes back from the grave—or seems to, puking up buckets of blood. Walsh kills Getz. Stalked by Walsh, McDormand saves herself by sticking a knife through his hand, then shooting him. Though far more convoluted, that, basically, is the plot. But in this film, it's style, not plot, that counts. And the Coen Brothers' style is riveting.

The Blood Spattered Bride

Europix, 1974; Color; 83 minutes
Director: Vicente Aranda
Producer: Jose Lopez Moreno
Writer: Vicente Aranda
With: Simon Andreu, Maribel Martin,
    Alexandra Bastedo

Umpteenth retelling of the Sheridan Le Fanu lesbian vampire fable, *Carmilla*, this time set in Spain. Bastedo is the sensuous

lesbian vampire whose yen for Martin is complicated by Martin's marriage to Andreu. Bastedo lets eroticism run its course and wins Martin over. In a vengeful rage, Andreu rips the women's hearts out, which is only fair as Bastedo, in addition to having broken quite a few hearts in her lifetime, has ripped the hearts from the chests of some of her male adversaries. How much of all this heart ripping you're likely to see depends on the print; most are truncated, leaving little but the frequent nudity.

Bloodsucking Freaks

Distributor unknown, 1976; Color; 88 minutes
Director: Joel M. Reed
Producer: Alan Margolin
Writer: Joel M. Reed
With: Seamus O'Brien, Louie de Jesus, Niles McMaster

Ultralow-budget gore film in the tradition of H. G. Lewis. O'Brien runs a Grand Guignol theater and white-slavery racket —he keeps his "merchandise" naked and caged up backstage. Another kidnap victim is a New York City ballerina, who, perhaps influenced by all the bloody goings-on front and backstage, develops a unique new dance step when she kicks a man to death. Filmed in "Ghoul-O-Rama," the film boasts such elaborate set pieces as having a woman's brains sucked out of her head with a straw! It is aka *The Incredible Torture Show*—it is definitely that, all right.

Bloodthirsty Butchers

Constitution Films, 1970; Color; 79 minutes
Director: Andy Milligan
Producer: William Mishkin
Writers: Andy Milligan, John Borske

With: John Miranda, Anabella Wood, Berwick Kaler

There's low budget and then there's *low* budget. At a cost of approximately $7,000, the incomparable Andy Milligan shot this epic in England to give it some class. Essentially, it's a modern retelling of the true story of Sweeney Todd, the demon barber of Fleet Street, who killed people for their money, then disposed of their bodies by turning them into meat pies. Yum! Yum! Stephen Sondheim's award-winning musical was inspired by the same crime—but not, I suspect, by this movie.

Bloody Birthday

Analysis Films, 1980; Color; 85 minutes
Director: Ed Hunt
Producer: Gerald T. Olson
Writers: Ed Hunt, Barry Pearson
With: Lori Lethrin, Susan Strasberg, Jose Ferrer, Elizabeth Hoy, Billy Jacoby, Andy Freeman

Canadian-made *Bad Seed* clone with a triple-threat band of murderous kids who are compelled to kill because their mothers gave birth to them during an eclipse; ever since, their combined horoscopes have been terrible. These kids (Hoy, Jacoby, Freeman) are a bad news lot, all right. They'll kill anyone, for *any* reason. They kill a teacher because she gives them too much homework; wipe out others with a bow and arrow; strangle a fellow classmate. Two of them are rounded up in the end, but angelic Hoy gets away to perpetrate more nefarious deeds, thus paving the way for a sequel, which the box-office failure of this dud prevented poor old Ed Hunt from inflicting upon us.

Bloody New Year

Academy Entertainment, 1987; Color;
90 minutes
Director: Norman J. Warren
Producer: Hayden Pearce
Writer: Frazer Pearce
With: Suzy Aitchison, Colin Heywood,
Catherine Brooks, Mark Powley

If it weren't for its unusually banal dialogue (even for a splatter movie), stiff acting, and inability to keep us interested in
what happens to the characters, *Bloody
New Year* might have been a winner. The
splatter FX are proficient and there are
some clever camera and editing tricks—
such as when an apparition jumps out of
a movie screen to claw a victim to death.
Five teens on an outing wreck their boat
and take refuge at a remote island hotel
that is decorated inside for a New Year's
Eve party circa 1959. Illusion and reality
blur (à la the *Elm Street* movies) as
the terrified teens experience an indoor
snowstorm, a marauding rope, and an array of violent poltergeist activity, and turn
into ghouls. It seems that back in '59, the
British government sent up a plane with
a device capable of altering time, and the
plane crashed near the hotel, trapping
everyone inside in a perpetual time warp.
Which is what happens to the teens as
well, despite their best efforts to get away.

Blue Monkey

SpectraFilm, 1987; Color; 96 minutes
Director: William Fruet
Producer: Martin Walters
Writer: George Goldsmith
With: Steve Railsback, Gwynyth
Walsh, John Vernon, Joe Flaherty,
Don Lake, Ivan E. Roth

An old codger cuts his finger on a bizarre
plant from some obscure island south of
Micronesia and is spirited to the county
hospital, which doubles as a high-tech
laser lab and was once an insane asylum.
He spits up a parasite in the nurses' faces.
Then some pesty little kids feed the parasite a hormonal growth compound that
just happens to be lying about, and the
parasite (which gives birth to its own mate)
mushrooms into a gigantic cross between
the creature in *Alien* and the ants in *Them.*
The hospital is quarantined, leaving those
trapped inside to contend with the beast.
Deadpan cop Railsback saves the day by
incinerating the mate and lasering the
oversized bug, which, due to murky lighting, we never get a good look at. The only
novel thing about this film is its meaningless title.

The Boogeyman

The Jerry Gross Organization, 1980;
Color; 86 minutes
Director: Ulli Lommel
Producer: Ulli Lommel
Writers: Ulli Lommel, (uncredited)
Suzanna Love and David
Herschel
With: Suzanna Love, Ron James,
Nicholas Love, John Carradine

A young girl (Ms. Love, who is also the
director's wife) returns to the scene of
her childhood, where she witnessed a
murder committed by her brother (Mr.
Love; this movie's a real family affair!).
Haunted by the incident, she is determined to rid herself of the nightmares
that have plagued her since childhood.
Instead, she comes in contact with a broken mirror that prompts people to kill. A
psychological thriller with lots of "creative deaths" including one by pitchfork.
Followed by a sequel, *Boogeyman II*
(1983).

Boogeyman II

Distributor unknown, 1982; Color; 79
minutes

Director: Bruce Starr
Producers: Ulli Lommel, Bruce Starr
Writers: Ulli Lommel, Suzanna Love
With: Suzanna Love, Ulli Lommel,
Shannah Hall

In *Boogeyman II*, extensive use is made of footage from the first *Boogeyman* in the form of flashbacks related by Lacey, a character common to both films. Sequels often include footage from earlier entries to bring the audience up to date, but in this case the film is half over before the flashbacks end and the new story gets under way. To make things worse, Lacey had no knowledge, during the first film, of much of the information she relates with such detail in the sequel. The new story is so predictable and Bruce Starr's direction so inept, that we begin to wish for a return to the flashback footage. The sequel can't even deliver decent splatter effects (unlike the original, which contained some well-executed gore). In the new story unimaginative deaths occur in quick succession with choppy editing, flashing lights, and loud music used to cover up incompetent effects. The first *Boogeyman* was a modest little thriller with some decent writing and clever filmmaking. Compared to the sequel, however, the first film begins to look like a masterpiece.—J. B.

Brain Damage

Paramount Pictures, 1988; Color; 89
  minutes
Director: Frank Henenlotter
Producer: Edgar Ievens
Writer: Frank Henenlotter
With: Rick Herbst, Gordon
  MacDonald, Jennifer Lowry, Theo
  Barnes, Lucille Saint-Peter

Henenlotter's follow-up to *Basket Case*, his first feature, is disappointing. It starts out well, then lapses into a replay of too many elements from *Basket Case* (to which

the director includes a blatant in-joke reference), culminating in a "mind blowing" finale that doesn't make much sense. A medieval foot-long creature called Aylmer (pronounced Elmer) escapes from its present owners, an elderly Jewish couple, and latches on to hero Herbst. Elmer injects a bluish liquid that induces euphoria into Herbst's brain. In return, Herbst must supply victims whose brains Elmer needs to suck out and eat to stay alive. Herbst suffers guilt, but as he's hooked on the euphoric states the drug provides, he is unable to fight back. One can interpret the film as a basic reworking of Jekyll and Hyde/Faust (or even *Little Shop of Horrors*) themes—or as a satiric metaphor about the perils of drug abuse. In any event, there's little suspense, the humor is too subdued, and Paramount appears to have trimmed some of the gore sequences, which are plentiful but not exceptional.

Breakfast at the Manchester Morgue

Distributor unknown, 1975; Color; 93
  minutes
Director: Jorge Grau
Producer: Edmondo Amati
Writer: Sandro Continenza
With: Ray Lovelock, Arthur Kennedy,
  Cristina Galbo

Set mainly in a hospital, this Spanish-made cannibal holocaust movie boldly apes Romero's *Night of the Living Dead*—in fact, it almost has the same plot. An experimental pesticide developed by the government succeeds in killing bugs but unhappily raises the dead in the process. The decomposing zombies prove just as gruesome as Romero's—and just as hungry. Lovelock is the hero who is consumed with revenge against the flesh-eating ghouls after they consume his girlfriend. He manages to ward off their attacks and kill quite a few in the process but is gunned down in the end by an ignorant, fascist cop (Kennedy). In a turnabout, however, he gets even by becoming a zombie himself and gorging himself on the flabby cop's innards. It is aka *Don't Open the Window*.

The Brood

New World Pictures, 1979; Color; 90 minutes
Director: David Cronenberg
Producer: Claude Heroux
Writer: David Cronenberg
With: Oliver Reed, Samantha Eggar, Art Hindle, Cindy Hinds, Robert Silverman, Susan Hogan

Under the care of experimental psychologist Reed, institutionalized psycho and child abuser Eggar develops the unique ability to manifest her inner demons in physical form. Whenever she approaches critical mass, her id creatures—the brood—come alive to do her murderous bidding. Though critically drubbed upon release and chastised for its perverse and repulsive gore (the climactic scene where Eggar gives birth to one of her id creatures will have you reaching for the nearest barf bag), *The Brood* is no grade-Z exploitation film. Among other things, it's a potent allegory about the effects of child abuse and the trauma of divorce. The gore is perfectly integrated with theme. One of Cronenberg's best.

The Burning

Filmways, 1981; Color; 85 minutes
Director: Tony Maylam
Producer: Harvey Weinstein
Writers: Peter Lawrence, Bob Weinstein
With: Brian Matthews, Leah Ayres, Brian Backer, Larry Joshua, Lou David

Counselors at a lakeside summer camp are being done in by a vengeful masked psycho brandishing pruning shears. Splatter movie in the *Friday the 13th* mold with effects by Tom Savini—many of which were cut prior to the film's release. Music by Rick Wakeman.

Caligula

Penthouse Films International, 1980; Color; 143 minutes
Directors: Tinto Brass, Giancarlo Lui, Bob Guccione
Producers: Bob Guccione, Franco Rossellini
Writer: Gore Vidal
With: Malcolm McDowell, Peter O'Toole, Teresa Ann Savoy, Helen Mirren, Sir John Gielgud, Guido Mannari

With credits such as "Adapted from a Screenplay by . . . ," "Additional sequences by . . . ," and "Edited by the Production," it's easy to tell why this lengthy sex and violence epic is a mess. Some of it is a bloody mess if you can sit through the rest. Early on, a drunken soldier is disemboweled after being force-filled with wine through a funnel. Then we're treated to some flagellation and impalement "aftermaths." Cal sucks some of his bride's blood from a small slit in her neck, and there's a pretty neat decapitation machine. Also, Cal throws up blood when he's got the fever, and a severed penis is thrown to a dog after a torture murder. Finally, Cal is cleaved in the head and stabbed in the belly with a sword and spears, his flunky's head is lopped off and kicked, his wife is stabbed, and his kid's head is stove in for a last bloody tableau. The effects are adequate, but the really graphic scenes go by fairly quickly. It's a lot of sexual chaff to go through for a little gory grain.—D. K.

Campsite Massacre

See The Final Terror

Cannibal Ferox

See Make Them Die Slowly

Cannibal Girls

American-International, 1972; Color;
   84 minutes
Director: Ivan Reitman
Producer: Daniel Goldberg
Writer: Robert Sandler
With: Andrea Martin, Eugene Levy,
   Ronald Ulrich, Randall Carpenter

An old-dark-house (or, rather, old-dark-restaurant) horror-comedy updated for the splatter generation. Girls whose car breaks down seek shelter at an old dark house, now turned into a restaurant where the bill of fare is human flesh. To add to the spoofery and send-up nature of the film, Reitman includes a William Castle-style gimmick: a warning bell that cues the audience that a gore scene is about to unfold ("When it rings—close your eyes if you're squeamish!"). Levy and Martin, of course, later became members of the popular Second City TV group. This film, in fact, is very much in the same satiric vein as that show.

Cannibal Holocaust

Distributor unknown, 1979; Color; 95
   minutes
Director: Ruggero Deodato
Producer: Franco Palaggi
Writer: Gianfranco Clerici
With: Francesca Cardi, Robert
   Kerman, Luca Barbareschi

Documentary filmmakers investigating the existence of cannibalism in the South American jungles push the natives too far in an effort to prove their thesis and get graphic scenes of munching and torture on film. As a result, they get chowed down. The film they shot is discovered and linked together with voice-over narration explaining in dire tones what's happening and how the moviemakers may have gotten what they deserved. Lots of impalements and disembowelings—plus animal violence for those who need their pot of grue fully stirred. Not to be confused with Umberto Lenzi's 1980 *Eaten Alive* (which, in turn, shouldn't be confused with Tobe Hooper's 1976 *Eaten Alive*), which has a similar plot and also features Kerman.

Cannibal Massacre

Distributor unknown, 1980; Color; 90
   minutes
Director: Anthony Dawson
Producers: Marizio Amati, Sandro
   Amati
Writers: Marizio Amati, Sandro
   Amati, Jose Luis Martinez Molla,
   Dardano Sacchetti
With: John Saxon, Cindy Hamilton,
   Elizabeth Turner

Quasi-allegory about the post war effects of the Vietnam experience on the American home front. GI Saxon returns from the jungles of Nam, where the Cong didn't get him but a cannibal did. Seems he was bitten by a fellow GI who'd developed a passion for human flesh. Now helplessly infected himself, Saxon joins with the GI who bit him, plus another cannibal compatriot, and the trio goes on a gluttonous orgy of flesh-eating, spreading the contagion to others. Eventually, the whole gang of ghouls is incinerated by the National Guard in the sewers of Atlanta. And that's about as allegorical as this Romero/Fulci clone gets. Vividly gruesome in the tradition of most Italian-made cannibal/

zombie movies—though the film was shot in Georgia. It is aka *The Cannibals Are in the Streets.*

The Cannibals Are in the Streets

See Cannibal Massacre

Carrie

United Artists, 1976; Color; 97 minutes
Director: Brian De Palma
Producer: Paul Monash
Writer: Lawrence D. Cohen
With: Sissy Spacek, Piper Laurie, William Katt, John Travolta, Nancy Allen, Amy Irving

Vastly overrated shocker based on the novel by Stephen King. Spacek is the withdrawn, put-upon teenager of the title who lives under the shadow of her sexually repressed, religion-crazed mother (Laurie). A vicious prank played on her as she is crowned queen of the senior prom unleashes her telekinetic powers in an orgy of destruction. Spacek is excellent, but De Palma's direction, a mixture of the exploitative, the derivative, and the tedious—the potentially most exciting scene in the film is made excruciatingly dull through languorous slow motion —sinks the film. Spacek and Laurie received Oscar nominations for their performances—a definite first (and last) for a splatter movie.

The Cars That Ate Paris

New Line Cinema, 1974; Color; 91 minutes
Director: Peter Weir
Producers: Hal McElroy, James McElroy
Writer: Peter Weir
With: Terry Camilleri, Melissa Jaffa, John Meillon, Kevin Miles

Crazies who worship automobiles trap unsuspecting motorists passing through their town of Paris, Australia, at night. The cars are then stolen, the drivers reduced to vegetables through surgery, and the vehicles turned into death-dealing road hogs. Wacked-out SF/splatter/thriller directed by the talented Peter Weir just prior to his big international success with *Picnic at Hanging Rock* (1975). For American release the film was retitled *The Cars That Eat People* and Aussie star Camilleri's voice was redubbed into Brooklynese!

The Cars That Eat People

See The Cars That Ate Paris

Cassandra

Cassandra Productions Pty. Ltd., 1987; Color; 94 minutes
Director: Colin Eggleston
Producer: Trevor Lucas
Writers: Colin Eggleston, John Ruane, Chris Fitchett
With: Shane Briant, Briony Behets, Kit Taylor, Lee James, Susan Barling, Tim Burns, Tessa Humphries

Cassandra, namesake of the psychic princess of Troy, is a famous photographer's daughter who has nightmares about a young woman committing suicide with a rifle at the behest of a demonic little boy in the Australian outback. She also sees visions of the throat-slashing murder of her father's pregnant mistress, and the attempted murder of her own mother, who turns out to be her aunt. Is the murderer her father's new sinister assistant or even her father himself? Cassandra can't tell because she sees her visions through the murderer's eyes. It turns out that the demonic little boy of Cassandra's dreams is her brother, now grown up, who's just escaped from a mental institution. After her father's head is lopped off with a shovel, Cassandra is drawn to the old family house in the outback. She is pursued by her aunt and a cop who catches an axe in the belly. Confronting her evil brother (if you care who he is, spend two bucks), Cassandra shoots and pours gas on him so he can immolate himself and burn down the house. This film is too complex for its own good and leaves a lot of loose ends. Gore fans will find the nearly bloodless murders anemic and badly in need of a splatter transfusion.—D. K.

Cathy's Curse

21st Century Pictures, 1980; Color;
    91 minutes
Director: Eddy Matalon
Producers: Eddy Matalon, N.
    Mathieu, Nicole Boisvert
Writers: Eddy Matalon, Myra
    Clement, A. Sens-Cazenave
With: Alan Scarfe, Beverly Murray,
    Roy Wiltham, Randi Allen

Yet another *Exorcist* rip-off in which a little girl (Allen) is possessed by the spirit of her long dead aunt, who was burned to death in a car crash. Not very effective Canadian-made shocker.

The Cat O'Nine Tails

National General Pictures, 1971;
    Color; 112 minutes
Director: Dario Argento
Producer: Salvatore Argento
Writer: Dario Argento
With: James Franciscus, Karl Malden,
    Catherine Spaak, Cinzia De
    Carolis, Carlo Alighiero

Reporter Franciscus is in pursuit of a particularly nasty mad slasher who kills because of an anomaly in his chromosomes (perhaps he caught this mysterious malady from Hywell Bennett in Roy Boulting's *Twisted Nerve* [1969], which offered the same medical explanation for Bennett's psychotic behavior). Blind ex-reporter Malden helps him. Characteristically stylish, gory, and narratively feeble Argento thriller. Not boring, though. Beware of TV prints, which are atrociously dubbed.

Cat People

Universal, 1982; Color; 118 minutes
Director: Paul Schrader
Producer: Charles Fries
Writer: Alan Ormsby
With: Nastassia Kinski, Malcolm
    McDowell, John Heard, Annette
    O'Toole, Ed Begley, Jr.

Overlong, overblown remake of Val Lewton's fragile B-movie classic. The Lewton film moved along at a brisk pace, allowing the viewer little or no time to ponder the essential silliness of the plot. But Schrader shows the cat people spectacularly bursting out of their human skins (courtesy of effects wizard Stan Winston), then plods along so that we can't help but ask ourselves how these folks keep metamorphosing back into their wrecked torsos again. Alan Ormsby's script also gets bogged down in detailing a convoluted cat people mythology, something Dewitt Bodeen wisely avoided in the original; he merely sketched in some details only when needed to propel the story along. Nudity, incest, and S&M flesh out the proceedings. Nicely shot on New Orleans locations, though.

The Challenge

Twentieth Century-Fox, 1982; Color;
112 minutes
Director: John Frankenheimer
Producers: Robert L. Rosen, Ron
Beckman
Writers: John Sayles, Richard
Maxwell, Ivan Moffat
With: Scott Glenn, Toshiro Mifune,
Donna Kei Benz, Atsuo
Nakamura

American Glenn gets involved in a Japanese family feud, takes up martial-arts training (one of the techniques is to bury him up to his neck in dirt and leave him there screaming), slaughters various folks with a lethal samurai sword, and finally beheads the bad guy. The real challenge is to sit through this interminable potboiler. Directed with flare but to no purpose by one-time Hollywood boy wonder Frankenheimer, whose output since the sixties has been spotty at best. Scott Glenn is so wooden an actor he should appear only in zombie flicks.

The Child

Valiant International, 1977; Color; 83
minutes
Director: Robert Voskanian
Producer: Robert Dadashian
Writer: Ralph Lucas
With: Richard Hanners, Laurel
Bennett, Frank Janson, Rosalie
Cole

A little girl (Cole), who perhaps has seen *Night of the Living Dead* one too many times, starts hanging around the local cemetery, where her mother is buried. Soon she makes friends with a number of flesh-eating ghouls, who also happen to be hanging around (in shreds), and uses her supernatural powers to make them do her bidding.

Children Shouldn't Play with Dead Things

Gemini, 1972; Color; 85 minutes
Director: Benjamin Clark
Producer: Benjamin Clark
Writer: Alan Ormsby, Benjamin Clark
With: Alan Ormsby, Valerie Mauches,
Anya Ormsby, Paul Cronin

A group of actors descends upon a supposedly deserted island to make a grade-Z horror movie (perhaps this one) and encounters corpses who rise from their graves to help lend a hand as extras. Half humor, half horror—in the *Night of the Living Dead* tradition—and all amateurish. Director Benjamin Clark now signs his films as Bob Clark. Filmed in Florida.

Chopping Mall

Trinity Films/Concorde Films, 1986;
Color; 76 minutes
Director: Jim Wynorski
Producer: Julie Corman
Writers: Jim Wynorski, Steve Mitchell
With: Kelli Maroney, Tony O'Dell,
Russell Todd, Karrie Emerson,
Suzee Slater

High-tech robots designed to act as security guards in a fabulous California shopping mall malfunction during an electrical storm and go berserk, attacking some teenage employees who've decided to stay after hours for a little partying and a lot of sex. Filled with movie-buff injokes (the sporting-goods store where the teens arm to the teeth to defend themselves is called "Peckinpah's"). The killer robots sound like the Martian death machines in George Pal's *War of the Worlds*. Paul Bartel, Mary Woronov, Dick Miller (who is called Walter Paisley, the name of his character in Roger Corman's classic *Bucket of Blood*), Mel Welles, and Gerrit

Graham appear in cameos. Not as funny as it might have been (nor as satiric as George Romero's *Dawn of the Dead*, to which it bears more than a passing resemblance), but fun nonetheless. Producer Julie Corman is Roger Corman's wife. It is aka *Killbots* (a much better title).

C.H.U.D.

Distributor unknown, 1984; Color; 87 minutes
Director: Douglas Cheek
Producer: Andrew Bonime
Writers: Parnell Hall, Shepard Abbott
With: John Heard, Daniel Stern, Kim Greist, Christopher Currey

The government secrets barrels of toxic radioactive waste in the sewers of a major city. The resulting contagion turns the derelicts sheltering there into Cannibalistic Humanoid Underground Dwellers, or C.H.U.D.s for short. At night—and even during the day sometimes—these mutant spawns rise up and chow down on the living. Paunchy Heard plays the city health inspector who takes the government to task—with the help of smart-mouthed activist Stern, who has most of the film's snappiest lines. The creatures look like fugitives from a grade-B fifties SF movie like *World Without End*. The mediocre effects are by John Caglione, who has done much better work.

Class of Nuke 'Em High

A Troma Team Release, 1987; Color; 84 minutes
Directors: Richard W. Haines, Samuel Weil
Producers: Lloyd Kaufman, Michael Herz
Writers: Richard W. Haines, Mark Rudnitsky, Lloyd Kaufman, Stuart Strutin
With: Janelle Brady, Gilbert Brenton, Robert Prichard, R. I. Ryan, James Nugent Vernon, Brad Dunker

This violent, anarchic, punk teen comedy employs a lot of gore makeup, prosthetic devices, and stage blood. The problem is that the effects are tossed off or thrown away like a bunch of slapstick one-liners at too fast a pace to be savored. Set in Tromaville, the radioactive and toxic-waste capital of the nation, the plot pits the good teens, Warren and Chrissy, against the Cretins (formerly the school honor society), the toughest punk gang on campus. At a wild party, the Cretins force Warren and Chrissy to smoke radioactive grass. Yet another reason to "just say no," kids. This causes our hero and heroine to (Gasp!) have sex. Chrissy becomes pregnant and gives birth to a mutant tadpolelike slime creature who becomes our protagonists' unwitting ally in their final battle with the Cretins. This is a movie with more ooze and slime than effective bloodletting.—D. K.

Code Name Trixie

See The Crazies

Color Me Blood Red

Box Office Spectaculars, 1964; Color; 74 minutes
Director: Herschell Gordon Lewis
Producer: David F. Friedman
Writer: Herschell Gordon Lewis
With: Don Joseph, Candy Conder, Scott H. Hall, Elyn Warner

Mad artist Adam Sorg (Joseph) uses human blood instead of Grumbacher Red to spice up his palette. This third entry in director Lewis's pioneering splatter trilogy (see *Blood Feast* and *2000 Maniacs*) contains enough worm-ridden corpses, shotgun-blasted faces, and lousy acting to satisfy the most ardent fan. Many have wondered whether this film was inspired by Roger Corman's similarly themed horror-comedy *Bucket of Blood* (1959). But Lewis says his real inspiration was the box-office receipts of his first two gore films. I believe him.

The Comeback

Bedford Films, 1977; Color; 100
   minutes
Director: Pete Walker
Producer: Pete Walker
Writer: Murray Smith
With: Jack Jones, Pamela Stephenson,
   David Doyle, Sheila Keith, Holly
   Palance, Richard Johnson

Crooner Jack Jones, who here gives one of the most lethargic performances in horror/splatter film history, plays a pop-music idol whose marriage drove an adoring fan to suicide. The girl's deranged parents (we don't know who they are until the unsurprising conclusion) set out to drive him mad when he sets up shop in an old mansion and tries to cut a new album. Many of his friends wind up getting cut instead. Yet another *Psycho* rip-off.

Conan the Barbarian

Universal, 1982; Color; 129 minutes
Director: John Milius
Producer: Edward Pressman
Writers: Oliver Stone, John Milius
With: Arnold Schwarzenegger, James
   Earl Jones, Sandahl Bergman,
   Gerry Lopez, Max Von Sydow

Milius's macho fantasy-adventure about the killer strong man of the Hyborean Age (drawn from the pulp novels and short stories of Robert E. Howard) is spectacular, violent . . . and dull! How could that be? Because John Milius made it, that's how! Schwarzenegger certainly looks the part of the muscle-bound hero, and Bergman makes a voluptuous, sword-wielding Valeria, but their characters, as the film itself, never really come alive.

The Confessional

Peter Walker (Heritage) Ltd., 1975;
   Color; 104 minutes
Director: Peter Walker
Producer: Peter Walker
Writer: David McGillivray
With: Anthony Sharp, Susan
   Penhaligon, Stephanie Beacham,
   Norman Eshley, Sheila Keith

An intense film about the darkest evil hiding beneath the official authority and trappings of the Catholic Church. Father Maldrum is an insane cleric who lusts after young women and takes the Lord's vengeance into his own hands. After the heroine tells him of her abusive boyfriend, he scalds the wrong man's face with boiling coffee, then corrects his mistake by killing the true offender with flaming incense. He then kills the suspicious mother of one of his girl victims with a poisoned host and strangles the heroine's sister with a rosary. After murdering his own mother, a helpless invalid, and slitting the throat of his housekeeper, who has loved him for thirty years, he convinces the sister's boyfriend, a disillusioned priest, to remain in the church, and sets out to eliminate the heroine in one of Walker's signature "up in the air" endings. The horror comes from the fact that the priest is above suspicion simply because he is a priest. The gore is subtly effective but not graphic or extensive.

— D. K.

Countess Dracula

Twentieth Century-Fox, 1970; Color;
93 minutes
Director: Peter Sasdy
Producer: Alexander Paal
Writer: Jeremy Paul
With: Ingrid Pitt, Nigel Green, Sandor
Eles, Maurice Denham, Lesley-
Anne Downe

Hungarian director Sasdy and producer Paal's tribute to that notorious Hungarian vampire countess Elizabeth Bathory, who slaughtered virgins and bathed in their blood to keep her complexion creamy. Lots of nudity and lots of blood, though chances are you won't see much of either if you catch this one on television. As always, Ms. Pitt makes a very seductive villainess.

The Crazies

Cambist Films, 1973; Color; 103
minutes
Director: George A. Romero
Producer: Al Croft
Writer: George A. Romero
With: Lane Carroll, W. G. McMillan,
Harold Wayne Jones, Lynn
Lowry, Richard Liberty

Romero's follow-up to *Night of the Living Dead* (he'd made two dissimilar films in between) is really quite good. The crash of a government plane carrying a deadly biological weapon unleashes the contaminant into the water supply of a Pennsylvania town. Pretty soon, the townspeople start to go crazy, killing their families, stabbing people with knitting needles, hanging themselves, etc. The military steps in to contain the madness and even more madness ensues (shades of the Vietnam War experience on the American home front) as people trying to flee the town are shot down in cold blood. Not as grisly as *Night*, but quite splattery nonetheless, the film suffers a bit from its too-frantic pacing. It certainly isn't boring, though. Due to terrible distribution, it flopped badly at the box office. For Romero fans, though, it's a must-see. It is aka *Code Name Trixie*.

Creepers

Dacfilm, 1983; Color; 82 minutes
Director: Dario Argento
Producer: Angelo Jacono
Writers: Dario Argento, Franco Ferrini
With: Jennifer Connelly, Donald
Pleasence, Daria Nicoldi, Dalila
Di Lazzaro

The generally inapt heavy-metal rock music blares on the sound track, a largely unknown cast overacts shamelessly, a mutant child (result of a tryst between a lunatic and a nurse at the asylum) runs amok skewering and slashing, maggots abound, a girl controls flies and other insects, a chimpanzee wields a straight razor, and Donald Pleasence takes the money and runs. What can it all mean? Why, it's nothing more nor less than one of Dario Argento's beautifully photographed and designed, but largely incomprehensible, "shock machine" movies. There's a bit more plot—mostly unrelated and all quite insane—than usual, one truly nauseating sequence, and (thanks to clever scripting) the world's longest telephone cord. The film *appears* to have been shorn of some sequences that might have verged on "kiddie porn" for U. S. release, but with Argento's utter lack of concern for coherence, who can tell? Fun in a brain-damaged fashion.—K. H.

Creepozoids

Titan Productions, 1987; Color; 72 minutes
Director: David DeCoteau
Producers: David DeCoteau, John Schouweiler
Writers: Burford Hauser, David DeCoteau
With: Linnea Quigley, Ken Abraham, Michael Aranda, Richard Hawkins, Kim McKamy, Joi Wilson

This movie is a pale, earthbound *Alien* clone. The film opens with the killing of a female scientist in a remote research complex at the hands, or should I say pincers, of a six-foot-tall black insectlike creature. Later, the complex, now deserted, is invaded by five deserters from a postapocalyptic war. The three men and two women play a deadly game of hide and seek with the creature and a couple of its smaller spawn in the labs and corridors of the complex. When bitten by the monster or its kids, the humans become violent and/or self-destruct. So, they are eliminated one by one until the last survivor kills the creature, which in death gives birth to a mutant human baby. The survivor also kills the baby, or does he? What any of this means is a mystery to me. The script, acting, and special effects are all adequate, but the film as a whole is too derivative to be anything more than a painless way to kill 72 minutes.—D. K.

Creepshow

Warner Brothers, 1982; Color; 122 minutes
Director: George A. Romero
Producer: Richard P. Rubinstein
Writer: Stephen King
With: Hal Holbrook, Adrienne Barbeau, Fritz Weaver, E. G. Marshall, Ted Danson, Stephen King, Carrie Nye, Viveca Lindfors

Romero and literary phenomenon King collaborated on this hymn to the popular EC horror comics of the fifties, which played no small part in the evolution of the splatter genre. The film consists of five separate stories each dealing with death, revenge, monsters, and such. Marshall's episode in which a man who hates bugs is ultimately done in by thousands of cockroaches is arguably the best—with "The Crate" running a close second due to Barbeau's wonderfully blowsy performance as the obnoxious wife of college professor Holbrook. Overlong and not as scary as it might have been, but good tongue-in-cheek fun nonetheless. As expected, Tom Savini's effects are not for the squeamish. Followed in 1987 by a sequel, *Creepshow 2*, directed by Michael Gornick, who photographed the first film.

Creepshow 2

New World Pictures, 1987; Color; 92 minutes
Director: Michael Gornick
Producer: David Ball
Writer: George A. Romero
With: George Kennedy, Lois Chiles, Dorothy Lamour, Tom Wright, Stephen King, Tom Savini (as "The Creep")

This follow-up to the eagerly awaited but disappointing Stephen King/George Romero team-up of 1982 was not so eagerly awaited and is a lot *more* disappointing. The first film was no multi-million-dollar extravaganza, but this one has a definite poverty row air about it (*Cheapshow 2?*). It has the same format: Animated EC-comics-style panels introduce the tales—but there are only three this time instead of five, all adapted again from stories by Stephen King. The first

("Chief Wood'nhead") is about a cigar-store Indian that comes to vengeful life when some punks rob the store and kill the owners. The second, "The Raft," is about a mysterious lake creature (which looks like a gigantic semisubmerged garbage bag) that scarfs down a quartet of teens when they drop in for a swim. The last episode, arguably the best (and funniest), is about a woman (Chiles) who accidentally runs down a hitchhiker and tries to get away with the crime—except that the dead fellow won't let her. Some nice effects by Howard Berger and Ed French, but not enough of them.

Cujo

Taft International, 1983; Color; 91 minutes
Director: Lewis Teague
Producers: Daniel H. Blatt, Robert Singer
Writers: Don Carlos Dunaway, Lauren Currier
With: Dee Wallace, Daniel Hugh-Kelly, Danny Pintauro, Christopher Stone, Ed Lauter

Bitten by vampire bats, a docile St. Bernard turns into a rabid, nearly unstoppable killing machine. The flimsy plot is really a setup for the film's last half hour, a genuine tour-de-force of splatter/terror, as Wallace and her young son (Pintauro) are trapped inside their broken-down car in the sweltering heat by the disease-crazed animal. The opening scene where the dog is accidentally lured into the bat cave by a fleeing rabbit is also a humdinger. Based on a novel by Stephen King.

The Curse

Trans World Entertainment, 1987; Color; 92 minutes
Director: David Keith

Producer: Ovidio G. Assonitis
Writer: David Chaskin
With: Wil Wheaton, Claude Akins, Malcolm Danare, Cooper Huckabee, John Schneider

Based on one of H. P. Lovecraft's best and most cinematic of stories, *The Color Out of Space* (filmed once before as *Die, Monster, Die* [1965] with Boris Karloff—though, luckily for H. P., there's no mention of his name anywhere in the film's credits. A meteor crashes in a field belonging to semi-impoverished farmer (and religious zealot) Akins. Its arrival at first appears to be a blessing. The well water tastes bad, but the chickens are growing fat and sassy and the fruits and vegetables are flourishing. Then everything goes to hell. The chickens try to kill a little girl. The tomatoes ooze juice that looks like blood. The apples are filled with maggots. Akins and family develop sores on their faces, start vomiting on each other, and finally take to killing one another with pitchforks and knives. All of this excitement is handled without an ounce of suspense, credibility, or coherence by actor David Keith (*An Officer and a Gentleman*), here making his directorial debut. Stick to acting, David.

Curtains

Distributor unknown, 1982; Color; 89 minutes
Director: Jonathan Stryker
Producer: Peter R. Simpson
Writer: Robert Guza, Jr.
With: Samantha Eggar, John Vernon, Linda Thorson

In the tradition of *The Flesh and Blood Show*, murder and mutilation befall a group of theatrical hopefuls—in this case, girls who are trying out for parts in a bizarre movie to be directed by Vernon at his eerie and remote (naturally) country estate. Eggar leads the disintegrating pack. The character Vernon plays in the film is Jonathan Stryker. Canadian director Richard Ciupka adopted the same name as a pseudonym for the film's credits. Whether this was to create a film-within-a-film motif or simply to escape blame for this flashy but incomprehensible mess, I don't know.

Daddy's Boys

Concorde Pictures, 1988; Color; 85 minutes
Director: Joe Minion
Producer: Roger Corman
Writer: Daryl Haney
With: Daryl Haney, Laura Burkett, Raymond J. Barry, Dan Shor

Fast and loose cheapie using sets left over from Corman's *Big Bad Mama II*. In fact, this film is little more than a gender reworking of Corman's two *Mama* flicks—mixed with *Bonnie and Clyde* and his own earlier *Bloody Mama*. Barry is big bad daddy, head honcho of a gang of bank robbers made up of his devoted sons. Sibling Jimmy (Haney) proves less devoted, and more enterprising, than the others and decides to strike out on his own with a gun-toting prostitute (Burkett), but irascible dad connives to bring him back to the fold under penalty of being crucified (literally). Lots of blood and gunplay and not bad considering its thrown-together origins. Minion, here making his directorial debut, wrote Martin Scorsese's *After Hours*, which this film resembles in its blackly humorous approach to violence.

Damien—Omen II

Twentieth Century-Fox, 1978; Color; 107 minutes
Director: Don Taylor

Writers: Stanley Mann, Mike Hodges
With: William Holden, Lee Grant, Lew Ayres, Robert Foxworth, Sylvia Sidney

Sequel to *The Omen* (1976), chronicling the devil child's adolescence. More "creative deaths" as Damien is groomed by villain Foxworth to take over Thorn (a little religious symbolism here?) Industries, a multinational company determined to hasten Armageddon by throwing the world into political and economic chaos. Cowriter Hodges was replaced as director due to "artistic differences." Followed by *The Final Conflict* (1981).

The Dark

Film Ventures, 1979; Color; 92 minutes
Director: John "Bud" Cardos
Producers: Dick Clark, Edward L. Montoro
Writer: Stanford Whitmore
With: William Devane, Cathy Lee Crosby, Richard Jaeckel, Keenan Wynn

Los Angeles skid-row murders perpetrated by an unknown killer, dubbed "the mangler" by the press, turn out to be the work of a werewolflike alien from outer space with glowing red eyes. Absolute junk.

Dawn of the Dead

United Film Distribution, 1979; Color; 126 minutes
Director: George A. Romero
Producer: Richard P. Rubinstein
Writer: George A. Romero
With: David Emge, Ken Foree, Scott Reiniger, Gaylen Ross

Romero's long-awaited (and long-avoided) sequel to *Night of the Living Dead* is a lengthy, suspenseful, action-filled, and deliciously comic extravaganza of gore and satire. To escape the zombie menace, four people hole up in a fabulous suburban shopping mall where everything is literally free for the taking—a consumer's paradise. Instinctively sensing familiar surroundings, the brain-dead zombies head there, too—followed by some murderous bikers—and after a while the place gets to look as crowded as Macy's at Christmas. Tom Savini's wall-to-wall special effects are astonishing. Romero and his wife, Christine Forrest Romero, have cameos at the beginning of the film—as a harried TV director and his assistant. Dario Argento provided some of the financial backing—as well as the score, by The Goblins. A masterpiece of splattery black humor.

Dawn of the Mummy

Harmony Gold, 1981; Color; 88 minutes
Directors: Frank Agrama, (uncredited) Armand Weston
Producer: Frank Agrama
Writers: Frank Agrama, Daria Price, Ronald Dobrin
With: Brenda King, Barry Sattels, George Peck, Joan Levy

A full-throttle splatter movie that pumps some badly needed blood into one of the most tired of all horror movie subgenres—the mummy movie. It was also filmed in Egypt, another first for a mummy movie, most of which have been shot on sound stages or in the American desert. The scarcely original plot is about the desecration of the tomb of a long-dead Egyptian prince—not by arrogant British Egyptologists this time, but by a fashion photographer and his bevy of luscious models, who are using the tomb as a backdrop for a photo spread. The mummy comes alive, resurrects his dead slaves (who were buried with him), and commands them to tear to pieces all those who cross their lumbering path. The flashback embalming scenes are also quite graphic. As witness the title (*Dawn of . . .*), the film works hard to recall Romero's zombie films. And from the standpoint of effects, it does.

Day of the Dead

United Film Distribution, 1985; Color; 102 minutes
Director: George A. Romero
Producer: Richard P. Rubinstein
Writer: George A. Romero
With: Lori Cardille, Terry Alexander, Joseph Pilato, Richard Liberty, Howard Sherman

Due to budgetary constraints, Romero was forced to scale down and revise his original script for this concluding episode in his zombie trilogy. As a result, many fans found it disappointing. I didn't. True, it lacks *Dawn of the Dead*'s epic grisliness and seems more as if it should be the middle episode rather than the last. But that's carping. This is an extremely well-crafted film full of ingenious special effects—courtesy of maestro Tom Savini. It's also very well acted—especially by Cardille, who could be another Jane Fonda if she gets the right breaks. (Cardille's dad, by the way, had a cameo in *Night of the Living Dead* [1968].) Howard Sherman's affecting performance as Bub, Romero's "zombie with a soul," is another high point.

Day of the Woman

See I Spit on Your Grave

Dead and Buried

Avco Embassy, 1981; Color; 92 minutes
Director: Gary Sherman

Producers: Ronald Schusett, Robert
Fentress
Writers: Ronald Schusett, Dan
O'Bannon
With: James Farentino, Jack
Albertson, Melody Anderson,
Dennis Redfield, Lisa Blount,
Nancy Locke Hauser

The dead rise in a New England town, courtesy of undertaker Albertson. Farentino plays the town sheriff, who's trying to find out who's killing people by sticking needles in their eyes—among other equally grisly modes of murder. Schusett and O'Bannon collaborated earlier on *Alien.*

Dead-End Drive-In

New World Pictures, 1986; Color; 92
minutes
Director: Brian Trenchard-Smith
Producers: Andrew Williams, Damien
Parer
Writer: Peter Smalley
With: Ned Manning, Natalie
McCurry, Peter Whitford

Set in Australia sometime in the 1990s. Worldwide inflation has soared out of sight, prompting the collapse of various economies and whole governments. In Australia, youth gangs—called Car Boys —prowl the city streets in psychedelic, souped-up jalopies, passing the time by crashing into each other. Seeking respite from all this mayhem, Manning and his girlfriend (McCurry) go to the local passion pit. While they're making out in the backseat, the cops who patrol the drive-in steal the wheels off the car, and Manning and his girl find themselves trapped. They're not alone. Seems the drive-in is really a government-sponsored concentration camp for disaffected youth and the unemployed, who are fed a steady diet of junk food and junk movies to keep them amused. Most of his fellow inmates have

never had it so good, but Manning wants out and begins planning his break, which he accomplishes in truly spectacular fashion. The film boasts some wild production design and is loaded with violence (though not much gore), but it sounds a lot better than it plays.

Deadly Eyes

Warner Brothers, 1982; Color; 87
minutes
Director: Robert Clouse
Producers: Jeffrey Schectman, Paul
Kahnert
Writer: Charles Eglee
With: Sam Groom, Sara Botsford,
Scatman Crothers

Oversized mutated rats terrorize a Canadian city. The police feed them puppies laced with poison to kill them, but nothing works. The climax takes place in a school—à la *The Birds*—as the rats pursue innocent children, as well as the hero and heroine, up the down staircase. The special effects are atrocious. The rats look like exactly what they are—dachshunds dolled up in size XL rat suits (their tails wag as they kill people). Based on British splatter/punk novelist James Herbert's debut book, *The Rats*, which is a lot scarier, more gruesome—and more convincing. The novel was set in England.

Deadly Friend

Warner Brothers, 1986; Color; 91
minutes
Director: Wes Craven
Producers: Robert M. Sherman,
Robert Crawford
Writer: Bruce Joel Rubin
With: Matthew Laborteaux, Kristy
Swanson, Michael Sharrett, Anne
Ramsey

Wiz kid Laborteaux's experiments with artificial intelligence produce a sophisticated robot called B-B, which reclusive, paranoid neighbor Ramsey blows apart with a shotgun. When his other neighbor (and girlfriend), Swanson, is killed by her brute father, Laborteaux implants B-B's artificial brain into the dead girl's head and resuscitates her. The result proves pretty nasty as the zombified girl goes about getting revenge (for herself and for B-B) by incinerating her dad and decapitating Ramsey with a basketball. The cops shoot her down in the end just as she is beginning to exhibit signs of her more human personality; then, in one of those meaningless shock epilogues so beloved of splatter moviemakers in general and Wes Craven in particular, B-B's metallic skull bursts through the dead girl's skin to make way for a sequel. Among the many, *many* holes in the plot that exist in this movie, one stands out: As the weeks go by, how come nobody at the hospital ever notices that Swanson's body is missing?

Dead of Night

See Deathdream

Dead Ringers

Twentieth Century-Fox, 1988; Color; 116 minutes
Director: David Cronenberg
Producers: David Cronenberg, Marc Boyman
Writers: David Cronenberg, Norman Snider
With: Jeremy Irons, Genevieve Bujold, Stephen Lack

Irons delivers a powerhouse performance (actually two of them) as twin gynecologists whose special bond spells doom for them both. They each pick up with druggie movie actress Bujold, but it is the less secure of the subtly twisted duo that gets hooked—in more ways than one. Som-

ber, perverse, and occasionally confusing, but fascinating to watch. Cronenberg plays with his own reputation for over-the-top splatter by setting us up for potentially ghoulish sequences, then not delivering them—only to hit us between the eyes with some very potent bits of grisliness when we least expect them. The split screen work is literally seamless. Based on the novel *Twins* by Bari Wood and Jack Greasland, which, in turn, was purportedly based on a true story.

Dead Time Stories

Cinema Group, 1987; Color; 83 minutes
Director: Jeffrey Delman
Producer: Bill Paul
Writers: Jeffrey Delman, Charles F. Shelton, J. Edward Kiernan
With: Scott Valentine, Melissa Leo, Nicole Picard, Matt Mitler

Bargain-basement anthology film reminiscent of *Creepshow*, in which baby-sitter Uncle Mike spins splatter yarns based on well-known fairy tales so that his horror-fan nephew will go to sleep. The ploy doesn't work on the nephew, but I found myself yawning more than once. The first episode, which boasts the film's best effects (by Bryant Tauser and Ed French), is about a resurrected witch named Magoga who feeds on human blood. The second, a modern retelling of "Little Red Riding Hood," is about a werewolf who pursues a luscious teen in a red jogging outfit to grandma's house because the teen accidently picked up his antiwerewolf prescription at the local drugstore. The third episode, the funniest and least sleep-inducing, is about a family of wackos (Mama, Papa, and Baby Baer) who run into a mass-murdering Goldilocks; she apparently saw *The Texas Chainsaw Massacre* one too many times.

Dear Dead Delilah

Avco Embassy, 1972; Color; 95
    minutes
Director: John Farris
Producer: Jack Clement
Writer: John Farris
With: Agnes Moorehead, Will Geer,
    Patricia Carmichael, Dennis
    Patrick, Michael Ansara

Moorehead is the wealthy but dying matriarch of a decaying southern clan whose heirs are being systematically butchered by an axe-wielding maniac. A prolific writer of horror/splatter novels (*All Heads Turn When the Hunt Goes By, Catacombs, The Fury*), John Farris made his directorial debut—and swan song—with this not very bold reprise of films similar to *Hush . . . Hush, Sweet Charlotte* (1964), which also costarred Agnes Moorehead.

Deathdream

Europix, 1972; Color; 90 minutes
Director: Bob Clark
Producer: Bob Clark
Writer: Alan Ormsby
With: Lynn Carlin, John Marley,
    Richard Backus, Henderson
    Forsythe, Anya Ormsby

A Vietnam-era reworking of W. W. Jacobs's classic tale, "The Monkey's Paw." Carlin learns of her son's death in the jungles of Nam and wishes him alive. Sure enough, he returns—as a catatonic, blood-drinking vampire. A genuinely haunting allegory about the effects of that cursed war on those who went to fight and die and those who were left behind to wait and worry. Backus is terrific as the undead vet. Tom Savini handled the gruesomely expert special effects. It is aka *Dead of Night* and *The Night Andy Came Home*. Not to be missed.

Death Line

See Raw Meat

Death Race 2000

New World Pictures, 1975; Color; 78
    minutes
Director: Paul Bartel
Producer: Roger Corman
Writers: Robert Thom, Charles B.
    Griffith
With: David Carradine, Sylvester
    Stallone, Simone Griffith, Louisa
    Moritz

Outrageous satire set in a futuristic America where hit-and-run driving has become the national sport and cross-country racers score points by achieving the highest body count. Stallone is particularly funny as "Machine Gun Joe," a souped-up gangster from Chicago who strives to cheat at every turn. Director Bartel says producer Corman cut most of the satiric elements out of the film prior to its release. It's still bloody good fun, though.

Death Sport

New World Pictures, 1978; Color; 83
    minutes
Directors: Allan Arkush, Henry Suso
Producer: Roger Corman
Writers: Henry Suso, Donald Stewart
With: David Carradine, Claudia
    Jennings, Richard Lynch, William
    Smithers, Jesse Vint

Semisequel to *Death Race 2000* (1975)—minus the laughs. Earth is a wasteland roamed by cannibal mutants and gladiators known as Range Guides, who do their fighting on motorcycles. Corman replaced director Henry Suso with New World vet Allan Arkush shortly after filming began. Artistic differences were not the cause. According to Corman, Suso just couldn't "hack it"—clearly a fatal flaw if you're supposed to be making a splatter movie.

Death Trap

See Eaten Alive

Death Valley

Universal, 1982; Color; 87 minutes
Director: Dick Richards
Producer: Elliott Kastner
Writer: Richard Rothstein
With: Paul Le Mat, Catherine Hicks, Stephen McHattie

Former TV-commercial director Richards has an undeniable flair for the visual, but that's about all. This film and his two previous features—*The Culpepper Cattle Company* (1972) and *March or Die* (1977)—are pictorially striking, but except for their exploitative scenes of sex and violence, they seem like glorified TV commercials—slick but empty. This one, about a young couple who are victimized by a deranged desert rat and must kill to survive, is no exception. Typical slasher fare.

Death Warmed Up

Distributor unknown, 1984; Color; 90 minutes
Director: David Blythe
Producer: Murray Newey
Writers: David Blythe, Michael Heath
With: Margaret Umbers, Michael Hurst, William Upjohn, Gary Day

Hurst is a semipsychotic superhero in the Mad Max tradition, who finds himself on an uncharted island where the evil doctor who created him is now involved in creating a race of mutant warriors in his image. Realizing that his superviolent superhero status is in jeopardy and that if the doc's plan succeeds he will become just another contorted face in the crowd, Hurst takes on the mad bunch in a fight to the death. Slick and sick.

Death Wish II

Columbia Pictures, 1982; Color; 93 minutes
Director: Michael Winner
Producers: Menahem Golan, Yoram Globus
Writer: David Engelbach
With: Charles Bronson, Jill Ireland, Vincent Gardenia, J. D. Cannon, Robert F. Lyons, Anthony Franciosa

After decimating a goodly portion of New York City slimeballs in his first *Death Wish* outing (which wasn't, nevertheless, a real splatter movie), avenger Bronson takes Horace Greeley's famous advice and goes west. He settles down in Los Angeles with his daughter, but their serenity proves short-lived when she is raped (again!) and killed by a vicious psycho (Lyons). Once again, Charlie goes on the warpath, shooting and bludgeoning his way through L.A.'s lowlifes to get to the killer. Followed by two more blood-rushing sequels set in different locales.

Death Wish 3

Cannon Films, 1985; Color; 90 minutes
Director: Michael Winner
Producers: Menahem Golan, Yoram Globus
Writer: Michael Edmonds
With: Charles Bronson, Deborah Raffin, Martin Balsam, Ed Lauter

Charles Bronson looks and acts tired. It may have been part of his characterization (shooting and killing dozens of hoodlums would wear anybody down), but it comes off as the actor who's had enough and not the character. The writer and director seem to be snoozing as well. The vigilante film has, to some degree, replaced the traditional Western, the lawless inner city substituting for the lawless frontier; the strong individual with a clear sense of right and wrong holding justice in his dead aim—A-man's-gotta-do-what-a-man's-gotta-do concept of righting wrongs whatever the personal cost. The problem is that the inner city presents too many real and complex social issues for such simpleminded, one-dimensional thinking. Some of the better vigilante films at least pay lip service to the issues, but in *Death Wish 3*, the punks have evolved into a human subspecies that must be exterminated (if ya can't reform 'em, shoot 'em). Director Michael Winner can't even muster the kinetic energy so essential for this type of film. In trying to top previous entries, the filmmakers get carried away with extremes. The "calling all gangs" climax is silly and the image of senior citizen Bronson walking around blowing away dozens of punks becomes not the stuff of legend but the fodder for lampoon.—J. B.

Death Wish 4: The Crackdown

Cannon Films, 1987; Color; 100 minutes
Director: J. Lee Thompson
Producer: Pancho Kohner
Writer: Gail Morgan Hickman
With: Charles Bronson, Kay Lenz, John P. Ryan, Perry Lopez

This latest installment in the saga of cinema's most popular vigilante boasts an aging Bronson performing more listlessly than he did in *Death Wish 3*—not that Chuck was ever one of the screen's most dynamic actors. But here when he takes on the violent young turks in hand-to-hand combat, the contrived staginess of the action that allows him to come out on top is painfully acute. In *Death Wish 4*, he assumes the role of Kurosawa's *Yojimbo*, playing two drug kingpins off each other, thereby destroying them both. However, the millionaire newspaper owner (Ryan) who hired him to do the job (supposedly the magnate's daughter died from a cocaine overdose) turns out to be yet another drug pusher who has duped Bronson into rubbing out the competition. Bronson doesn't like being duped, though, and he blows Ryan away in the film's most spectacular splatter set piece. Electrocutions, blood-spattering firepower, and gory knifings add to the frolic. Bronson goes about his killing business with such effortless ease, however, that there's never an ounce of suspense.

Deep Red

Mahler Films, 1976; Color; 98 minutes
Director: Dario Argento
Producer: Salvatore Argento
Writer: Giuseppe Basan
With: David Hemmings, Daria Nicolodi, Gabriele Lavi, Macha Meril

Hemmings witnesses the murder of a mind reader and sets out to track down the killer. This stylish and bloody thriller (the beheading by elevator scene is a real showpiece) ranks among director Argento's best, which is not saying much unless one is a devoted fan. He simply cannot tell a coherent story, but he sure knows how to use the camera. Music by The Goblins. It is aka *The Hatchet Murders*. Daria Nicolodi is Mrs. Argento in real life.

Deep Space

Trans World Entertainment, 1988;
  Color; 90 minutes
Director: Fred Olen Ray
Producers: Alan Amiel, Fred Olen
  Ray
Writers: Fred Olen Ray, T. L. Lankford
With: Charles Napier, Ann Turkel,
  Ron Glass, James Booth, Bo
  Svenson, Julie Newmar, Peter
  Palmer

Centaur One, carrying a space-based U. S. biological warfare weapon, goes awry and crashes in California. Two teens come upon the wreckage and the weapon, a large brown blob that is described as looking like a roach egg but looks more like a gigantic stool specimen. The egg cracks open, tentacles spring out, and the teens are eaten by the warlike creature inside —which quickly grows up to look like a cross between Giger's *Alien* design and Godzilla. Cops Napier and Glass are assigned to the case but prove totally incompetent. Psychic Newmar picks up the creature's vibes and the police track it to a warehouse where they take it on with chain saws, guns, and a jar of "special gas," accompanied by a flashing light display stolen from *Alien.* Former L'il Abner Palmer plays a medical examiner. Nice photography by Gary Graver, who worked on Orson Welles's uncompleted film, *The Other Side of the Wind.* All in all though, this is just another bad Fred Olen Ray tribute to bad SF movies of the fifties.

The Demon Lover

21st Century Pictures, 1976; Color;
  85 minutes
Directors: Donald G. Jackson, Jerry
  Younkins
Producers: Donald G. Jackson, Jerry
  Younkins
Writers: Donald G. Jackson, Jerry
  Younkins
With: Gunnar Hansen, Val Mayerik,
  Christmas Robbins, Tom Hutton

Michigan-made independent about an occultist who conjures up a hideous demon to do his bidding but then must deal with the Beast when it turns on him. A must-see for those who enjoyed Hansen as "Leatherface" in *The Texas Chainsaw Massacre* (1974). Full of movie-buff in-jokes (à la the films of Joe Dante) featuring characters named (Forrest) Ackerman, (George A.) Romero, (Alan) Ormsby—well, you get the idea.

Demons

Ascot Entertainment Group, 1985;
  Color; 89 minutes
Director: Lamberto Bava
Producer: Dario Argento
Writers: Dario Argento, Lamberto
  Bava, Dardano Sacchetti, Franco
  Ferrini
With: Urbano Barberini, Natasha
  Hovey, Karl Zinny, Fiore Argento,
  Paolo Cozzo

This gore extravaganza from the son of late Italian splatter master Mario Bava starts out promisingly enough but then degenerates into a clone of *Dawn of the Dead* and *The Evil Dead.* A mysterious figure with a half-metal face passes out freebie tickets to the premiere of an unnamed film at a haunted theater called the "Metropole." The film is about some teens who unearth a book about demons from the tomb of Nostradamus and unleash these demons upon the "reel" world. The same events are quickly played out in the theater as several unlucky patrons become taloned blood- and slime-spewing creatures who are determined to slaughter the others in every graphically horrible way possible. The impressive gore effects by Rosario Prestopino are as wall-to-wall as those in *The Evil Dead*. Pop songs by Billy Idol, Motley Crue, Rick Springfield, and others fill out the throbbing heavy-metal sound track.

Demons 2

Imperial Entertainment, 1987; Color; 88 minutes
Director: Lamberto Bava
Producer: Dario Argento
Writers: Dario Argento, Lamberto Bava, Franco Ferrini, Dardano Sacchetti
With: David Knight, Bobby Rhodes, Asia Argento, Virginia Bryant

Whereas *Demons* drew its inspiration from Romero's zombie films and Sam Raimi's *The Evil Dead*, *Demons 2* appears to be a nod to Cronenberg's *They Came from Within*. Residents of a high-rise apartment complex who are watching a TV documentary about the events in *Demons* find themselves at the mercy of another plague of demons when one of the creatures emerges from a TV set, claims a victim, and starts spreading the contagion from floor to floor. Even animals aren't immune from demonitis. A physics student and his pregnant wife (no, she *doesn't* give birth to a demon come the final fadeout!) are the ostensible leads who, taking their cue from *Demons*, head for the roof to survive. Lots of pulsating veins in this one, as well as blood and gore dripping from ceilings and through plumbing fixtures, plus a fairly wild demon versus body-builder melee in the complex's parking garage—but otherwise, the Argento/Bava team seems to have run out of steam. A disjointed and disappointing sequel—even Rosario Prestopino's retread FX fail to score strongly.

Deranged

American-International, 1974; Color; 82 minutes
Directors: Jeff Gillen, Alan Ormsby
Producer: Tom Karr
Writers: Jeff Gillen, Alan Ormsby
With: Roberts Blossom, Cosette Lee, Robert Wagner, Brian Sneage

The exploits of everybody's favorite cannibal-killer of the fifties, Wisconsin's own late but unlamented Ed Gein (pronounced *Geen*), have almost become a mini cottage industry for filmmakers. Ed's exploits (he murdered several women, ate parts of their bodies, and wore their skins around his farmhouse) have formed the basis for *Psycho*, *The Texas Chainsaw Massacre*, and *Three on a Meathook*. The Gillen/Ormsby entry (with makeup effects by Tom Savini) is probably the most clinical and closest to the truth—though Ed's name is changed to Ezra Cobb. It matches the macabre humor of the others, though—especially the scene where Cobb has his mummified victims keep his mummified mommy company at dinner.

Desperate Living

New Line Cinema, 1977; Color; 90 minutes
Director: John Waters
Producer: John Waters
Writer: John Waters
With: Liz Renay, Mink Stole, Susan Lowe, Edith Massey, Mary Vivian Pearce, Jean Hill

Released from a mental hospital, socialite Mink Stole later runs off with her 400-pound maid (Hill) when the maid kills Mink's husband by sitting on him and squashing him to death. The pair then holes up in a town called Mortville, which is populated by criminals and run by an Idi Amin-worshiping fat lady (Massey).

Typical John Waters fare—which is to say atypical of the work of almost any other director.

The Devil's Rain

Bryanston Pictures, 1975; Color; 85 minutes
Director: Robert Fuest
Producers: James V. Cullen, Michael S. Glick
Writers: Gabe Essoe, James Ashton, Gerald Hopman
With: Ernest Borgnine, Eddie Albert, Ida Lupino, William Shatner, Keenan Wynn

Satanism and witchcraft flourish in a dusty southwestern town (actually Mexico), which is also the gateway to Hell. Hero Shatner tries to abscond with the devil's guest register. In the end, the title rain turns all the satanists into something resembling either (1) road accidents or (2) melting pizzas. Look for John Travolta in a small role.

The Devil's Wedding Night

Dimension Pictures, 1973; Color; 85 minutes
Director: Paul Solvay
Producer: Ralph Zucker
Writers: Ralph Zucker, Alan M. Harris
With: Mark Damon, Sara Bay

An archaeologist discovers a mysterious ring that has the power to draw young girls to the foreboding Transylvania castle near which it was found. The ring, it turns out, belongs to that queen vampire, Countess Elizabeth Bathory (Bay), who enjoys bathing in virgins' blood. Ample splatter. Ample skin. What more could one ask?

The Devil Wears Clodhoppers

See This Stuff'll Kill Ya!

Dr. Butcher, M.D.

Aquarius Releasing, Inc., 1981; Color; 80 minutes
Director: Frank Martin
Producer: Terry Levine
Writer: Frank Martin
With: Ian McCulloch, Alexandra Cole, Donald O'Brian, Sherry Buchanan

Moreau-style jungle doctor performs backwoods brain surgery on still-conscious victims, stifling their screams by severing their vocal chords prior to each operation. But wait, that's not all; there are also cannibals running amok, gobbling up the tourists. *Tourists?* The M.D. stands for "medical deviate." As graphic as they come. Looks like a film by Lucio Fulci, but director Frank Martin is actually Francesco Martino.

Dr. Gore

Majestic International Pictures, 1972; Color; 90 minutes
Director: J. G. "Pat" Patterson
Producer: J. G. "Pat" Patterson
Writer: J. G. Patterson, Jr.
With: J. G. Patterson, Jenny Driggers, Roy Mehaffey, Linda Faile, Jan Benfield, Jeannine Aber, Candy Furr, Vickie O'Neal

This twisted takeoff on *Bride of Frankenstein* is the only solo effort by a veteran of several Herschell Gordon Lewis films. Dr. Don Brandon (Patterson) with the help of his hunchbacked assistant (Mehaffey) murders and dismembers five young women to bring his dead wife, Anitra (Driggers), back to life as the perfect woman. There are gobs of Lewis-style gore as limbs are severed and eyeballs are cut out. We're also treated to some pretty good mad lab scenes considering the obviously low budget. The doctor finally succeeds in creating his own personal Frankenstein, a perfect woman who is hot to trot with any man, even the hunchback. When the doctor discovers their dalliance, he splits the hunchback's hump with an axe and dumps his body in an acid vat. The film ends with Dr. Don cooling his heels in jail, while his creation catches a ride out of town with a passing motorist. A wandering plot that sometimes gets lost and inane dialogue (Example: "Be sure to wear your jacket, so they won't know you're a hunchback.") put this picture in Ed Wood, Jr., territory as well as Lewis land. So bad it's good, if you're in the right mood.—D. K.

Dr. Jekyll and Mr. Blood

See The Man with Two Heads

Dr. Jekyll's Dungeon of Death

Rochelle Films, 1979; Color; 91 minutes
Director: James Wood
Producer: James Wood
Writer: James Mathers
With: James Mathers

Ultra low-budget monster-in-the-basement (the film looks like it was shot in one, too) flick about the grandson of you know who performing his ancestor's famous experiment on unsuspecting victims who come his way.

Dolls

Empire Pictures, 1987; Color; 77 minutes
Director: Stuart Gordon
Producer: Brian Yuzna
Writer: Ed Naha
With: Stephen Lee, Guy Rolfe, Hilary Mason, Carrie Lorraine, Ian Patrick Williams

Stuart Gordon's third film is a little gem of homage to James Whale's *The Old Dark House,* combined with fascinating elements of the old Warner Brothers cartoons such as *Toy Town Tonight,* in which toys come to life, and a bit of *Hansel and Gretel* thrown in for good measure. Unfortunately, this unlikely combination of elements seems to have escaped most critics, who happily trashed the film as nothing more than a sillier than usual splatter film, without regard for its effective atmosphere and unbridled imagination. Guy Rolfe (famous to horror aficionados from William Castle's *Mr. Sardonicus,* and, because of which, he was probably cast here) is wonderful as the somewhat less campy Ernest Thesiger character from *The Old Dark House;* and Stephen Lee is a refreshing change-of-pace hero in a role obviously patterned on Charles Laughton's from the same film. The story is simple enough—travelers dropping in at Guy Rolfe and Hilary Mason's mysterious house because of a bad storm, where they are, in essence, judged—by Rolfe, Mason, and their vast array of occasionally murderous dolls—as good or evil by whether or not they are children at heart. Ed Naha's script is unfailingly bright (sometimes hilarious) and insightful, and Gordon's direction gets the most out of it. The doll effects may sound foolish, but they are splendidly achieved and presented with such an admirably straight face that they succeed on nearly every level, generating a surprising amount of suspense and unflinchingly bloody violence. Gordon proves once again that his is a very special talent, but one that, alas, is like caviar and Cordon Rouge to an audience wanting Big Macs and Coca-Cola.—K. H.

The Doll Squad

Gemini, 1973; Color; 101 minutes
Director: Ted V. Mikels
Producer: Ted V. Mikels
Writers: Jack Richesin, Pamela Eddy,
    Ted V. Mikels
With: Francine York, Michael Ansara,
    Anthony Eisley, Lisa Todd, Tura
    Satana, Jean London

Low-octane "thriller" (it was rated PG!)
about an all-girl army of assassins called
"The Doll Squad" who are called into action by CIA chief Anthony Eisley (whose
career seems to have taken a precipitous
nosedive following his stint on the fifties
TV detective show, "Hawaiian Eye") to
put an end to the nefarious career of a
renegade CIA operative (Ansara) who's
been monkeying with the U.S. space pro-
gram and is out to enslave the world. As
has often been noted, Mikels's film pre-
dates the hit TV series "Charley's Angels,"
which bears more than a passing resemblance to *The Doll Squad* (Doll Squad
leader York is even named Sabrina, the
leader of the Angels)—except that the individual episodes of the TV show were
slicker and shorter. Doll Squad member
Satana starred in Russ Meyer's bloodier,
sexier, and far more exciting *Faster, Pus-
sycat! Kill! Kill!* It is aka *Hustler Squad.*

Don't Answer the Phone

Crown International Pictures, 1980;
    Color; 95 minutes
Director: Robert Hammer
Producer: Robert Hammer
Writers: Robert Hammer, Michael
    Castle
With: James Westmoreland, Flo
    Gerrish, Nicholas Worth, Ben
    Frank, Pamela Bryant

Physical-fitness enthusiast and nutso
strangler Worth prowls the hills of Hollywood in search of victims (there is no
shortage), then calls into a local radio talk
show to discuss his hang-ups with the
female psychiatrist host. Based on the
novel *Nightline* by Michael Curtis, a fic-
tionalized account of the Los Angeles
Hillside Strangler case. A cheap but gritty
and tough-minded shocker whose only
drawback in credibility is that Worth is so
obviously wacko, it's hard to believe that
no one suspects him of being the killer.
But then again, maybe that's the film's point.
It is aka *The Hollywood Strangler.*

Don't Go in the House

Film Ventures, 1980; Color; 82
    minutes
Director: James Ellison
Producer: Ellen Hammill
Writers: Ellen Hammill, James Ellison,
    Joseph Masefield
With: Dan Grimaldi, Robert Osth,
    Ruth Dardick

Tormented by his mom, a young boy gets
his revenge by murdering her and then
cremating her body, an act that drives
him psycho but also instills him with an
ambition: to become an incinerator
worker. He does this, then lures unsuspecting young women to his place of business so that he can pretend they're mom
and burn them up all over again. In the
end, he gets plenty burned up himself
when he imagines all these old flames
coming back to life to revenge themselves
on him. Not exactly a hot one.

Don't Look in the Basement

Hallmark Releasing, 1973; Color; 95
    minutes
Director: S. F. Brownrigg
Producer: S. F. Brownrigg
Writer: Tim Pope

With: William McGee, Annie MacAdams, Rosie Holotik, Gene Ross, Jesse Lee Fulton

Inmates of a Florida asylum for criminally bad filmmakers plot to take over the studio—er, nuthouse—in this criminally bad and bloody shocker from the distributors of *Last House on the Left* (1972).

Don't Open the Window

See Breakfast at the Manchester Morgue

Dracula Is Dead and Well and Living in London

See The Satanic Rites of Dracula

Dracula's Dog

Crown International Pictures, 1977; Color; 88 minutes
Director: Albert Band
Producers: Charles Band, Frank Ray Perilli
Writer: Frank Ray Perilli
With: Michael Pataki, Jan Shutan, Libbie Chase, Reggie Nalder, Jose Ferrer

An explosion uncovers the tomb of one of Dracula's servants (Nalder), along with the dead count's vampire dog Zoltan. Together, they head for America where the last of Dracula's relatives (Pataki) lives. There, they draw more victims into their late and lamented master's cult. Nalder does the planning while Zoltan, taking his cue from the Hound of the Baskervilles, does most of the dirty work. Albert Band directed the miniclassic (but nonsplatter) *Face of Fire* (1959) based on Stephen Crane's novella, *The Monster*. Check that out instead and skip this one.

Dracula's Last Rites

Cannon Films, 1980; Color; 88 minutes
Director: Dominic Paris
Producer: Kelly Van Horn
Writer: Dominic Paris
With: Patricia Lee Hammond, Gerald Fielding, Victor Jorge, Mimi Weddell

Story of a village of vampires lorded over by a mortician named Lucard—that's Dracula spelled backward minus the letter *a*—who perpetuates their race by draining the blood of traffic-accident victims (planned accidents, that is) who wind up on his slab. Routine vampire story shot in New York, the Empire (not Vampire) State. It is aka *Last Rites*.

The Dream Master

See A Nightmare on Elm Street Part 4

The Dream Warriors

See A Nightmare on Elm Street Part 3

Dressed to Kill

Filmways, 1980; Color; 105 minutes
Director: Brian De Palma
Producer: George Litto
Writer: Brian De Palma
With: Michael Caine, Angie Dickinson, Nancy Allen, Keith Gordon

Caine is a New York City psychiatrist whose chief clients include a housewife (Dickinson) with sexual problems and a transsexual named Bobbi, who is about to take the "big step" but then panics with murder on his/her mind. The film is so derivative that it cannibalizes its structure (and some dialogue) from *Psycho* (1960) and lifts whole scenes from that film as

well as Hitchcock's *Vertigo* (1958) and *Rear Window* (1954). Effective, but it leaves you with the feeling that you've been ripped off by a real pro.

Driller Killer

Rochelle Films, 1979; Color; 90 minutes
Director: Abel Ferrara
Producer: Rochelle Weisberg
Writer: Nicholas St. John
With: Jimmy Laine (Ferrara), Carolyn Marz, Baybi Day, Tony Coca-Cola and The Roosters

First feature by New York University grads Ferrara and St. John about a frustrated artist who goes bonkers and starts slaughtering people with a carpenter's drill. Kinetic sleaze.

Drive-in Massacre

New American Films, 1976; Color; 78 minutes
Director: Stuart Segall
Producer: Stuart Segall
Writers: John Goff, Buck Flower
With: Jake Barnes, Adam Lawrence, Douglas Gudbye

A restless crowd and a bad double feature lead to two brutal killings at a drive-in where a dollar a carload proves to be no bargain. Best to see at a drive-in, if you can find one that still shows movies and hasn't been turned into a parking lot or an outdoor church.

Eaten Alive

New World Pictures, Mars Production Corp., 1976; Color; 89 minutes
Director: Tobe Hooper
Producers: Mardi Rustam, Alvin L. Fast
Writers: Mardi Rustam, Alvin L. Fast, Kim Henkel, Tobe Hooper
With: Neville Brand, Mel Ferrer, Marilyn Burns, Carolyn Jones, William Finley

The main body of critics, still foaming at the mouth over the Museum of Modern Art's addition of *The Texas Chainsaw Masscare* to its permanent collection, helped bury Hooper's follow-up film before it was even released, reporting that the new film was an unscary, tasteless (of course) disaster, that Hooper had proved himself an inept amateur, etc. As a result, Hooper's bizarre, utterly stylized redneckish variation on *The Old Dark House–Psycho* school of horror has all but been overlooked. Too bad, because the film—despite some badly meandering stretches whenever it moves away from Neville Brand's "old dark motel"—is probably the best cinematic attempt to date to capture the other-worldly madness of the death of the amateur-night-in-Dixie brand of the American Dream. Brand's sleazy motel, complete with tatty roadside animal attractions (most of which, except his giant man-eating alligator—or crocodile—are dead or dying), is a worthy southern-fried successor to the Bates Motel. Unlike those modern maestros of hayseed tomfoolery, the Coen Brothers, Hooper neither romanticizes nor celebrates ignorance, but savages its narrow-minded, macho meanness with the incisiveness of a kind of splatter film William Faulkner. One need only see the outrageous moment where Brand, in a righteous fury, shoots himself in the leg (a wooden leg, it turns out) and gulps down the good ol' boy's cure-all, a BC powder, to set himself to rights, to realize that Hooper knows of what he speaks. By no means a great film, *Eaten Alive* is nonetheless a more accomplished work than its obscurity suggests. It is aka *Death Trap, Horror Hotel Massacre,* and *Starlight Slaughters.* —K. H.

Eaten Alive

Distributor unknown, 1980; Color; 90
  minutes
Director: Umberto Lenzi
Producer: Antonio Crescenzi
Writer: Federico Zanni
With: Ivan Rassimov, Janet Agren,
  Robert Kerman, Paola Senatore

Agren and Kerman head for South America in search of Agren's missing sister when they get a hot tip as to her whereabouts. The clue is a bizarre film left behind by a south-of-the-border hitman who gets rubbed out on the streets of New York, courtesy of a truck. The hitman's film shows scenes of sadistic torture and cannibalism and features a cameo by long-lost sis. (Speaking of cameos, yes, that *is* Mel Ferrer in a small role.) Rassimov plays a Jim Jones figure who runs the cannibal cult and forces suicide upon his followers. Brutal and unpleasant entry in the Italian cannibal movie subgenre; made by the director of the equally unpleasant *Make Them Die Slowly.*

The Ecology of a Crime

See Twitch of the Death Nerve

The Eerie Midnight Horror Show

21st Century Pictures, 1974; Color;
  87 minutes
Director: Mario Gariazzo
Producer: Juston Reed
Writer: Ambrogio Molteni
With: Stella Carnacina, Chris Awram,
  Lucretia Love, Gabriele Tinti

Post-*Exorcist* conglomeration of obsession/possession themes coupled with religious metaphors about Satan, Barabbas, and other bad and good guys from the Bible—plus a weak story about a statue that hornily comes to life. It is aka *The Tormented.*

Enemy Territory

Empire Pictures, 1987; Color; 89
  minutes
Director: Peter Manoogian
Producers: Cynthia DePaula, Tim
  Kincaid
Writers: Stuart Kaminsky, Bobby
  Liddell
With: Gary Frank, Ray Parker, Jr.,
  Jan-Michael Vincent, Frances
  Foster

Promised a hefty commission, white insurance man Frank takes his life in his hands by going into a dangerous ghetto neighborhood near dark to get a $100,000 policy signed. The holder, a retired teacher, lives in a run-down apartment complex that's been turned into a nocturnal combat zone by a vicious all-black youth gang called the Vampires. Frank incurs the gang's wrath (no difficult task). The Vampires declare war on the "white ghost" and anyone who tries to help him—a small group that includes the teacher, her granddaughter, a telephone repairman, and a crippled Vietnam vet who has turned his apartment into a bunker, complete with spear-throwing wheelchair and enough ordnance to take out a small army. The blood flows thick and fast as Frank and the repairman use knives, guns, and a baseball bat to fend off the gang—whose leader is called the Count and whose second in command is appropriately nicknamed "Psycho."

The Entity

Embassy Pictures, 1983; Color; 125
  minutes
Director: Sidney J. Furie
Producer: Harold Schneider

Writer: Frank de Felitta
With: Barbara Hershey, David
Lablosa, Jacqueline Brooks, Ron
Silver

Hershey gives a convincing performance
as a put-upon middle-class divorcée and
mother whose life is further complicated
when an unseen supernatural presence
enters her bedroom and rapes her. She
moves, but the malevolent ectoplasmic
sex fiend follows her and rapes her again
and again. Psychologists are in a quan-
dary as to what to do—is she simply sexually frustrated, or what? Not on your life.
Enter a team of open-mouthed parapsy-
chologists who install Hershey and a rep-
lica of her apartment in the university lab
in the hopes of capturing the demon on-
camera, freezing it, and destroying it.
Purportedly, writer de Felitta, who adapted
from his own best-selling novel, based this
pyrotechnical display of sound, fury, and
demon rape on a true case. Its rambling
length and repetitive graphic depictions
of spectral rape tend to diminish the film's
intensity and effectiveness; it might have
been better if it had been half as long.

Eraserhead

A Libra Films Release, 1978; B&W;
90 minutes
Director: David Lynch
Producer: David Lynch
Writer: David Lynch
With: Jack Nance, Charlotte Stewart,
Jeanne Bates, Laurel Near

Appropriately disgusting but also down-
beat, dreamlike (or *nightmarelike* if you
prefer) tale of a fishlike monster baby
whose birth turns its parents' lives upside
down (not that their lives were all that
right side up in the first place). The film
spins wildly out of control with allegor-
ical/symbolic/nonsensical fantasy images
of grotesque doings. Made by the cheer-

less David Lynch (with partial backing from
the American Film Institute), who went
on to ruin *The Elephant Man* (1980).

Eternal Evil

Distributor unknown, 1988; Color; 85
minutes
Director: George Mihalka
Producer: Pieter Kroonenburg
Writer: Robert Geoffrin
With: Winston Rekert, Karen Black,
John Novak, Patty Talbot

Canadian-made police procedural/super-
natural opus shot in 1985 by *My Bloody
Valentine* director Mihalka and released
on video three years later, following limited theatrical distribution. TV-commercial
producer Rekert's hobby is the study of
out-of-body experiences, or astral projec-
tion. Experiments on himself enable him
to "see" several murders being carried
out by an unknown serial killer. Rekert's
knowledge of the killings puts him under
suspicion. In typical Hitchcock tradition,
he, therefore, must set out on his own to
prove his innocence and bring the real
perpetrator to justice. Mihalka goes a bit
overboard with the simulated astral pro-
jection "bird's-eye view" shots.

The Evil Dead

Renaissance Pictures, 1983; Color; 86
minutes
Director: Sam Raimi
Producer: Robert G. Tapert
Writer: Sam Raimi
With: Bruce Campbell, Ellen
Sandweiss, Hal Delrich, Betsy
Baker, Sarah York

Although *The Evil Dead* has since been
eclipsed by Raimi's far more accomplished sequel/rehash, *The Evil Dead II*,
the original film has a screwy cheesiness
that is hard to resist. The plot is your
average "kids on an outing in the woods

encounter something nasty" routine, but the decidedly unsociable evil spirits of *The Evil Dead* were a welcome change from the run of brain-dead slashers and malevolent hillbillies so popular at the time, especially since the spirits here seem to belong to Larry, Moe, and Curly's wicked twins. One by one, the young cast are assaulted and/or taken over by the demons (unleashed by their foolhardy playing of a tape recording designed for the purpose, which was left by the previous tenant-victim) in a variety of tasteless and comic ways. Raimi's major accomplishment here lies in his uncanny ability to build the film to a fever pitch (however ludicrously) and then take it further and further with ever more elaborate gore effects (by Bart Pierce and Tom Sullivan) and strikingly vertiginous camera work (by Tim Philo). More clever than good, *The Evil Dead* succeeds on sheer energy. Clips from it appear on a TV screen in Wes Craven's *A Nightmare on Elm Street*.—K. H.

The Evil Dead II

Renaissance Pictures, 1987; Color; 85 minutes
Director: Sam Raimi
Producers: Robert G. Tapart, Bruce Campbell
Writers: Sam Raimi, Scott Spiegel
With: Bruce Campbell, Sarah Berry, Dan Hicks, Kassie Wesley, Theodore Raimi

Slapstick comes to splatter with Sam Raimi's engaging, often hysterically funny "bad taste" sequel to his own *The Evil Dead*. Rather than pick up the story line from the original, this backtracks and provides us with a miniature version (with a vastly reduced cast) of it at breakneck speed. Once again, the misguided professor's conveniently tape-recorded incantations from the vaguely Lovecraftian *Necro-*

nomicon Di Morti are foolishly played back, and once again the "wood demon" and his friends run riot in a nonstop series of ever-more ghastly possessions, body-hurtlings, blood-spewings, chain-sawings, and assorted demonic mischief. This round, Raimi has an obviously bigger budget and uses it to produce some genuinely brilliant images and outstanding vertiginous camera acrobatics in the midst of homages to everybody from his friends the Coen Brothers to the Three Stooges and *The Wizard of Oz* (and you thought Dorothy ran afoul of some unpleasant trees!). Despite a telegraphed ending and a rather disappointing materialized "wood demon," the film is too inventive and cheerfully nasty to carp—a treat for splatter connoisseurs.—K. H.

The Exorcist

Warner Brothers, 1973; Color; 121 minutes
Director: William Friedkin
Producer: William Peter Blatty
Writer: William Peter Blatty
With: Ellen Burstyn, Jason Miller, Linda Blair, Max Von Sydow, Lee J. Cobb

A pyrotechnical wonder designed to pulverize audiences into a single gagging mass. Virginal Blair is possessed by the devil and becomes a foul-minded, foul-mouthed, vomit-spewing little monster. Miller and Von Sydow are the exorcists who are called in to drive the demon out. Dick Smith's still-astonishing makeup and prosthetic effects are the real stars. The film does not wear well, however, because once one becomes inured to the shocks, the plot and characters leave little else to chew on. No question though, it's one of the most influential splatter movies ever made. Followed in 1977 by the nonsplattery *Exorcist II—The Heretic,* an absurd sequel that left audiences' heads spinning the way Blair's did in the first film.

The Exterminator

Avco Embassy, 1980; Color; 101
  minutes
Director: James Glickenhaus
Producer: Mark Buntzman
Writer: James Glickenhaus
With: Robert Ginty, Christopher
  George, Samantha Eggar, Steve
  James

Out-of-work Vietnam vet Ginty finds his
true calling when a friend is nearly beaten
to death by a gang of New York City street
thugs. Taking his cue from Charles Bronson (Bernard Goetz hadn't arrived on the
scene yet), he goes on a revenge spree,
rubbing out the culprits and other un-
savories with his trademark weapon, a
blowtorch. George is the cop who must
bring Ginty to justice even though he sort
of admires the guy for helping to rid
the streets of scumballs. Eggar, a good
actress who always seems to be cast in
irrelevant, thankless roles, is cast in
yet another irrelevent, thankless role as
George's classy-looking but long-suffering
girlfriend. Followed in 1984 by a sequel,
Exterminator II, directed by producer
Buntzman.

Eyes of a Stranger

Warner Brothers, 1980; Color; 85
  minutes
Director: Ken Wiederhorn
Producer: Ronald Zerra
Writers: Mark Johnson, Eric L. Bloom
With: Lauren Tewes, John Disanti,
  Peter Durge, Jennifer Jason Leigh

TV reporter Tewes (of TV's "Love Boat"
fame) discovers that the psychotic killer
whose escapades she's been headlining
each night lives in the apartment across
the way from her. The question is: how
to prove it so that the police will be convinced? She decides to smoke him out on
her own. Occasionally tense tale laced with

graphic gore (courtesy of Tom Savini, most
of whose ultraviolent effects Warner
Brothers left on the cutting-room floor
to avoid an X rating), weakened by some
wild implausibilities toward the end.

Eyes of Fire

Elysian Pictures, 1984; Color; 90
  minutes
Director: Avery Crounse
Producer: Philip J. Spinelli
Writer: Avery Crounse
With: Dennis Lipscomb, Guy Boyd,
  Rebecca Stanley, Sally Klein

An eerie, occasionally haunting and beautifully photographed story about . . . well,
that's just the trouble; the script is such
a jumbled mishmash that I'm not sure
what the story's about. In flashback, a girl
tells a Colonial officer (the film takes place
in eighteenth-century America) about
being trapped, along with some other set-
tlers, in a mysterious valley populated
by tree spirits and other supernatural
creatures. She and two small children
manage to escape thanks to help from
another member of their group, a girl
named Leah, who turns out to have supernatural powers. Good makeup FX by
Annie Maniscalco—though there are a few
too many scenes of tree and mud spirits
spitting up green slime.

The Eyes of Laura Mars

Columbia Pictures, 1978; Color; 103
  minutes
Director: Irvin Kershner
Producer: Jon Peters
Writers: John Carpenter, David Zelag
  Goodman
With: Faye Dunaway, Tommy Lee
  Jones, Brad Dourif, Raul Julia,
  René Auberjonois

Fashion photographer Dunaway, who
chicly combines scenes of eroticism with

violence in her *Vogue* spreads, gets a taste of the real thing when she starts "seeing" in her mind's eye the violent mutilation murders of various women. Able to predict the murders but not identify the killer (naturally!), she seeks solace in the arms of the detective (Jones) assigned to the case, but she gets a big surprise instead. Designed as a high-class thriller, this is really a low-class exploitation film full of sleazy noncharacters and contrived situations, including an ending that's downright unbelievable. Carpenter wrote the original story (though he disavows what was done to it) and Jack Harris (*The Blob* [1958]) executive produced. Dunaway should have shot her cameraman; she looks positively anemic throughout.

Fade to Black

Compass International Pictures, 1980; Color; 100 minutes
Director: Vernon Zimmerman
Producers: George Braunstein, Roy Hamady
Writer: Vernon Zimmerman
With: Dennis Christopher, Linda Kerridge, Tim Thomerson, Morgan Paull, Marya Small

Deranged film fan Christopher goes over the edge and starts killing folks who've victimized him, modeling his murders after scenes from his favorite movies. A promising idea insufficiently realized. Kerridge is probably the definitive Marilyn Monroe look-alike.

Faster, Pussycat! Kill! Kill!

Russ Meyer Associates, 1966; B&W; 83 minutes
Director: Russ Meyer
Producer: Russ Meyer
Writer: Jack Moran

With: Tura Satana, Haji, Lori Williams, Susan Bernard, Stuart Lancaster

A trio of buxom "good-time girls" led by the psychotic Satana goes on a rampage in the desert, kidnapping a girl and killing her boyfriend—actually, they break his back and leave him to the buzzards. After that, they hide out with a crippled man and his two sons, who have a small fortune in cash stashed away. Determined to get at the loot, the pussycats try to seduce the men into revealing its whereabouts. When that fails, Satana grinds the old man to a pulp under the wheels of a car. The other boys (one of whom is named Vegetable, giving you a fair idea of his mental agility) turn on the pussycats and some knifings, karate kicks, and other mayhem ensue—until Satana is run over by a truck driven by the girl she kidnapped. Writer Moran, a former actor, had a small role in William Wyler's *The Best Years of Our Lives*. Music by the Bostweeds. A Russ Meyer classic!

Fatal Pulse

Great Entertainment Group, 1987; Color; 90 minutes
Director: Anthony J. Christopher
Producer: Anthony J. Christopher
Writer: James Hundhausen
With: Michelle McCormick, Ken Roberts, Joe Phelan, Alex Courtney

Yet another "mad slasher loose on campus" flick; this time he's carving his way through the AOK sorority—if you can believe *that* name! There are plenty of suspects, all with a capital *S*—a disturbed, moronic Vietnam vet, a sniveling chemistry professor with terminal jitters, an unlucky-in-love slob of a student, the boyfriend of one of the victims, and another student who's hooked on drugs and "Petticoat Junction." The police are no help because they don't bother questioning anyone. They're also too incompetent to find the lead suspect even though no one else seems to have the slightest difficulty finding him. The gore murders—via electrocution, drowning, and knife—are standard stuff. For some reason, however, the slasher is compelled to bare his victims' breasts before doing them in; perhaps he was just being egged on by a voyeuristic director. A who-cares whodunit that moves so slowly you'll be asleep long before the "surprise finish."

Fear No Evil

Avco Embassy Pictures, 1981; Color; 99 minutes
Director: Frank La Loggia
Producers: Frank and Charles M. La Loggia
Writer: Frank La Loggia
With: Stefan Arngrim, Elizabeth Hoffman, Kathleen Rowe McAllen, Frank Birney

High school student Arngrim is the incarnation of the devil; when his teachers and fellow students pick on him, he kills them. Turns out that another classmate (McAllen) and an old woman (Hoffman) are incarnations of the archangels Gabrielle and Mikhail, whose metaphysical mission is to overthrow the Great Beast. The final battle takes place on a remote island with the dead rising from their graves to do the devil's bidding. La Loggia's debut feature, made in Rochester, New York, strives for significance, but like *The Omen* and many other devil-child movies, it winds up simply wallowing in blood, gore, and nudity. Many of these elements—plus the film's overbearingly intrusive and jarring use of then current rock 'n' roll hits—weren't Frank's idea, however; they were imposed on him by Embassy, who felt the film's loftier aims

alone wouldn't grab the teens. *Blood Simple*'s Joel Coen worked on the editing.

The Female Butcher

Distributor unknown, 1972; Color; 85 minutes
Director: Jorge Grau
Producer: Jose Maria Gonzalez Sinde
Writers: Juan Tebar, Sandro Continenza
With: Ewa Aulin, Lucia Bose, Espartaco Santoni, Franca Grey

"Documented in the pages of the Guinness Book of World Records," this is the story of a medieval noblewoman who reputedly slaughtered over 600 young girls and bathed in their blood to keep her complexion creamy smooth and wrinkle-free. In other words, it's the familiar story of history's favorite vampire countess, Elizabeth Bathory (*Countess Dracula*, et al.), here played by Bose—though most of the actual murders are carried out by her undead husband (Santoni). The film plays fast and loose with the facts, but there are enough decapitations and throat slashings to take your mind off the inaccuracies. Made in Spain. It is aka *Legend of Blood Castle*.

Female Trouble

New Line Cinema, 1974; Color; 92 minutes
Director: John Waters
Producer: John Waters
Writer: John Waters
With: Divine, David Lochary, Mary Vivian Pearce, Mink Stole, Edith Massey

Dawn Davenport (Divine) pursues her life of crime as if it was a form of show business, determined to win a cherished Oscar for best performance by a mass murderer in an electric chair. A film in amusing bad taste from the unhinged director of *Pink Flamingos* (1972).

The Final Chapter

See Friday the 13th—The Final Chapter

The Final Conflict

Twentieth Century-Fox, 1981; Color;
  108 minutes
Director: Graham Baker
Producer: Harvey Bernhard
Writer: Andrew Birkin
With: Sam Neill, Rossano Brazzi, Don
  Gordon, Lisa Harrow

After murdering dozens of innocent people in his two previous film escapades, *The Omen* (1976) and *Damien—Omen II* (1978), the son of the devil (Neill) is at last given his comeuppance. One expects Armageddon at the very least, but, alas, Damien goes out with a whimper instead. Producer Bernhard had planned yet another opus in the series, *Armageddon 2000,* but it was shelved when it became clear from the box-office receipts for this film that audiences had had enough.

The Final Terror

Distributor unknown, 1981; Color; 82
  minutes
Director: Andrew Davis
Producer: Joe Roth
Writers: Jon George, Neill Hicks,
  Ronald Schusett
With: Rachel Ward, Darryl Hannah,
  John Friedrich, Adrian Zmed

Routine *Friday the 13th/Deliverance* vacationers-in-peril movie with minimal gore—due, perhaps, to the film's less than minimal budget. The vacationers this time around are a group of young forest rangers and their sweethearts out to do some camping and canoeing. Instead, they run afoul of a lunatic backwoodsman and his even more lunatic mom (who gave birth to her benighted son after being raped). Led by Friedrich, a former Vietnam vet (naturally!), the vacationers struggle to make it out of the woods alive as mad mom launches her campaign of terror. To add to the tedium, most of them do survive. Obviously the folks who made this movie didn't realize that in madslasher flicks it's the body count that counts. It is aka *Campsite Massacre.*

Flavia Priestess of Violence

Worldwide Entertainment Corp.,
  1976; Color; 95 minutes
Director: Gianfranco Mingozzi
Producer: Gianfranco Mingozzi
Writers: Gianfranco Mingozzi,
  Raniero di Giovanbattista, Sergio
  Tau, Francesca Vieltri, Fabrizio
  Onofri, Bruno de Geronimo
With: Florinda Bolkan, Anthony
  Corlan, Maria Casares

After being unjustly imprisoned in a nunnery, Flavia (Bolkan) revolts against the sexist and repressive political climate into which she's been born (fifteenth-century Italy) and escapes to join an invading army intent on conquering her homeland. Victimized and brutalized both within the nunnery's walls and without, she becomes a vengeful she-devil, beheading and castrating all her male enemies. Her zeal eventually proves too much even for her compatriots, who, at the film's gruesome conclusion, proceed to skin her alive. With six screenwriters at work inventing "creative deaths," *Flavia* really piles on the splatter. It is aka *The Rebel Nun.*

Flesh and Blood

Orion Pictures, 1985; Color; 126
  minutes
Director: Paul Verhoeven

Producer: Gys Versluys
Writers: Paul Verhoeven, Gerard
Soetman
With: Rutger Hauer, Jennifer Jason
Leigh, Tom Burlinson, Jack
Thompson, Ronald Lacey

Medieval bloodbath about a marauding band of cutthroats led by Hauer who kidnap Princess Leigh (no, not Leia) on her way to be married to Prince Burlinson. As it's a marriage of convenience, Burlinson is not in love with the girl, but after she's kidnapped, her absence apparently makes his heart grow fonder and he goes after her with a band of his own warriors. The final showdown takes place at an old castle, where limbs and other body parts soon proliferate. The twist is that sultry, diminutive Leigh (who reveals most of the film's flesh when she is raped by practically everybody) finally falls for Hauer, too. She's a survivor, though, and plays both suitors against each other. Burlinson wins, but Hauer escapes with his life (he gets even with her, though, in *The Hitcher*). Well-acted and drenched in atmosphere (as well as blood), the film, strangely, isn't very involving or exciting. Verhoeven was apparently warming himself up for *Robocop*.

The Flesh and Blood Show

Entertainment Ventures, 1973; Color;
97 minutes
Director: Pete Walker
Producer: Pete Walker
Writer: Alfred Shaughnessy
With: Jenny Hanley, Ray Brooks, Luan
Peters, Patrick Barr, Robin
Askwith, Judy Matheson

A group of actors is called to audition for a Grand Guignol stage production, but it's all a ruse perpetrated by a madman who plans to kill the troupe as an act of revenge against *all* actors. Shot partially

in 3-D. Walker reigned for a time as Britain's premier splatter director, but his best film is the nonsplatter *House of the Long Shadows* (1983), an amusing and affectionate tribute to the "old dark house" movies of the twenties and thirties and the Hammer gothics of the fifties and sixties.

The Flesh Eaters

Distributor unknown, 1964; B&W; 88
minutes
Director: Jack Curtis
Producers: Jack Curtis, Terry Curtis,
Arnold Drake
Writer: Arnold Drake
With: Martin Kosleck, Rita Morley,
Byron Sanders, Ray Tudor

A diverse group of unfortunates is shipwrecked on an island inhabited by everybody's favorite movie Goebbels, Martin Kosleck, a mad scientist who is experimenting with flesh-eating fish. Early post-*Blood Feast* splatter independent is not as gory as the Lewis film, but it has its flesh-munching moments (courtesy of the fish).

Flesh Feast

Viking International Pictures, 1970;
Color; 72 minutes
Director: B. (Brad) F. Grinter
Producers: Veronica Lake, B. F.
Grinter
Writer: Thomas Casey
With: Veronica Lake, Phil Philbin,
Heather Hughes, Chris Martell

Former Hollywood glamour queen Lake's last screen appearance. She plays a scientist (and ex-inmate of a mental asylum) who's discovered a technique for restoring youth to aged flesh. The technique involves maggots, which she uses to tear away the old wrinkled flesh, thus paving the way for the new stuff. When, courtesy of some helpful neo-Nazis, she finally gets the chance to try her revolutionary technique out on a needy subject, she finds the patient to be none other than Adolf Hitler! Even she won't go that far to get a write-up in the *New England Journal of Medicine*, and so, suffering a crisis of conscience, she lets the maggots make a hot lunch of Der Führer instead. Martell had a featured role in H. G. Lewis's *The Gruesome Twosome*.

Flesh for Frankenstein

See Andy Warhol's Frankenstein

The Fly

Twentieth Century-Fox, 1986; Color; 96 minutes
Director: David Cronenberg
Producer: Stuart Cornfield
Writers: Charles Edward Pogue, David Cronenberg
With: Jeff Goldblum, Geena Davis, John Getz

Dynamite remake (*rethinking* is probably more apt) of the 1958 Vincent Price howler that owes as much to Franz Kafka as it does to George Langelaan's original story. Goldblum's experiment in teleportation goes awry when a fly gets trapped in his telepod with him, turning the device into a gene splicer. As he slowly and gruesomely succumbs to *fly-dom*, losing all sense of identity and humanity, the film reaches emotional highs not often attained, or even strived for, in most splatter movies. Goldblum is sensational as the luckless scientist and Davis is equally good as his bereft girlfriend. And in a wonderful turnabout, John Getz's "villain" becomes a good guy. Chris Walas won an Oscar for his special effects. Cro-

nenberg's best film to date. (Look for the director's cameo as a gynecologist in a grisly dream sequence.)

The Fog

Avco Embassy, 1980; Color; 91 minutes
Director: John Carpenter
Producer: Debra Hill
Writers: John Carpenter, Debra Hill
With: Hal Holbrook, Janet Leigh, Adrienne Barbeau, Jamie Lee Curtis, John Houseman, Nancy Loomis

A ghost ship whose crew was murdered for the gold on board returns in the fog, the dead crew members seeking vengeance on the descendants of those who killed them. Transparent characters and telegraphed scares, not to mention an ending that seems tacked on for its shock value alone, sink this contemporary ghost story from the director of *Halloween* (1978). Some good effects, though. Director Carpenter appears in a cameo as a church janitor.

Folks at the Red Wolf Inn

Intercontinental, 1972; Color; 83 minutes
Director: Bud Townsend
Producer: Michael Macready
Writer: Allen J. Actor
With: Linda Gillin, John Neilson, Arthur Space, Mary Jackson

A genuine "meat movie" played for laughs. Jackson and '50s SF movie veteran Space are aging cannibals who run the Red Wolf Inn, where the bill of fare is—you guessed it—the guests. Winsome Gillin is next on the menu, but the plot gets complicated when the couple's son (Neilson) falls for the girl—and the girl herself, unwilling to be hung up in the meat locker or have her body parts stored in the fridge, quits playing the defenseless heroine and strikes back. Producer Macready (who plays a cameo role) is the son of late, great movie villain George Macready (*Paths of Glory*, et al.). It is aka *Terror House*.

Forbidden World

See Mutant

Forced Entry

Productions 2, 1981; Color; 88 minutes
Director: Jim Sotos
Producers: Jim Sotos, Henry Scarpelli
Writer: Henry Scarpelli
With: Tanya Roberts, Ron Max, Nancy Allen

The title tells you what kind of violence to expect from this clinker. It's about a stuttering grease monkey who gets enraged, rapes and kills women who are repelled by his cloddishness. In the course of the film, he rapes and kills three women—being impotent, he uses a liquor bottle to help out—but the fourth (Roberts), a housewife with marital problems, finally carves him up. The movie has a somber atmosphere that is made even more somber by the psycho's non-stuttering voice-over diatribes against city filth and whores (reminiscent of De Niro's patter in *Taxi Driver*) and an unbelievably slow pace. To pad out the running time, the murders are shown in slow motion (one of them is shown *twice*) and there are endless shots of people driving around, drinking coffee, taking showers, etc. Nancy Allen is third-billed, but her part as a hitchhike victim lasts about two minutes. A real el cheapo—filmed on location in Staten Island and New Jersey.

Forever Evil

B & S Productions/FrameWork Films, 1987; Color; 107 minutes
Director: Roger Evans
Producers: Jill Clark, Hal Payne
Writer: Freeman Williams
With: Charles Trotter, Howard Jacobsen, Red Mitchell, Tracey Huffman, Kent Johnson, Diane Johnson

Mark Denning (Mitchell) and Reggie Osborn (Huffman), the sole survivors of two separate mass murder incidents, join forces against the perpetrator, an ancient god named Yag Kothag, whom we never get to see. Yag is fronted by Nash (Jacobsen), an evil realtor, who sells the victims homes whose locations form a pentagram. The hero and heroine spend most of the picture fighting Nash's minions, a zombie servant and a devil dog. The plot is further, and unnecessarily, complicated by a fortune-teller who's killed off before the credits roll, the hero's nightmares of a demon baby, and talk of the cycles of pulsing quasars. A helpful cop (Trotter) is only around to become Yag fodder. Mark eventually saves Reggie by dispatching Nash with a ceremonial dagger. The acting is poor, the pace is nonexistent, the gore effects and makeup are crude, and the optical effects are bargain basement.
—D. K.

Four Flies on Grey Velvet

Paramount Pictures, 1971; Color; 100 minutes
Director: Dario Argento
Producer: Salvatore Argento
Writers: Dario Argento, Luigi Cozzi, Mario Foglietti
With: Michael Brandon, Mimsy Farmer, Bud Spencer, Francine Racette

Argento updates the old wives' tale about the image of a murderer being captured on the retina of his/her victim—a theory, incidentally, that pathologists actually explored at the time of the Jack the Ripper murders, but to no avail. A phantom slasher is slaughtering Brandon's male and female friends. Using laser technology, the victims' eyes are photographed in the hope that they will reveal the image of the killer. The resulting image looks like a cross between an ink blot and "four flies on grey velvet," thus the title. Typical Argento psychofilm, full of graphically presented nasty murders, colorful decor, and a not too surprising twist finish.

Frankenstein and the Monster from Hell

Paramount Pictures, 1974; Color; 93 minutes
Director: Terence Fisher
Producer: Roy Skeggs
Writer: John Elder
With: Peter Cushing, Shane Bryant, Madeline Smith, Dave Prowse, Bernard Lee, Charles Lloyd-Pack

This last entry in Hammer's long-running (since 1957) Frankenstein series is by far the goriest. Dr. F. (Cushing) has been consigned to a mental asylum, which he quickly takes over so that he can stitch together his latest creature (Prowse), a Neanderthal with a propensity for sticking shards of glass in people's faces. In the end, the inmates—not a few of whose body parts have gone into making the beast—literally tear the creature apart, tossing its innards all over the place. By no means the best of the series, but not the worst, either. Cushing, as usual, is excellent. Fisher, whose last film this was, died of cancer in 1980 at age seventy-six. European prints run ninety-nine minutes.

Frankenstein's Castle of Freaks

Cinerama Releasing, 1973; Color; 89 minutes
Director: Robert H. Oliver
Producer: Robert Randall
Writer: Mario Francini
With: Rossano Brazzi, Michael Dunn, Edmund Purdom, Christine Royce, Gordon Michael

A potpourri of creatures runs riot over the countryside thanks to more handiwork from the mad Dr. F. and his latest life-creating device, the Electric Accumulator—a good name for a rock group. More nudity than splatter. It is aka *House of Freaks*.

Freddy's Revenge

See A Nightmare on Elm Street Part 2

Friday the 13th

Paramount Pictures, 1980; Color; 95 minutes
Director: Sean S. Cunningham
Producer: Sean S. Cunningham
Writer: Victor Miller
With: Adrienne King, Betsy Palmer, Harry Crosby, Joseph Zito

A summer camp that was closed down after two counselors were brutally murdered prepares to reopen for business. One by one, the new counselors are stalked and slaughtered by a relentless killer. This is the controversial box-office smash that propelled the independent, low-budget splatter movie into the big time, spawning a host of sequels and gruesome imitations—as well as a syndicated television series that had absolutely nothing to do with its progenitor except the title. Effects by Tom Savini. Director Cunningham, the producer of *Last House on the Left* (1972), has since left the directing chores on most of his films to others. You might call him the George Lucas of low-budget splatter.

Friday the 13th—Part II

Paramount Pictures, 1981; Color; 87
  minutes
Director: Steve Miner
Producers: Steve Miner, Dennis
  Murphy
Writer: Ron Kurz
With: Amy Steel, John Furey,
  Adrienne King

Jason returns to get even with the counselor (King) who killed his murderous mom. Then he goes back to camp to take up where mom left off. Steve Kirshoff handled the gore effects this time. In this and most subsequent *Friday the 13th* flicks, the MPAA insisted on cuts and Paramount agreed to avoid an X rating. Still fairly splattery, though.

Friday the 13th—Part III

Paramount Pictures, 1982; Color; 95
  minutes
Director: Steve Miner
Producer: Frank Mancuso, Jr.
Writers: Martin Kitrosser, Carol
  Watson
With: Dana Kimmell, Paul Kratka,
  Tracie Savage, Jeffrey Rogers,
  Richard Brooker

This third entry in the saga of the indomitable Jason (Brooker) was shot in 3-D to separate it a bit from the pack. The 3-D effects are good—especially the scene where Jason pops out the eyeball of one of his victims and it seemingly lands in the audience's lap. The film is not in 3-D on video or television prints, however.

The plot is standard Jason fare. The story takes up where Part II left off, as yet another band of unwitting teens enters the badlands of Camp Crystal Lake. This time around, they encounter not just Jason but some murderous bikers. Not at all discriminatory, Jason proceeds to decimate both groups before going up in flames. Martin Becker handled the gore effects in this one and they're just as good as ever.

Friday the 13th—The Final Chapter

Paramount Pictures, 1984; Color; 91
  minutes
Director: Joseph Zito
Producer: Frank Mancuso, Jr.
Writer: Barney Cohen
With: E. Erich Anderson, Kimberly
  Beck, Judie Aronson, Corey
  Feldman, Crispin Glover, Richard
  Brooker

Though killed in his previous outing, Jason (Brooker) rises from his slab in the morgue like some supernatural creature to go on yet another spree. In this episode, the screen's most prolific and versatile mass murderer is vengefully chopped up into little pieces by a monster makeup enthusiast named Tommy (Feldman), who shaves his head to make himself look like Jason. Though subtitled *The Final Chapter*, the film ends with the implication that the emotionally disturbed Tommy, seasoned by his massacre of Jason, will assume Jason's role in future films. And sure enough, *Friday the 13th: A New Beginning* followed a year later.

Friday the 13th—Part V: A New Beginning

Paramount Pictures, 1985; Color; 92
  minutes
Director: Danny Steinmann

Producer: Timothy Silver
Writers: Martin Kitrosser, David
Cohen, Danny Steinmann
With: John Shepard, Melanie
Kinnaman, Richard Young,
Shavar Ross

Though only a year separated the release of *The Final Chapter* and *A New Beginning*, Tommy Jarvis, Jason's prepubescent executioner in the previous film, has somehow managed to grow into a teenager (Shepard)! Released from a state hospital, where he has been undergoing therapy for traumas incurred in *The Final Chapter*, he is placed in a private hospital located out in the boondocks. He's plagued by night and daymares about Jason's return—and, after one of Tommy's fellow patients is axed to death by another "inmate," the old boy returns with a vengeance, knocking everybody off, one by one. With as much nudity and as gore-filled as the others in the series (Martin Becker once again handles the FX, which by this time are getting more than a bit repetitive), Part V strives to be a whodunit—or, rather, a whoisit—but director Steinmann gives the killer's identity away early on (he practically puts a neon sign on him!). The ending, where the physically and emotionally battered Tommy finally dons Jason's mask for the next sequel, comes as no surprise, either. Easily one of the worst installments in the series.

Friday the 13th—Part VI: Jason Lives

Paramount Pictures, 1986; Color; 87 minutes
Director: Tom McLoughlin
Producer: Don Behrns
Writer: Tom McLoughlin
With: Thom Mathews, Jennifer Cooke, David Kagan, Renee Jones, C. J. Graham

Writer-director McLoughlin either didn't see Part V or decided to forget about how it ended. In Part VI, Tommy Jarvis (this time played by Thom Mathews) returns not as Jason (which the ending of Part V implied), but as the hero, who digs Jason (C. J. Graham) up to make sure he's dead and inadvertently brings him back to life, courtesy of a bolt of lightning. There's a lot more humor mixed with the gore effects in this outing. The opening credits include an amusing parody of the James Bond logo, as Jason, seen through a gun barrel, walks across the screen and hurls a knife, blood dripping down the screen. The best line in the film belongs to the alcoholic gravedigger who comes upon Jason's opened tomb and opines: "Why did they go ahead and dig up Jason? Some folks sure have a *strange* idea of entertainment!"

Friday the 13th—Part VII: The New Blood

Paramount Pictures, 1988; Color; 92 minutes
Director: John Buechler
Producer: Iain Paterson
Writer: Gary Drucker
With: Lar Park Lincoln, Kevin Blair, Kane Hodder

This latest installment in the long-running series contains no surprises. In fact, even the gore is less explicit, due to more stringent controls from the ratings board. The filmmakers have the killings down to a science. The camera cuts away at exactly the right moment so that we think we've seen more than what is really shown (in fact, so tightly timed are these shots that if you happen to blink at just the right moment, you may end up thinking you've seen much *less* than is actually the case). In any event, in this outing, it's "Jason's back and Carrie's got 'im," as writer Gary Drucker, attempting to inject some freshness into the tired conventions, pits our ever-changing "hero" against a young woman with telekinetic powers. You might call it a classic conflict of mind over splatter. Who wins? Paramount Pictures. They reap the profits.—J. B.

Frightmare

A Pete Walker Production (Miracle), 1974; Color; 86 minutes
Director: Peter Walker
Producers: Peter Walker, Tony Tenser
Writer: David McGillivray
With: Rupert Davies, Sheila Keith, Deborah Fairfax, Paul Greenwood, Kim Butcher, Fiona Curzon, Noel Johnson, Leo Genn

This film is about an English family with a mother who's a cannibal. She's just been released from the asylum, supposedly cured, but everyone's wondering whether she's up to her old culinary tricks again. Is her loyal, loving husband shielding her from the authorities as he did the last time? Is one of the two daughters following in mom's footsteps? The potentially provocative climax, which pits the normal sister against the rest of her abnormal family, isn't played out to its full potential. It's like a half-hour TV show where the audience is left to imagine its own ending. The gore, whether caused by electric drill, hot poker, or other means, is minimal and indirectly observed. The highlight is the good sister's psychiatrist boyfriend being killed with a pitchfork. A good idea for a film that is never brought to a satisfying conclusion. It is aka *Once Upon a Frightmare.*—D. K.

Frightmare

Screenwriters Production Company, Inc., 1982; Color; 86 minutes
Director: Norman Thaddeus Vane

Producers: Patrick Wright, Tallie Wright
Writer: Norman Thaddeus Vane
With: Ferdinand Mayne, Luca Bercovici, Nita Talbot, Leon Askin, Jennifer Starrett, Barbara Pilavin, Jeffrey Combs

This film about the death of a malevolent aging horror star and the revenge he wreaks on the college horror-film society members who steal his body as a prank starts out strong but degenerates into a rotting corpse of a movie, lacking sufficient connective tissue. After murdering his present and past directors, Conrad Ragsov (Mayne) is interred in a mausoleum with video replay and a neon star over the door. Seven students (four boys and three girls) lift his body for a macabre dinner party. His wife and mistress, a medium, bring him back to life. He kills off the collegians one by one by strangulation and tongue ripping, fire from his glaring eyes, toxic fumes, face smashing with his levitated coffin, decapitation by sword (the best and bloodiest death, suffered by Jeffrey Combs of *Re-Animator* and *From Beyond* fame), and cremation while still alive. The mistress gets hers in the end after trying to steal the "dead" star's jewelry. A lack of vital characterization turns the victims into "just bodies" even before they're dead.—D. K.

Fright Night

Columbia Pictures, 1985; Color; 105 minutes
Director: Tom Holland
Producer: Herb Jaffe
Writer: Tom Holland
With: Chris Sarandon, Roddy McDowall, William Ragsdale, Amanda Bearse, Stephen Geoffreys

Veteran splatter scriptwriter Holland (*The Beast Within, Psycho II*) made his directorial debut with this inexplicably well-received nod to the vampire films of yore (particularly those made by Hammer), coupled with trendy gore effects. Sarandon is a vampire who moves next door to teenager Ragsdale. To put an end to this neighborhood scourge, Ragsdale enlists the help of late-night-TV horror movie host McDowall, who used to play a vampire hunter in Hollywood B movies. Thinking the kid nuts at first, McDowall is gradually convinced—especially when one of Ragsdale's pals (Geoffreys) becomes a victim of the vampire. Sarandon makes a good vampire, though his dialogue tends to get a bit garbled when he's wearing his fangs.

Frissons

See They Came from Within

From Beyond

Empire Pictures, 1986; Color; 85
   minutes
Director: Stuart Gordon
Producer: Brian Yuzna
Writers: Dennis Paoli, Brian Yuzna,
   Stuart Gordon
With: Jeffrey Combs, Barbara
   Crampton, Ken Foree, Carolyn
   Purdy-Gordon, Ted Sorel

"A mind is a terrible thing to waste," claimed the ads for this follow-up film by the fine folks who brought us *Re-Animator*, and the altered hero (Jeffrey Combs) of *From Beyond* obviously took the message to heart. He doesn't waste them; he sucks them out through the victim's eye! Just as inventive as the first film, this surprisingly faithful adaptation of H. P. Lovecraft's short story about a device that allows one to see—and, unfortunately, be seen by—unpleasant forces and creatures that inhabit another dimension is a little more straight-faced and

ambitious (the latter possibly due to budgetary advantages of shooting in Italy). The cast is again letter-perfect (especially Jeffrey Combs, looking increasingly like a pint-sized, more manic Tony Perkins), and Gordon's direction is smooth and assured, deftly blending the old Universal-style horror fantasy with the newer splatter techniques in a way no other current genre specialist even attempts. Shorn of a few bits of gore, this one managed to squeak by on an R rating, assuring slightly better distribution, but Gordon's work, despite its high quotient of blood and guts, has yet to receive the attention it deserves from any but a handful of admirers. A colorful, flamboyant gem.—K. H.

The Funhouse

Universal, 1981; Color; 94 minutes
Director: Tobe Hooper
Producers: Derek Powers, Steven
   Bernhardt
Writer: Larry Block
With: Elizabeth Berridge, Cooper
   Huckabee, Largo Woodruff, Miles
   Chapin, Kevin Conway, Sylvia
   Miles, William Finley

Four teenagers decide to spend the night in a carnival funhouse and encounter all manner of horrors, including a deformed monster that wears a Frankenstein mask to hide an even uglier visage beneath. Atmospheric and genuinely scary. Effects by Rick Baker and Craig Reardon.

The Fury

Twentieth Century-Fox, 1978; Color;
   117 minutes
Director: Brian De Palma
Producer: Frank Yablans
Writer: John Farris
With: Kirk Douglas, John Cassavetes,
   Carrie Snodgress, Andrew
   Stevens, Amy Irving, Fiona Lewis

Two young psychics are pursued by government agents and international terrorists who want to put their powers to use as the ultimate weapon. Lots of bleeding nostrils, pulsating veins, exploding heads, and a spectacular death by Lewis, who becomes a whirling dervish of blood. Farris adapted from his own novel.

Future-Kill

An International Film Marketing Release, 1986; Color; 83 minutes
Director: Ronald W. Moore
Producers: Gregg Unterberger, John H. Best
Writer: Ronald W. Moore
With: Edwin Neal, Marilyn Burns

Ronald W. Moore makes the most of a limited budget, starting with a clever but ambitious premise. A group of peaceful antinuclear demonstrators have made their home in a decaying section of an inner city. Ed Neal, in a surprising departure from his *Texas Chainsaw* character, plays Splatter, a member of the group who was disfigured by a nuclear accident. He is too violent for the others. Splatter kills the group leader and blames a gang of frat boys who have come into the area looking for kicks. Low on gore (though Splatter has a neat mechanical hand with spring-blade "claws" for a weapon) but high on imagination, Moore creates a number of interesting scenes. The dialogue is concise and dramatic. Colored lighting, carefully placed shadows, and a few strategically placed foreground props make the locations appear to be more decrepit and foreboding than was actually the case (a maximum effect for a minimum investment). Unfortunately, the limited budget begins to show during an extended climactic chase/fight scene that the filmmakers simply don't have the resources to fully realize. Well worth the time, though.—J. B.

Gates of Hell

An MPM Release, 1983; Color; 93 minutes
Director: Lucio Fulci
Producer: Giovanni Masini
Writers: Lucio Fulci, Danny Sacchetti
With: Christopher George, Robert Sampson, Kathleen MacColl

Unofficial cannibal/zombie sequel to Fulci's box-office hit *Zombie*, it is set in the mythical Lovecraftian town of Dunwich, Massachusetts, where the suicide of a village priest opens the gates of hell, releasing the hungry dead. Fulci offers virtually no plot this time around, concentrating on the kind of over-the-top gore effects that made his previous film such a success. There's no needle-through-the-eye scene this time around, but there is a sequence (inspired, perhaps, by Romero's screwdriver scene in *Dawn of the Dead*) where a victim is skewered ear-to-ear with a power drill. In the end, the zombies are incinerated and the gates of hell are closed. A movie with guts. And lots of 'em. It is aka *Twilight of the Dead*.

Ghost Story

Universal, 1981; Color; 108 minutes
Director: John Irvin
Producer: Bud Weissbourd
Writer: Lawrence D. Cohen
With: Fred Astaire, Melvyn Douglas, Douglas Fairbanks, Jr., John Houseman, Alice Krige, Craig Wasson

Four old-timers who committed an act of manslaughter in their youth are haunted in their waking and nonwaking moments by the vengeful ghost of the victim whose body they tried to conceal. Jack Cardiff's stunning atmospheric photography of northern New York State and Vermont's wintery landscapes, Alice Krige's otherworldly performance as the spiteful spirit, and Dick Smith's makeup effects are the only elements that work in this otherwise plodding, disjointed, and not very frightening adaptation of Peter Straub's popular, though overrated, best-seller.

Ghoulies

Empire Pictures, 1984; Color; 81 minutes
Director: Luca Bercovici
Producer: Jeffrey Levy
Writer: Luca Bercovici
With: Lisa Pelikan, Peter Liapis, Jack Nance, Michael des Barres

Empire Pictures, run by splatter maven Charles Band and his father, Albert, is fast becoming the AIP of the eighties, turning out one low-budget, fast-profit exploitation pic after another. Some of them are good (*Re-Animator*), some not so good. This one—about a young man who performs a Satanic ritual that unleashes the title creatures on unsuspecting earthlings—is not so good. Similar to Joe Dante's *Gremlins,* released the same year (giving you a good idea of how fast Band and Company can grab on to a successful formula and rush it through production to release), most of the ghoulies—puppetlike critters from another dimension—are supposed to be cuddly and cute. Here, the humans dish out most of the splatter, prompting the ghoulies to hide their eyes. The effects, however, look cheap—which they no doubt were. Empire's studios are located in Italy, where this film was made.

God Told Me To

New World Pictures, 1975; Color; 91 minutes
Director: Larry Cohen
Producer: Larry Cohen
Writer: Larry Cohen
With: Tony Lo Bianco, Sandy Dennis, Deborah Raffin, Richard Lynch, Sam Levene, Sylvia Sidney

Thoughtful but confused hybrid of *The Omen* and *Chariots of the Gods*, it was made by the prolific triple threat Larry Cohen, whose ambitions always manage to exceed his grasp. Lo Bianco plays a deeply religious New York City cop with a firm faith in God, though he doesn't know why. Several people go on a mass-murder binge. When they're brought down, each confesses that the reason he was driven to kill was that "God told me to." Lo Bianco's investigation leads to an androgynous creature (the product of an alien's mating with a female earthling) who professes to be the second coming, who is set on inspiring devotion through fear this time around. In the not-so-surprising surprise finish, Lo Bianco discovers the reason for his abiding faith (he is the bloodthirsty creature's far more Godlike brother) and slays the beast in mankind's behalf. Fairly soft-core in the gore department, but gruesome enough. The film is dedicated to composer Bernard Herrmann.

Goodnight God Bless

ABC Pictures, 1987; Color; 98 minutes
Director: John Eyres
Producers: Geoff Griffiths, Zafar Malik
Writer: Ed Ancoats
With: Emma Sutton, Frank Rozelaar Green, Jared Morgan, Jane Price

There are so many shots of feet in this movie—running, stalking, tiptoeing up stairs—you'd swear it was made by a bunch of foot fetishists. The plot concerns a psycho priest who opens fire in a British schoolyard, killing several children. Identified by a little girl whose life is saved when he runs out of ammo, the killer puts aside his gun for a knife and goes after the girl and her mother. As the police

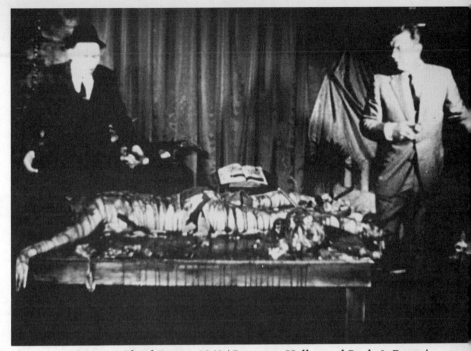

Blood Feast—1963 (Courtesy, Hollywood Book & Poster)

2000 Maniacs—1964 (Courtesy, Hollywood Book & Poster)

Color Me Blood Red—1964
(Courtesy, Hollywood Book & Poster)

The Exorcist—1973
(Copyright © 1973 Warner Bros., Inc./
Courtesy, Hollywood Book & Poster)

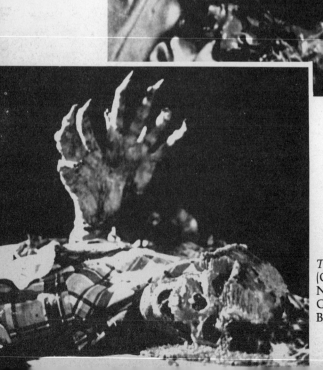

The Evil Dead—1983
(Copyright © 1983
New Line Cinema/
Courtesy, Hollywood
Book & Poster)

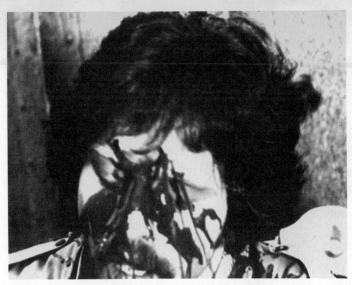

Dawn of the Dead—1979
(Copyright © 1978 Dawn Associates/K. Kolbert/
Courtesy, Hollywood Book & Poster)

Day of the Dead—1985
(Copyright © 1985 Dead Films Inc./Richard and Susan Golomb/
Courtesy, Hollywood Book & Poster)

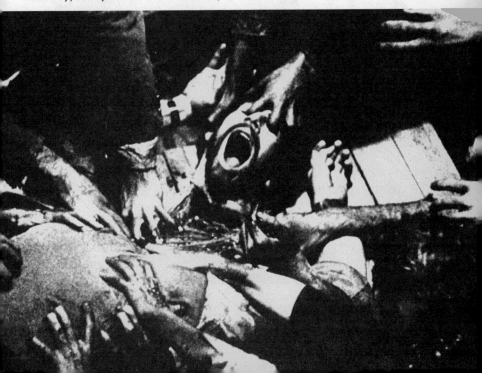

The Boogeyman—1980
(Copyright © 1980 The Jerry
Gross Organization/Courtesy,
Hollywood Book & Poster)

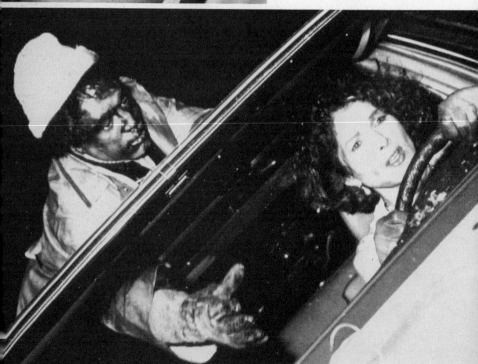

Creepshow 2—1987
(Copyright © 1986 New World Pictures/Courtesy,
Hollywood Book & Poster)

Cujo—1983
(Copyright © 1983 Warner
Bros., Inc./Courtesy,
Hollywood Book & Poster)

Alien—1979
(Copyright © 1979 Twentieth
Century-Fox/Courtesy,
Hollywood Book & Poster)

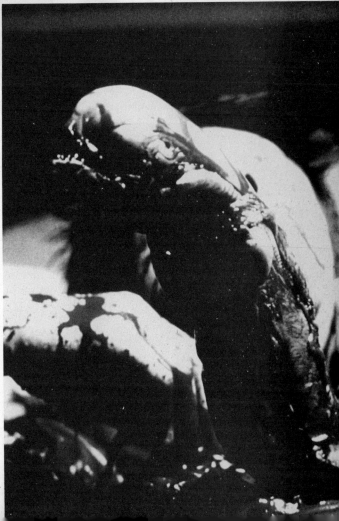

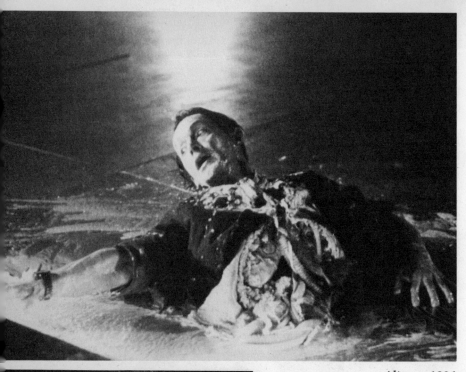

Aliens—1986
(Copyright © 1986 Twentieth
Century-Fox/Courtesy,
Hollywood Book & Poster)

*An American Werewolf in
London*—1981 (Copyright © 1981
Universal City Studios, Inc./
Courtesy, Hollywood Book &
Poster)

Mark of the Devil—1970
(Courtesy, Hollywood Book & Poster)

Raw Meat—1973
(Copyright © 1973 American-International)

Sisters—1973
(Copyright © 1973 American-International)

chief stares out of his office window hoping a clue will float by, the cops assigned to protect the girl and her mother are easily dispatched via throat slashing and impalement. But the mother's boyfriend, an American cop assigned to the case, arrives in time to blow the butcher away. Amateurish, slow-moving slasher flick full of scenes that go on *forever!* One of them, a ponderous interrogation sequence shot at a distance in total silence, is a sure cure for insomnia. Made by people with no discernible talent whatsoever.

The Gore Gore Girls

A Lewis Motion Picture Enterprises
    Release, 1972; Color; 90 minutes
Dirctor: Herschell Gordon Lewis
Producer: Herschell Gordon Lewis
Writer: Alan J. Dachman
With: Frank Kress, Amy Farrell, Henny
    Youngman

Splattery whodunit about a psycho slayer-mutilator of go-go dancers who work for nightclub owner Youngman. Plenty of suspects here—including a Vietnam vet who draws faces on melons, then pulverizes them with his fist. Other nice scenes include the scalding of a victim whose face is pushed into a bowl of boiling oil. As (intentionally) funny as it is disgusting, this remains Lewis's swan song as a splatter director—unless those rumors of a *Blood Feast II* come to pass.

Gore-Met, Zombie Chef from Hell

Swanfilms, 1986; Color; 90 minutes
Director: Don Swan
Producer: Don Swan
Writers: Don Swan, Jeff Baughn,
    William Highsmith
With: Theo Depuay, Kelley Kunicki, C.
    W. Casey, Alan Marx, Michael
    O'Neill, Joy Merchant, Jeff Pillars,
    Jeff Baughn, Chuc Clubb, Billy
    Scott

This film has absolutely nothing going for it. The direction is nonexistent. The script is replete with a clichéd and virtually formless plot, lifeless characters (no pun intended), vacuous, uncompelling dialogue and sophomoric humor. The cast is composed exclusively of nonactors. The cinematography is mostly single-point-of-view porn loop style filled with ragged pans and jerky unmotivated zooms. The lighting is harsh, flat, and ugly. The sound track is full of dropouts and camera noise. The gore effects are pitiful. They're poorly executed and are mostly "aftermath" stuff. We hardly ever get to see anything really happening. To call this mess amateurish would be giving it too much dignity.
— D. K.

The Graduation

See The Prowler

Graduation Day

Bedford Films, 1981; Color; 85
    minutes
Director: Herb Reed
Producer: Herb Reed
Writers: Anne Marisse, Herb Reed
With: Christopher George, Patch
    MacKenzie, E. Danny Murphy,
    Michael Pataki, E. J. Peaker

Death on campus as track stars are stalked and killed by a standard mad slasher whose face is concealed until the not-too-surprising finish. *Halloween* and *Friday the 13th* clone. Take note all of you who keep insisting that splatter movies boast an antifeminist message: A woman (by the name of Jill Rockow) created the mutilation makeups for this one. And a good job she does, too.

Graveyard Shift

Cinema Ventures, Inc., 1986; Color;
89 minutes
Director: Gerard Ciccoritti
Producer: Michael Bockner
Writer: Gerard Ciccoritti
With: Silvio Oliviero, Helen Papas,
Cliff Stoker, Dorin Ferber, Dan
Rose, John Haslett Cuff, Don
James

This present-day erotically oriented vampire tale has a lot more stylish sensuality than good plot sense. As the film unreels, it becomes increasingly difficult to follow the story line and keep the characters straight, and the ending is a total anticlimax. The vampire hero is a driver for the Black Cat Cab Company on the (you guessed it) graveyard shift. He has a harem of female vampire victims, including a stripper and a cop. The heroine is a video director with a fatal disease who somehow gives our hero the courage to want to end his undead existence. The movie's only interesting idea, a spiritual bond of sensations between the vampires à la the Corsican brothers, never really pays off. The traditional stake-through-the-heart finish, which takes place on a graveyard set meant for one of the heroine's videos, looks cheap and contrived. There is a fair amount of blood, but none of the special effects are very special. The ending is the ultimate cliché: The heroine replaces the hero as a vampire cabbie.
—D. K.

Gremlins

Warner Brothers, 1984; Color; 106
minutes
Director: Joe Dante
Producer: Michael Finnell
Writer: Chris Columbus
With: Zach Galligan, Phoebe Cates,
Hoyt Axton, Polly Holliday, Dick
Miller, Keye Luke, Jackie Joseph

Screwball inventor Axton picks up a furry pet for his son (Galligan) in Chinatown and gives it to him for Christmas. The pet, called a Mogwai, comes with special instructions. It can't get wet, shouldn't be fed after midnight, etc. Naturally these instructions aren't followed and the Mogwai sprouts furballs, which grow into murderous gremlins with a delightfully vicious sense of humor. The myriad gremlins go on the rampage, terrorizing and killing folks and turning the picture-postcard town upside down. Overlong, overdone, and sometimes overcute, but any film that trashes Frank Capra's treacly *It's a Wonderful Life* as solidly as this one does can't be all bad. The gremlins are fun—especially Spike, the chain-saw-wielding leader. Dante fills the film with movie-buff in-jokes, serving up people such as writer Richard Matheson and animator Chuck Jones in cameos.

The Grim Reaper

Film Ventures, 1981; Color; 87
minutes
Director: Joe d'Amato
Producer: Oscar Santaniello
Writers: Joe d'Amato, Lewis (Luigi)
Montefiori
With: Tisa Farrow, Saverio Vallone,
Vanessa Steiger, George Eastman

Shipwrecked with his family on a picturesque but remote Greek island, Eastman (alias cowriter Montefiori) must devour the corpses of his wife and kid to survive. The strain of it all drives him round the bend. As the years go by and the island develops a modest tourist trade, the now completely deranged and hideous cannibal, having long since lost any shred of hospitality or social grace, kills and consumes anyone who ventures upon the island. Farrow and Vallone are the latest unlucky pair, but after a grueling duel with axes and other weapons, Eastman's territorial imperative is overcome and he's hacked to pieces.

The Gruesome Twosome

A Mayflower Pictures Inc. Release, 1967; Color; 72 minutes
Director: Herschell Gordon Lewis
Producer: Herschell Gordon Lewis
Writer: Allison Louise Downe
With: Elizabeth Davis, Chris Martel, Gretchen Welles, Rodney Bedell

Wigged-out son (Martel) of equally wigged-out wig-shop owner Davis scalps young women with a battery-operated electric knife and other handy tools in order to collect their hair for mom's business. Ultrarealistic gore effects mixed with absurdism make for a passably funny ghoulish "comedy" in the Lewis tradition. Lewis added a ridiculous (and interminable) prologue with two talking balloon heads because his original cut was too short to release as a feature film.

Halloween

Compass International Pictures, 1978; Color; 90 minutes
Director: John Carpenter
Producer: Irwin Yablans
Writer: John Carpenter
With: Jamie Lee Curtis, Donald Pleasence, Nancy Loomis, P. J. Soles

A psychotic masked killer—and stand-in for the boogey man—busts out of the asylum where he was sent after murdering his sister some years back and returns to the scene of the crime, his old hometown. His target this time: a trio of delectable baby-sitters. Carpenter's nod to *Psycho* (the Pleasence character is named Sam Loomis after the part played by John Gavin in the Hitchcock classic) became one of the most successful independent films ever made and is considered by many to be a classic scare show.

Halloween II

Universal Pictures, 1981; Color; 92 minutes
Director: Rick Rosenthal
Producers: John Carpenter, Debra Hill
Writers: John Carpenter, Debra Hill
With: Jamie Lee Curtis, Donald Pleasence, Charles Cyphers, Jeffrey Kramer

Takes up immediately where the original left off. The Shape goes to the hospital to finish off recuperating Curtis, the lone survivor of his initial onslaught. Feeling he'd already made this film once (which indeed he had), Carpenter handed over the directorial reins to film-school grad Rick Rosenthal after seeing a slick student film of Rosenthal's called *The Toyer*, a thriller in the mold of the original *Halloween*. Rosenthal's final cut didn't have enough gore, though, so Carpenter went back and inserted some graphic murders to please the fans.

Halloween III: Season of the Witch

Universal, 1983; Color; 98 minutes
Director: Tommy Lee Wallace
Producers: Debra Hill, John Carpenter
Writer: Tommy Lee Wallace
With: Tom Atkins, Stacey Nelkin, Dan O'Herlihy

In this third episode of John Carpenter's *Halloween* series, Michael Myers is replaced by villainous mask maker Dan O'Herlihy, whose specially designed Halloween masks have the power to take over the minds of those who wear them and turn them into killers. It's all part of a diabolical plot to take over the world. Nigel Kneale wrote the original screenplay, but it was altered so much that he requested that his name be removed from the credits. Tepid re-hash of elements from *Invasion of the Body Snatchers*.

Halloween 4: The Return of Michael Myers

Galaxy Releasing, 1988; Color; 88 minutes
Director: Dwight H. Little
Producer: Paul Freeman
Writer: Alan B. McElroy
With: Donald Pleasence, Ellie Cornell, Danielle Harris, Michael Pataki, Sasha Jenson, George Wilbur

After a hiatus of seven years during which Jason Vorhees stole most of his thunder, the indomitable Michael Myers returns to Haddonfield on Halloween night to put the knife to his niece Jamie (Harris). Pleasence also returns as Sam Loomis, the obsessed doctor who refers to the masked killing machine as "it" rather than "he." *Halloween 4* dispenses with the tongue-in-cheek elements of the *Elm Street* and *Friday the 13th* series to concentrate on serious scares, but the end-product is just another retread of stalk and slash clichés as Jason—I mean Michael—goes about his bloody business, puncturing people's heads with his thumb and impaling them with shotguns. The "surprise" conclusion (which echoes the ending of *Friday the 13th—The Final Chapter*) neatly paves the way for a *Halloween 5*. But this formula is so shopworn by now that it's hard to get excited at the prospect.

Hands of the Ripper

Universal, 1971; Color; 85 minutes
Director: Pater Sasdy
Producer: Aida Young
Writer: L. W. Davidson
With: Eric Porter, Angharad Rees, Keith Bell, Jane Merrow, Dora Bryan

Freudian disciple Porter discovers the waifish daughter of Jack the Ripper (Rees) living with an oppressive medium/madam who is subsequently skewered with a fireplace poker. Porter knows Rees is the killer but takes her into his home anyway, determined to understand and cure her. Instead (shades of Hitchcock's *Marnie*), he falls in love with her and gets a sword stuck through him for his efforts. Extremely gory, though thematically intriguing, Hammer thriller with a great performance by Porter, who is clearly as much of a psychosexual case as his murderous patient. Beware of TV prints, which are not only severely cut (the gore, obviously) but have extraneous scenes added (shot in Hollywood) to pad out the running time.

Happy Birthday to Me

Columbia Pictures, 1981; Color; 108 minutes
Director: J. Lee Thompson
Producers: John Dunning, Andre Link
Writers: John Saxton, Peter Jobin, Timothy Bond
With: Melissa Sue Anderson, Glenn Ford, Tracy Bregman, Jack Blum, Laurence Dane

Returning to college after recuperating from a car crash that killed her mother and put her in the hospital, Anderson finds herself experiencing blackouts—following which, some of her friends start turning up slain. One is actually shish-kebabed to death. Is she the guilty party? It takes a party to find out—her birthday party, that is—during which the mad shish-ke-baber is finally revealed in an ending so poorly established that it virtually makes no sense at all. Hollywood vet Ford must have been hard up for cash to have allowed himself to appear in a piece of junk like this.

Hatchet for a Honeymoon

Distributor unknown, 1969; Color; 83 minutes
Director: Mario Bava
Producer: Manuel Cano Sanciriaco
Writers: Mario Bava, Santiago Moncada, Mario Musy
With: Stephen Forsythe, Dagmar Lassander, Laura Betti, Jesus Puente

This typically stylish Mario Bava psychofilm, though made in 1969, was not released in the United States until the early seventies when, to capitalize on the success of *Mark of the Devil*, its distributor gave it a "V for Violence" rating and promoted the hell out of it. Bava's film is perhaps not as disgusting as *Mark*, but there are enough axe murders in it to satisfy splatter fans one and all. Forsythe plays the psychopath, an impotent designer who can't consummate his own marriage and so decides to take his frustration out on various brides-to-be who come into his store to buy their wedding gowns. It is aka *The Red Sign of Madness*.

The Hatchet Murders

See Deep Red

Hell Night

Compass International Pictures, 1981; Color; 100 minutes
Director: Tom DeSimone

Producers: Irwin Yablans, Bruce Cohn Curtis
Writer: Randolph Feldman
With: Linda Blair, Vincent Van Patten, Peter Barton, Kevin Brody, Jenny Neuman

Just when you thought it was safe to go back to the frat house . . . it turns out to be the very spot where a fellow frat brother witnessed his father slay his family many years before. Needless to say, the concept of hell night (hazing) triggers the prankster in him and he starts killing off his brothers as well as some sisters from an associate sorority. Not a bad dead-teenager movie, but nothing special, either—with the most spectacular splatter saved for the villain's demise on a spiked fence.

Hello Mary Lou—Prom Night II

Virgin Vision, 1988; Color; 97 minutes
Director: Bruce Pittman
Producer: Peter Simpson
Writer: Ron Oliver
With: Michael Ironside, Wendy Lyon, Justin Louis, Richard Manette

This one doesn't just provide a catalogue of nods to other splatter movies—it's a virtual encyclopedia of knowing winks to the entire splatter/horror genre. Characters have names such as Hennenlotter and Dr. Poelzig; scenes and dialogue are lifted from the *Elm Street* series, *Carrie, The Exorcist, Martin,* etc; camera moves and color scheme are straight out of *The Shining;* and the possessed characters are described as suffering from Linda Blair-itis. The plot is the standard splatter revenge theme. About to be crowned prom queen, vixenish Mary Lou is accidentally torched by her jilted boyfriend. Thirty years later, another aspiring prom queen unleashes her vengeful spirit. The film takes an interminable amount of time (and exposition) to get to the prom-night massacre, but there are a few flamboyant set pieces involving a malevolent blackboard and the crushing of a victim inside a row of lockers, which fold up like an accordion. The post-*Carrie* shock epilogue has the newly possessed Ironside drive off in a car with the license plate "Mary Lou 2," suggesting a sequel. Coproducer Ray Sager starred as H. G. Lewis's *The Wizard of Gore* and worked on a number of other Lewis films.

Hellraiser

New World Pictures, 1987; Color; 94 minutes
Director: Clive Barker
Producer: Christopher Figg
Writer: Clive Barker
With: Andrew Robinson, Clare Higgins, Ashley Laurence, Sean Chapman

"I have seen the future of horror and his name is Clive Barker," Stephen King has written. I don't know, Steve. Judging from this, the "future" looks like the same old thing to me: sex and slime and blood and gore. Robinson and Higgins move into the ex-home of Robinson's sleazy, hedonistic brother, Frank, unaware that his putrefying remains are under the floorboards in the attic. Seems that in his pursuit of pleasure (and pain), Frank made contact with a wrongo group of unearthlies—including a bizarre acupuncture creature—that put him to death. Robinson cuts his hand and the blood oozes through the floorboards, putting some flesh back on Frank's bones. While her unsuspecting husband goes back and forth to work, Higgins lures men to their home so that Frank (now a Freddy Kreuger lookalike) can add to his body weight by draining them of their blood. All ends badly,

of course—especially for Frank, whom the vengeful unearthlies tear apart with chains and hooks. The creepiest thing about the film is Robinson (the flamboyant psycho in Don Siegel's *Dirty Harry*), who comes across as slightly screwy even when he's playing a good guy.

The Hidden

New Line Cinema, 1987; Color; 98 minutes
Director: Jack Sholder
Producers: Robert Shaye, Gerald J. Olson, and Michael Meltzer
Writer: Bob Hunt
With: Kyle MacLachlan, Michael Nouri, Claudia Christian, Clarence Felder

Outer-space detective MacLachlan assumes the role of an FBI agent to track down a marauding psychopath from their home planet (Altair). The trouble is, the villainous alien, who has a penchant for guns, Ferraris, and heavy-metal music, keeps changing shapes (à la *The Thing*), invading one unwitting host after another. The sluglike creature accomplishes this by oozing out of the mouth of one host into that of another. Nouri is the at-first-uncomprehending L.A. police inspector who becomes MacLachlan's partner in the chase. The two of them eventually develop a strong camraderie and exchange a lot of snappy lines. The splatter is relegated mostly to graphic "bullet hits," but fans won't be disappointed, as there's enough firepower in this movie to rival *Robocop*. Fast paced and exciting, though not much plot—what plot there is, however, bears more than a passing resemblance to Hal Clement's classic SF novel *Needle,* which was also about an alien detective and his prey who assume human shapes on earth to carry out a deadly game of cat and mouse.

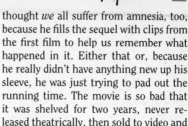

The Hills Have Eyes

Vanguard Releasing, 1977; Color; 90
  minutes
Director: Wes Craven
Producer: Peter Locke
Writer: Wes Craven
With: James Whitworth, John
  Steadman, Janus Blythe, Dee
  Wallace, Susan Lanier, Michael
  Berryman, Martin Speer

Suburban middle-class vacationers taking a shortcut through the desert meet up with a murderous clan of deranged desert rats and must fight for survival when their car breaks down. Ghoulishly funny (and suitably gross) reworking of the Sawney Bean cannibal-killer case, one of the most celebrated in the annals of Scottish crime. This not-to-be-missed splatter movie was followed in 1985 by a sequel, *The Hills Have Eyes—Part II*, which is so awful it's hard to believe it was made by the same director.

The Hills Have Eyes—Part II

Hills Two Corporation, 1985; Color;
  88 minutes
Director: Wes Craven
Producers: Barry Cahn, Peter Locke
Writer: Wes Craven
With: Michael Berryman, John
  Laughlin, Tamara Stafford, John
  Bloom, Janus Blythe

Desert rat Ruby (Blythe), who turned on her cannibal family in *The Hills Have Eyes*—even killing one of her brothers with a rattlesnake—returns in this wretched sequel as a pert teenager apparently suffering from amnesia. She and her newfound friends go back to the desert to party and race dirt bikes and run smack into more hill folks, including Berryman, another survivor from the earlier film. Writer-director Craven must have

thought *we* all suffer from amnesia, too, because he fills the sequel with clips from the first film to help us remember what happened in it. Either that or, because he really didn't have anything new up his sleeve, he was just trying to pad out the running time. The movie is so bad that it was shelved for two years, never released theatrically, then sold to video and pay TV to help recoup some of its cost.

The Hitcher

Embassy Pictures, 1986; Color; 97
  minutes
Director: Robert Harmon
Producers: Kim Ohman, David Bombyk
Writer: Eric Red
With: Rutger Hauer, C. Thomas
  Howell, Jennifer Jason Leigh,
  Jeffrey DeMunn

Serial-killer Hauer is picked up by Howell and thereafter won't leave the kid alone; he even tries to pin the killings on Howell so that the kid can't go to the police. Leigh plays a waitress who tries to help Howell, but the demented Hauer ties her to a couple of trucks and splits her in half. Howell digs into a plate of french fries and finds them "finger lickin' good." Homophobic psychofilm in which Hauer is (a) trying to seduce Howell into becoming just like him, or (b) just trying to seduce him. Your guess is as good as mine. It's hard to believe but the graphic violence in Red's original screenplay was actually toned down for the film! Ghastly, but undeniably suspenseful—even if totally preposterous.

Hollywood Chainsaw Hookers

Camp Motion Pictures, 1988; Color;
  90 minutes
Director: Fred Olen Ray

Producer: Fred Olen Ray
Writers: Dr. S. Carver, B. J. Nestles,
    Fred Olen Ray, T. L. Lankford
With: Gunnar Hansen, Linnea
    Quigley, Jay Richardson, Michelle
    McLellan

Whether intended to be or not, all of Fred Olen Ray's pictures are camp. This time, so that we'll know, an onscreen title card announces it as a Camp Motion Picture. Richardson plays a wisecracking but dim-witted gumshoe in search of a runaway (Quigley) who has joined up with a religious cult of chainsaw–worshiping hookers led by stout, bearded Gunnar Hansen (of *Texas Chainsaw Massacre* fame). The hookers seduce and slice up their "Johns" as part of a ritual sacrifice to the Great Chainsaw God (the police label one of them "The Cuisinart Queen.") Quigley has infiltrated the group to revenge the death of a friend ("I didn't tell my mother," she tells the P.I., "because I was afraid of being grounded.") At the final midnight sacrifice, the chain-saw groupies drink sacremental motor oil. The cops arrive to save the day, but some of the baddies get away to leave room for a sequel (the possibly upcoming *Student Chainsaw Nurses,* or "Bad to the Bone.") Hansen's deft handling of his dialogue shows why, as Leatherface, he wasn't given any in *Texas Chainsaw Massacre.*

The Hollywood Strangler

See Don't Answer the Phone

Horror Hotel Massacre

See Eaten Alive

Horror on Snape Island

See Tower of Evil

Horror Planet

See Inseminoid

Horror Rises from the Tomb

Avco Embassy, 1973; Color; 80
    minutes
Director: Carlos Alonso Aured
Producer: Profils
Writer: Jacinto Molina (Paul Naschy)
With: Paul Naschy, Emma Cohen, Vic
    Winner, Helga Line, Christine
    Suriana, Luis Ciges

Spirit of a villainous knight, who was beheaded for his crimes, returns to plague his descendant, possessing him and forcing him to reenact his gruesome deeds. Made-in-Spain splatter epic by horror/splatter cult actor Paul Naschy—who also penned the script under his real name: Jacinto Molina. Most American prints are invariably (and terribly) dubbed as well as cut.

Hospital Massacre

See X-Ray

House of Freaks

See Frankenstein's Castle of Freaks

House of Psychotic Women

Independent International Pictures,
    1973; Color; 85 minutes
Director: Carlos Aured
Producer: Jose Giner
Writer: Jacinto Molina (Paul Naschy)
With: Paul Naschy, Diana Lorys,
    Maria Perschy, Eva Leon

A cat-and-mouse game—or battle of the sexes—vaguely reminiscent of Don Siegel's *The Beguiled,* but a lot gorier. Naschy plays an ex-convict who gets a job as stud and all-round handyman for three women living in an old house. All three appear to be quite deranged, though each in a different way, their maladies ranging from nymphomania (which provides a good excuse for some graphic sex scenes) to murder (which provides a good excuse for some graphic slice-and-dice and eye-gouging scenes). Naschy thinks he's got it made, but the murderess among his entourage has other plans, and soon the body parts start to proliferate. Cheap, incoherent, but very splattery psycho-drama.

House of Whipcord

American-International, 1974; Color; 102 minutes
Director: Peter Walker
Producer: Peter Walker
Writer: David McGillivray
With: Barbara Markham, Patrick Barr, Ray Brooks, Ann Michelle, Sheila Keith, Dorothy Gordon, Robert Tavman

"This film is dedicated to those who are disturbed by today's lax moral codes and who eagerly await the return of corporal and capital punishment . . ." reads the ironic title at the start of this movie about justice and punishment gone mad. A blind, senile, and almost deaf former judge and his mistress, a former warden discharged for malfeasance, run their own clandestine free-lance prison where they punish "indecent" young women. Their bastard son, using the name Mark E. Desade, supplies them with girls who have escaped official justice. A sadistic guard dispenses discipline by solitary confinement, flogging, and hanging. A French model, who posed nude in public, is the lead victim. Although the limited gore is all "aftermath" stuff, a scene of Keith admiring her handiwork on the back of a flogging victim is still chilling. The violence, care-

fully kept just out of camera range, allows the viewer's imagination to run riot. Unlike some of his other films (*The Confessional* and *Once Upon a Frightmare*), which leave the audience hanging, Walker manages to give this one a definite ending.—D. K.

The House on Sorority Row

Artists Releasing Corporation, 1983; Color; 90 minutes
Director: Mark Rosman
Producers: Mark Rosman, John G. Clark
Writer: Mark Rosman
With: Kathryn McNeil, Eileen Davidson

A veritable compendium of splatter movie clichés. A sorority house provides an excellent stomping ground for a mad slasher: all those young, mostly female victims in various stages of dress and undress engaging in various sexual acrobatics. But how many ways can the same plot elements be shifted about before obvious repetitions begin to occur? Early on in the film, one develops a strong sense of déjà vu. From its opening flashback (depicting the birth of a child who grows up into a psychotic killer) through the masked slasher opening his eyes after he is presumed dead, the film is obvious and predictable. Not only does writer-director Mark Rosman fail to provide any originality or variety, he also neglects to tie up a number of loose ends—exactly what was the experiment performed on the housemother resulting in the slasher son, for example—leaving the viewer with more questions than answers.—J. B.

The Howling

Avco Embassy, 1981; Color; 91 minutes
Director: Joe Dante

Producers: Michael Finnell and Jack Conrad
Writers: John Sayles, Terence H. Winkless
With: Dee Wallace, Patrick MacNee, Dennis Dugan, Christopher Stone, Dick Miller, John Carradine

Sexy werewolf tale that mixes comedy and splatter much more successfully than *An American Werewolf in London* (1981) but to just as little purpose. Rob Bottin's werewolf transformation effects are the film's highpoint; they're as good as those in *Werewolf,* which won Rick Baker an Oscar. One of Dante's in-jokes is giving his characters the names of well-known horror filmmakers—George Waggner, R. William Neill, Terry Fisher, Fred Francis, Erle Kenton, and so on. Based (very loosely) on Gary Brander's novel of the same title. Followed by a sequel, *The Howling II,* which had nothing to do with either this film or the novel.

The Howling II

Hemdale, 1984; Color; 91 minutes
Director: Philippe Mora
Producer: Steven Lane
Writers: Robert Sarno, Gary Brander
With: Christopher Lee, Annie McEnroe, Reb Brown, Sybil Danning

Subtitled "Your Sister Is a Werewolf." At the funeral of the character played by Dee Wallace in the first film, her brother (Brown, a Ryan O'Neal look-alike) and another reporter (McEnroe) meet occult investigator Lee, who persuades them that the world is going to the wolves—werewolves. The good news is that the head werewolf's (Danning) lunar birthday is approaching. When it does, all the werewolves in the world will reveal themselves—an ideal time to kill them off. Off to Transylvania the intrepid trio goes, armed with silver bullets, stakes,

and garlic (yes, the film does get its werewolf and vampire mythology mixed up a bit). The transformation scenes are mediocre, but there's plenty of effective blood and gore—flesh ripping, arms being lopped off, exploding heads, the gamut, plus a fair amount of werewolf sex. Danning does little but hiss, bare her breasts, and flex her pecs—a shot that's repeated at least six times in the closing credits! A truly dreadful sequel. Poor Chris Lee. Does he really need the work this badly?

The Howling III

Bancannial Pictures, 1987; Color; 94 minutes
Director: Philippe Mora
Producers: Charles Waterstreet, Philippe Mora
Writer: Philippe Mora
With: Barry Otto, Imogen Annesley, Max Fairchild, Frank Thring, Leigh Biolos, Michael Pate

Arms talks between the Russians and the United States break down—apparently due to a "werewolf gap." A Russian ballerina defects to the Australian outback to mate with a hulk who looks like one of the inbred clan members in *The Hills Have Eyes.* A female werewolf sleeps with an assistant movie director, gives birth to the first marsupial human, stuffs it in her pouch, and skips to Hollywood to win the Academy of Laser Arts and Sciences best actress award. The Pope and the President agree to a worldwide ban on killing lycanthropes. Chubby Frank Thring (director of *Shape Shifters—Part 8,* the film that gives the wolfwoman her Hollywood break) does an amusing caricature of the aging Hitchcock. The werewolf transformations seem inspired by "Little Red Riding Hood." Shot primarily in the Australian outback, this fairy tale, satire, splatter-cum-"save the werewolves" movie appears to have been dreamed up in the ozone layer.

Human Experiments

Crown International Pictures, 1980;
Color; 82 minutes
Director: J. Gregory Goodell
Producers: Summer Brown, J.
Gregory Goodell
Writer: Richard Rothstein
With: Linda Haynes, Geoffrey Lewis,
Ellen Travolta, Aldo Ray, Jackie
Coogan, Lurene Tuttel

Psychiatrist in a women's prison rids inmates of their criminal impulses through
brainwashing and other techniques that
erase their memories. Ellen Travolta is
John's sister. Writer-director Goodell is
the author of an excellent book on independent filmmaking. No doubt he
learned a lot making this country and
western splatter pic.

Humanoids from the Deep

New World Pictures, 1980; Color; 82
minutes
Director: Barbara Peeters
Producers: Martin B. Cohen, Hunt
Lowry
Writer: Frederick James
With: Doug McClure, Ann Turkel, Vic
Morrow

A California fishing village is terrorized
by a modern ecological horror that is half-
man, half-fish, and all horny: sea beasts
that are compelled to mate with village
women in order to preserve their species.
Absurd splattery SF with some good effects by Rob Bottin.

Humongous

Embassy Pictures, 1981; Color; 93
minutes
Director: Paul Lynch

Producer: Anthony Kramreither
Writer: William Gray
With: Janet Julian, David Wallace,
John Wildman, Janet Baldwin

Another dead-teenager movie from the
director of *Prom Night*. This time around,
the kids, who have been shipwrecked on
a remote island, are being stalked and
killed by the island's possessive resident
—a seven-foot-tall mutant with the mind
of a child (sort of a murderous Baby Huey)
and the appetite of a starving wolf. Seems
the mutant's mom was raped—by
something—years before, which explains
his existence, bizarre appearance, and lack
of social grace. Lynch tries for suspense
as well as gore, but the gore wins out
because it's hard to get worked up over
the potential demise of characters you
don't give a shit about.

Hunter's Blood

Concorde Pictures, 1987; Color; 102
minutes
Director: Robert C. Hughes
Producer: Myrl A. Schreibman
Writer: Emmett Alston
With: Samuel Bottoms, Kim Delaney,
Clu Gulager, Ken Swofford, Joey
Travolta

Five sportsmen—one of them a city slicker
from "way up north"—head into the
backwoods of Arkansas for a weekend
hunting trip and run smack into an inbred
tribe of degenerates straight out of *Deliverance*, *The Hills Have Eyes*, and *The
Texas Chainsaw Massacre*. Seems these
grotesques are illegally slaughtering deer
and selling the venison steaks to the Razorback Meat Company for shipment to
"one o' them thar burger chains." Two
forest rangers save the sportsmen's bacon
and arrest some of the tribe. But on the
way to the hoosegow, the rangers are captured and killed—one is gutted like a deer,

the other beheaded. Instead of hightailing it out of the woods like sensible people, the sportsmen press on with their hunting trip, confirming an earlier statement made by one of rangers that, ". . . yer a die-hard bunch o' hunters." If you ask me, they're also pretty stupid—'cause you just know those hill folks ain't gonna let them out o' the woods alive. You can count on lots of graphic killings in this one—and, amazingly, a fair degree of suspense as well.

The Hunting Party

United Artists, 1971; Color; 108 minutes
Director: Don Medford
Producer: Lou Morheim
Writers: Lou Morheim, Gilbert Alexander, William Norton
With: Candice Bergen, Oliver Reed, Gene Hackman, Simon Oakland, L. Q. Jones, G. D. Spradlin

Outlaw Reed kidnaps and rapes the wife (Bergen) of cattle baron and hunting enthusiast Hackman, who likes to tour the nineteenth-century Texas countryside in a bordello-equipped train accompanied by a score of sharpshooters. Possessive Gene and his men go after Reed and his gang, and, one by one, the sharpshooters whittle the outlaws down. Supersplattery western made in the wake of *The Wild Bunch*, which it outdoes in violence but nothing else. When Gene learns that Reed and Bergen have fallen in love, he truly goes berserk and kills Bergen by shooting her in the breasts and crotch. He also subjects Reed to a lingering death by shooting him in the shoulders, blowing off his kneecaps, etc. And people think Jason Vorhees is sadistic!

Hustler Squad

See The Doll Squad

I Dismember Mama

Europix, 1974; Color; 81 minutes
Director: Paul Leder
Producer: Leon Roth
Writer: William Norton
With: Zooey Hall, Joanne Moore Jordan, Greg Mullavey, Marlene Tracey

With this one, the title really does tell all. A deranged young man (Hall), sick and tired of his domineering mom, decides to chop her and others up into little bitty pieces. Not exactly original, but you've gotta admit: The title's a gem.

I Drink Your Blood

Cinemation, 1971; Color; 88 minutes
Director: David Durston
Producer: Jerry Gross
Writer: David Durston
With: Jadine Wong, Bashkar, Ronda Fulz, Lynn Lowry, George Patterson

A rabid splatter-venereal comedy about a vengeful young man whose father is killed by some hippies who slipped him an overdose of LSD. The boy gets even by slipping the hippies rabies-ridden meat. The hippies, in turn, go on to infect others. Definitely a cautionary tale.

Ilsa—Harem Keeper of the Oil Sheiks

Cambist Films, 1976; Color; 93 minutes
Director: Don Edmonds
Producer: William J. Brody
Writer: Langton Stafford
With: Dyanne Thorne, Michael Thayer, Wolfgang Roehm, Sharon Kelly

"Ilsa's Back—More Sadistic Than Ever!" the ads for this sequel screamed. I'm not sure she could be more sadistic than she was in her first outing (see following entry), but the plot of this truly wacked-out sequel goes many steps beyond. This time around, Ilsa deals in white (and black) slavery, supplying nubile women for the titular Harem Sheiks to maim and torture. One unfortunate victim has an explosive diaphragm inserted that's set to go off upon orgasm. Imaginative, huh? American secret agent Thayer arrives to see what he can do about lowering oil prices, and succeeds in putting an end to Ilsa's scam as well. The brutalized harem girls are released and go on an orgy of castration against their tormentors. Ilsa is buried alive in shit. Dean Cundey, onetime cinematographer for John Carpenter, cophotographed the film. He has since gone on to bigger, though not always better, things.

Ilsa—She Wolf of the SS

Cambist Films, 1974; Color; 72 minutes
Director: Don Edmonds
Producer: Herman Traeger
Writer: Jonah Royston
With: Dyanne Thorne, Sandi Richman, Wolfgang Roehm, Jo Jo Deville

Buxom Thorne plays Ilsa, the sadistic head torturer of a Nazi concentration camp where all manner of grisly (and purportedly true, if you believe producer Traeger's ominous voice-over introduction) genetic and deviant experiments are being carried out. Ilsa really enjoys her work and indulges in it on and off hours. She also knows how to throw a party. At one, for a visiting German dignitary (Roehm), instead of the old girl-in-the-cake routine, she has a girl stand on a block of ice with a rope around her neck. As the ice melts, she slowly strangles. Other Ilsa tricks include castrating male prisoner lovers who don't measure up to her sexual

standards. The females, she merely electrocutes. In the end, she's killed by her own German high command, who fear her more than they do the Allies. *They Came from Within*'s Joe Blasco handled the very convincing—and very stomach-churning—special effects. The camp exteriors, incidentally, were shot on old "Hogan's Heroes" sets. But that Ilsa, she's no Colonel Klink!

The Incredible Melting Man

American-International, 1978; Color; 84 minutes
Director: William Sachs
Producer: Samuel F. Gelfman
Writers: William Sachs, Rebecca Ross
With: Alex Rebar, Burr DeBenning, Myron Healey, Rainbeaux Smith

Astronaut Rebar returns to earth suffering from a rare disease contracted while he was in outer space. Seems the temperature change, combined with the virus, is causing him to melt. But that's not the worst of it. He's also developed a powerful hunger—and only human flesh will do. As space scientists and the authorities try to find and stop him before he consumes the local populace, Rebar melts into the backwoods, looking for victims to satisfy his insatiable appetite. Good effects by Rick Baker. Look for director Jonathan Demme in a cameo role.

The Incredible Torture Show

See Bloodsucking Freaks

Indiana Jones and the Temple of Doom

Paramount Pictures, 1984; Color; 118 minutes
Director: Steven Spielberg
Producer: Robert Watts

Writers: Willard Huyck, Gloria Katz
With: Harrison Ford, Kate Capshaw, Amrish Puri, Roshan Seth, Philip Stone, Ke Huy Quan

The intrepid Jones sets out to retrieve a precious gem that has been stolen from an East Indian village and rescue the villagers' children who have been taken captive and put to work in the mines by a bizarre group of cultists straight out of *Gunga Din.* Capshaw is a nightclub singer who unwittingly tags along. This prequel to the megahit *Raiders of the Lost Ark* is even more fast and furious than the first film and boasts even more scenes designed to make your stomach heave. There's a dinner sequence where the bill of fare includes monkey brains and slithery eels—the latter consumed by one of the diners in a single stomach-churning gulp. There's also lots of equally slimy bugs crawling around—and a scene where a man gets his pulsating heart yanked from his chest, which resulted in a national outcry for the MPAA to create a new movie rating (PG–13). Ky Huy Quan's "Short Round," Indiana's diminutive helper, is strident and thoroughly obnoxious.

Inferno

Twentieth Century-Fox, 1980; Color; 107 minutes
Director: Dario Argento
Producer: Claudio Argento
Writer: Dario Argento
With: Leigh McCloskey, Alida Valli, Daria Nicoldi, Eleanora Giorgi

Lots of plot (all senseless), gallons of blood (all red), rafts of acting (all ripe), tons of mystery (possibly intentional), and volumes of production design (all gorgeous) signal another typical Dario Argento opus. Love Argento's slapdash story sense or hate it, this is probably his most beautiful film. Alas, it is also very likely his most

incomprehensible (no mean feat), and it offers a climax that is a huge letdown. The plot—as far as can be discerned—has something to do with the Three Mothers (forces of evil) living in (or under) lavish art deco apartment houses in three parts of the world. Narration and time-location titles clarify nothing. Along the way are a handful of noteworthy sequences, including an unintentionally hilarious one where a woman is savaged by cats (you can almost *see* the stagehands tossing the flying felines into frame), which are later drowned in sacks by an antique dealer, who is being devoured for his pains by rats during a lunar eclipse, until a maniacal greasy-spoon cook happens along to put him out of his misery with a couple well-aimed blows of his butcher knife! Wow! All this and Keith Emerson's rip-off of Jerry Goldsmith's *Omen* score, too.
—K. H.

Innocents from Hell

See Sisters of Satan

Inseminoid

Shaw-Jupiter, 1981; Color; 86 minutes
Director: Norman J. Warren
Producers: Richard Gordon, David Speechley
Writers: Nick and Gloria Maley
With: Judy Geeson, Robin Clark, Jennifer Ashley, Stephanie Beacham, Victoria Tennant

High body count *Alien* clone that takes the malevolent extraterrestrial theme a provocative step further by having outer-space scientist Geeson impregnated by a slime creature and giving birth to half-human/half-alien and all cannibalistic offspring. Tyro British splatter director Warren, working with a good cast, good FX—and *no* budget—knows when to divert our attention from the film's shortcomings by piling on the gore: namely, every other scene. A full-throttle gross-out replete with a disgusting alien birth sequence and scores of murders as Geeson and her trapped outer-space pals wipe each other out and, in turn, get wiped out. It is aka *Horror Planet*.

Invasion of the Blood Farmers

NMD Film Distributing Company, 1972; Color; 80 minutes
Director: Ed Adlum
Producer: Ed Adlum
Writers: Ed Adlum, Ed Kelleher
With: Norman Kelley, Tanna Hunter, Bruce Detrick, Jack Neubeck, Paul Craig Jennings

How ya gonna keep 'em down on the farm after they've been pureed? A half-baked religious sect modeled after the Druids cooks up a wild scheme to keep its catatonic, anemic, dying queen alive by using ritual sacrifices involving gallons of human blood. The ads for this film were not misleading. "See what really happens on a TERROR FARM!" they screamed. "We warn you! Don't eat before you see this show and you'll have nothing to lose."

Invasion of the Body Snatchers

United Artists, 1978; Color; 115 minutes
Director: Philip Kaufman
Producer: Robert H. Solo,
Writer: W. D. Richter
With: Donald Sutherland, Brooke Adams, Leonard Nimoy, Jeff Goldblum, Veronica Cartwright

Creepy remake (with an urban setting this time around) of the 1956 Don Siegel classic. This version's a little too long, a bit too overblown, and far too slowly paced to achieve classic status itself. But don't get me wrong; it's still quite good. As in the original, pod creatures from the stars are taking over humans, draining them of their emotions and turning them into McCarthyesque witch-hunters. Unlike the original, this film had a real budget, so the special effects are a lot better—and, of course, a lot more disgusting. I also like the revised ending, where Sutherland realizes that to live in a town taken over by pod people he must mimic them, and he identifies his only surviving friend (Cartwright) in order to appear convincing—in short, he becomes a pod anyway. Look for cameos by Kevin McCarthy, Don Siegel, and Robert Duvall.

The Island

Universal, 1980; Color; 113 minutes
Director: Michael Ritchie
Producers: Richard Zanuck, David Brown
Writer: Peter Benchley
With: Michael Caine, David Warner, Angela Punch-McGregor

News-magazine reporter Caine and his incredibly snotty son fly to the Bahamas to investigate a series of unsolved missing-persons cases and stumble upon a cult of pirate cutthroats, descendants of the infamous buccaneers, who are still living in the old style, plundering and killing unsuspecting tourists for booty. A piece of farfetched drivel in which Caine literally sleepwalks through his role, and the pirates, who speak in a patois of gibberish, are about as fearsome as The Three Stooges.

Island of the Alive (It's Alive III)

Warner Brothers, 1986; Color; 95 minutes
Director: Larry Cohen

Producer: Paul Stader
Writer: Larry Cohen
With: Michael Moriarty, Karen Black,
　　Laurene Landon, Gerrit Graham

Larry Cohen's films have always been a
mixed bag. They usually begin with an
interesting—if offbeat—premise, but fall
apart somewhere along the line. *Island
of the Alive,* the third of the *It's Alive*
movies is, as might be expected, an eccentric concoction. Mutant babies are
placed on an island to isolate them from
society. They grow up (at an accelerated
rate) and—are you ready for this?—have
mutant babies of their own. If that's not
far-out enough, it turns out the adult mutants aren't such bad folks after all—just
misunderstood. Michael Moriarty is on
hand, as he often seems to be in Cohen's
movies, playing yet another character on
the edge. Some gore as the babies attack
various victims (before we find out how
nice they are deep down inside).—J. B.

Island of the Twilight People

See Twilight People

I Spit on Your Grave

The Jerry Gross Organization, 1980;
　　Color; 98 minutes
Director: Meir Zarchi
Producers: Joseph Zbeda, Meir Zarchi
Writer: Meir Zarchi
With: Camille Keaton, Aaron Tabor,
　　Richard Pace, Anthony Nichols

Keaton (reputedly a relative of the late
Buster) is raped by a quartet of thugs.
After recuperating, she exacts her revenge on them—with castration being a
favored method. Often compared to *Last
House on the Left* (1972), the film really
has more in common with John Boor-

man's *Deliverance* (1972) and, particularly, Sam Peckinpah's *Straw Dogs* (1971).
Reportedly even John Waters admits he
was grossed out by it. Ultrasleazy and disturbing splatter flick that is by no means
the brainless exploitation vehicle many
critics have accused it of being. It is aka
Day of the Woman.

It's Alive

Warner Brothers, 1974; Color; 91
　　minutes
Director: Larry Cohen
Producer: Larry Cohen
Writer: Larry Cohen
With: John P. Ryan, Sharon Farrell,
　　Andrew Duggan, Guy Stockwell,
　　Michael Ansara

Farrell gives birth to a mutant baby that
makes quick work of everyone in the operating room. Distraught father Ryan must
track junior down as the hungry tot crawls
about the city feasting on milk-truck drivers and various other people. Excellent
effects by Rick Baker and a terrific score
by Bernard Herrmann make this low-key
splatter pic a winner. Followed by two
sequels, *It Lives Again* (1978) and *Island
of the Alive* (1986).

It's Alive II

See It Lives Again

It's Alive III

See Island of the Alive

It Lives Again

Warner Brothers, 1978; Color; 91
　　minutes
Director: Larry Cohen
Producer: Larry Cohen

Writer: Larry Cohen
With: Frederic Forrest, Kathleen
    Lloyd, John P. Ryan, John Marley,
    Andrew Duggan

Sequel to *It's Alive* (1974). Turns out that Ryan's deadly tot wasn't the only one. There's more—a veritable army of them. He tries to warn pregnant Lloyd and her husband (Forrest) that they're about to add to the list, but they don't believe him until it's too late. Essentially, this is just a rehash of the original, though not as exciting. Effects are minimal. The excellent score by the late Bernard Herrmann was fashioned by Herrmann disciple Laurie Johnson (of TV's "The Avengers") out of used and unused tracks from the first film. It is aka *It's Alive II.*

Jack's Back

Palisades Entertainment, 1988; Color;
    97 minutes
Director: Rowdy Herrington
Producer: Tim Moore
Writer: Rowdy Herrington
With: James Spader, Cynthia Gibb,
    Rod Loomis, Rex Ryan

Capitalizing on the Jack the Ripper centennial (1888–1988), writer-director Herrington updates the grisly exploits of history's legendary serial killer. The locale is modern Los Angeles, where prostitutes are being killed and mutilated on the exact dates the original Ripper struck. Several med students fall under suspicion. They don't get along too well with each other. When one of them (Spader) is murdered, his twin brother (Spader also), who witnessed the crime in a dream, decides to get to the bottom of it all. Plodding whodunit that telegraphs its "surprise ending" way too early. Surely the infamous and venerable Jack deserves more memorable commemorative treatment than this!

Jack the Ripper

Cineshowcase, 1978; Color; 105
    minutes
Director: Jesus Franco
Producer: Peter Baumgartner
Writer: Jesus Franco
With: Klaus Kinski, Josephine Chaplin,
    Herbert Fux, Lina Romay

The phantom killer of the London fog strikes again in this el cheapo production shot on West German and Swiss locations that look absolutely nothing like London. Kinski makes a somnolent Jack, slicing up the ladies and dropping their bodies in the Thames.

Jack the Ripper of London

Distributor unknown, 1971; Color; 87
    minutes
Director: José Luis Madrid
Producer: José Luis Madrid
Writers: José Luis Madrid, Jacinto
    Molina, Sandro Continenza
With: Paul Naschy, Patricia Loran,
    Rensso Marinano, Orquidea de
    Santis

Spanish horror-film star Naschy took time out from playing his continuing werewolf character, Waldemar Daninsky, and various other movie monsters to play that true-life monster, Jack the Ripper—though actually he's only a suspect in the Ripper's mutilation murders of London's prostitutes. (The film updates the crimes to the seventies.) The real Ripper turns out to be a cop. The film combines this tidbit of actual Ripper lore (the cop theory has never been taken very seriously) with other, more unsavory bits—such as having the Rip clip off the ears of his victims and perform other such acts, all shown in fairly graphic detail. Naschy also co-wrote the script of this seldom-shown Spanish cheapie under his given name, Jacinto Molina.

Jason Lives

See Friday the 13th—Part VI: Jason Lives

Jaws

Universal, 1975; Color; 124 minutes
Director: Steven Spielberg
Producers: Richard Zanuck, David Brown
Writers: Peter Benchley, Carl Gottlieb
With: Roy Scheider, Richard Dreyfuss, Robert Shaw, Lorraine Gary, Murray Hamilton

Depending upon how you look at it, this is either a poor man's *Moby Dick* (1956) or a rich man's *Creature from the Black Lagoon* (1954). A twenty-five-foot great white shark invades the waters off Amity Island at the outset of the summer tourist season and starts gobbling up the swimmers. Police chief Scheider wants to close the beaches, but mayor Hamilton won't let him. As a result, the team of Scheider, Dreyfuss, and Shaw must venture out in a boat and try to kill the shark at sea. Expertly directed, nail-biting thriller.

Jaws 2

Universal, 1978; Color; 116 minutes
Director: Jeannot Szwarc
Producers: Richard Zanuck, David Brown
Writers: Howard Sackler, Carl Gottlieb
With: Roy Scheider, Lorraine Gary, Murray Hamilton

Another great white shark descends on Amity Island, arguably to revenge the death of its mate at the hands of Steven Spielberg. Scheider is quite good as the police chief, a thankless role this time around, but the film is little more than a rehash of the original—which was not all that "original" to begin with. Szwarc (it rhymes with shark) replaced John Hancock as director shortly after filming began. He gives the shark so many close-ups that you can see it's a fake.

Jaws 3-D

Universal, 1983; Color; 99 minutes
Director: Joe Alves
Producer: Rupert Hitzig
Writers: Richard Matheson, Carl Gottlieb
With: Bess Armstrong, Dennis Quaid, Simon MacCorkindale, Lou Gossett, Jr.

More attacks from yet another great white; which has invaded a Sea World-style attraction in Florida. Quaid plays the grown-up son of Amity sheriff Roy Scheider (who declined to participate in any future *Jaws* sequels after being contractually bound to star in the unfortunate *Jaws 2*), who tries to stop the shark from putting the bite on all the tourists. Director Alves served as production designer on the first film. Originally the film was to be a comedy titled *Jaws 3—People 0*. Mild gore.

Jaws the Revenge

Universal, 1987; Color; 87 minutes
Director: Joseph Sargent
Producer: Joseph Sargent
Writer: Michael de Guzman
With: Michael Caine, Lorraine Gary, Lance Guest, Mario Van Peebles

Amity police chief Brodie has died of a heart attack, leaving his younger son, Sean, to take over. During the Christmas holidays, Sean is gobbled up by a great white shark. Mrs. Brodie (Gary) is convinced the attack was personal and that her older son, Michael (Guest), a researcher for the

Bahamian Fishery Department, may be next on the shark's menu. She's right, of course. Caine plays a pilot who falls for the widow and helps her and Michael stave off the beast—but not before it eats his plane. Once again, too many close-ups of "Bruce" the mechanical shark allow you to see how phony it looks and therefore kill the suspense. The low-gore theatrical release was rated PG–13. The videocassette contains approximately three minutes of graphic shark-chomping footage cut from the theatrical version. They don't help much. A sucker for reading final credits, I got a chuckle out of this one: Marine Coordinator—John "Moby" Griffin.

Just Before Dawn

Distributor unknown, 1980; Color; 90
    minutes
Director: Jeff Lieberman
Producers: David Sheldon, Doro
    Vlado Hreljanovic
Writers: Mark Arywitz, Gregg Irving
With: George Kennedy, Chris
    Lemmon, Deborah Benson

Not to be confused with an old William Castle flick of the same title, this cross between *Friday the 13th* and *The Hills Have Eyes* involves a group of luckless campers who run into some inbred hill folks with saws who don't like anyone treading on their property. Kennedy plays a forest ranger who helps out in the nick of time. Chris Lemmon is the son of actor Jack Lemmon.

Keep My Grave Open

Distributor unknown, 1980; Color; 80
    minutes
Director: S. F. Brownrigg
Producer: S. F. Brownrigg
Writer: F. Amos Powell
With: Camilla Carr, Gene Ross

Brownrigg's follow-up (seven years later!) to his *Don't Look in the Basement* is an atmospheric but confusing (as well as tedious) blood feast about a bizarre woman who lives in an old mansion—she goes by the name "The Lady of the Mansion," strangely enough—and lures passersby to the secluded house so that a mysterious force can murder them. The film opens with a nosy hitchhiker getting skewered with a sword. Things go rapidly and gruesomely uphill or downhill from there, depending upon your point of view.

Killbots

See Chopping Mall

The Killer Behind the Mask

See Savage Weekend

Killer Fish

Associated Films, 1979; Color; 101
    minutes
Director: Anthony Dawson (Antonio
    Margheriti)
Producer: Alex Ponti
Writer: Michael Rogers
With: Lee Majors, Karen Black, James
    Franciscus, Margaux Hemingway,
    Marisa Berenson

Heist movie in which the haul winds up in piranha-infested waters. Various sorts set out to retrieve the goods, which at least provides some motivation for getting them into the water so that they can be eaten in glorious Technicolor. Is it my ears, or does Margaux Hemingway speak with a pronounced lisp? Made in Brazil.

Killer Party

A Polar Film & Marquis Production,
    1986; Color; 92 minutes
Director: William Fruet

Producer: Michael Lepiner
Writer: Barney Cohen
With: Martin Hewitt, Ralph Seymour, Elaine Wilkes, Paul Bartel, Sherry Willis Burch, Alicia Fleer, Joanna Johnson

The opening of this picture takes off in three different surprising directions before settling down to its story of three college coeds who are determined to get into the exclusive Sigma Alpha Pi sorority. After that, it turns into a pretty standard version of the old "who's killing the teenage partygoers in the old dark house" melodrama. Who is the killer? Is it one of the supersnooty Sigma Alpha Pi sisters? Is it one of the cruelly sexist Beta Tau boys? Is it the practical-joking, ugly-duckling pledge? Or, is it the spirit of the fatal hazing victim from years past? I'm not telling. The plot keeps twisting and turning and the pace is brisk. The acting, by the mostly young cast, is consistently good, with an interesting turn by director/actor Paul Bartel as a professor. Splatter fans may be somewhat disappointed because the gore in this film is a long time coming and isn't very graphic or extensive.—D. K.

Killer's Moon

Distributor unknown, 1978; Color; 90 minutes
Director: Alan Birkinshaw
Producers: Gordon Keymer, Alan Birkinshaw
Writer: Alan Birkinshaw
With: Anthony Forrest, Tom Marshall, Georgine Kean, Nigel Gregory

Gritty, British low-budgeter about four crazies who escape from a mental home where they are being experimentally treated with LSD (not a good idea, as anyone who lived through the sixties will admit). Anyway, the brains of the homicidal foursome are now completely scrambled, but their killer instincts are still intact. They head for the scenic English countryside, where, predictably, they meet up with some teenage schoolgirls on an outing and launch a campaign of terror, butchering their way through them. Made two years before *Friday the 13th,* but of the same school. Shot in Ken Russell country, the gorgeous Lake District, which provides a scenic backdrop to the graphic bloodletting.

The Kindred

An FM Entertainment Release, 1986; Color; 92 minutes
Directors: Jeffrey Obrow, Stephen Carpenter
Producer: Jeffrey Obrow
Writers: Stephen Carpenter, Jeffrey Obrow, John Penny, Earl Ghaffari
With: David Allen Brooks, Amanda Pays, Kim Hunter, Rod Steiger

An interesting change of pace from the psycho/slasher films which have dominated the horror scene since *Halloween* in 1978. Rod Steiger and especially Kim Hunter remind us of what good acting is, and it is a credit to the rest of the cast that they are able to hold their own against these two pros. The script not only provides the cast with believable characters and realistic dialogue but also tells a compelling story. The film leaves some unanswered questions—just what is Rod Steiger doing with a dungeon/torture chamber under his lab?—but these problems aren't too serious. There are some decent gore effects, but they take a backseat to the story. The scene in which a character turns into a bizarre amphibian creature, complete with working gills, is very effective, as is the climactic scene when the monster goes through a total metamorphosis.—J. B.

La Lama Nel Corpo

See The Murder Clinic

La Lupa Mannera

See Legend of the Wolfwoman

Last House on Dead End Street

Cinematic Films, 1977; Color; 90
   minutes
Director: Victor Juno
Producer: Norman F. Kaiser
Writer: Brian Lawrence
With: Credits unavailable

Many people have accused splatter movies of being little more than fantasized "snuff films." Some have even gone so far as to accuse a few of being real "snuff films." *Last House on Dead End Street* perversely invites—even inflames—this controversy. It's about a bunch of sleazoid filmmakers who make "snuff films" that their distributor doesn't know are "snuff films"—until the filmmakers slaughter the distributor and some other people on film and use the scenes to make another "snuff film." A genuinely over-the-top gore epic that's rapidly achieving cult status.

Last House on the Left

Hallmark Releasing, 1972; Color; 91
   minutes
Director: Wes Craven
Producer: Sean S. Cunningham
Writer: Wes Craven
With: David Hess, Lucy Grantham,
   Sandra Cassel, Marc Sheffler, Ada
   Washington, Jeremy Rain, Fred
   Lincoln

Trio of degenerates rape and mutilate two young girls in the woods. Unwittingly, they stop off at the home of one of the victims. When the parents catch on to what's happened, they start laying the groundwork for revenge via castration and a chain saw. Intense and disturbing watershed splatter movie with an almost documentary feel, which director Craven now considers so grim that it even shocks him. Loosely based on Ingmar Bergman's *The Virgin Spring* (1960), this is one of anti-splatter film critic Roger Ebert's avowed "guilty pleasures."

Last Rites

See Dracula's Last Rites

The Legacy

Universal, 1979; Color; 100 minutes
Director: Richard Marquand
Producer: David Foster
Writers: Jimmy Sangster, Patrick Tilley,
   Paul Wheeler
With: Katharine Ross, Roger Daltrey,
   Sam Elliot, Charles Gray, John
   Standing

Ross is drawn, along with some other guests, to one of those secluded mansions so beloved of uninspired screenwriters. There, she finds herself the prey of the house's virtually mummified owner, who wheezes in hiding behind the folds of an oxygen tent. Turns out the old geezer is the head of a devil cult and he wants to enthrone Ross at its head before he wheezes into the Great Beyond. Before that not-too-exciting revelation jolts us awake, however, Ross and company are treated to a string of clichéd scares (shadowy disappearing shapes and so on). There are also some diverting "creative deaths" in the tradition of *The Omen*—drownings, impalements, etc.—but nothing flamboyant enough to lift the film above the norm.

Legacy of Blood

See Blood Legacy

Legend of Blood Castle

See The Female Butcher

Legend of the Wolfwoman

Dimension Pictures, 1976; Color; 100
   minutes
Director: Rino Di Silvestro
Producer: Diego Alchimeded
Writers: Renato Rossini, Rino Di
   Silvestro
With: Annik Borel, Frederick Stafford,
   Renato Rossini, Dagmar
   Lassander, Osvaldo Riggieri

Possessed by the spirit of a long-dead female werewolf, a young girl (Borel) becomes a lycanthrope herself. The
transformation scenes allow her ample
opportunity to strip. When she starts
chomping away at the community, police
detective Stafford is called in to investigate. It is aka *Wolfwoman* and *La Lupa
Mannera.*

Lifeforce

Cannon Films, 1985; Color; 101
   minutes
Director: Tobe Hooper
Producers: Menahem Golan, Yoram
   Globus
Writers: Dan O'Bannon, Don Jakoby
With: Peter Firth, Steve Railsback,
   Frank Finlay, Mathilda May,
   Michael Gothard

Astronaut Railsback discovers an alien life
form (May) in the tail of Halley's Comet
and brings it back to earth. Turns out
she's a vampire with a penchant for walking around in her birthday suit, and she
kisses people and shrivels them up. Some

victims even crack apart like hammered
stone. Soon all of London is in peril. Firth
is the Scotland Yard inspector who does
little but stand around. Though the effects (by John Dykstra) are good, this is
an astonishingly boring and laughable
alien invasion flick that retains little of
Colin Wilson's excellent SF novel, *The
Space Vampires,* upon which it is based.

The Long Riders

United Artists, 1980; Color; 100
   minutes
Director: Walter Hill
Producer: Tim Zimmermann
Writers: Bill Bryden, Steven Phillips
   Smith, Stacy and James Keach
With: David, Keith, and Robert
   Carradine; Stacy and James
   Keach; Randy and Dennis Quaid;
   Christopher and Nicholas Guest

What do you do when you're saddled with
yet another retelling of the too-often-told
saga of Jesse James and his boys? You
gimmick it up, swipe plot devices and set
pieces from the works of other, better
filmmakers (such as Robert Altman and
Sam Peckinpah to name two), and lay on
the bloody special effects; in short, you
make a splatter Western. At least, that's
what Walter Hill did here. No doubt about
it: The film is exciting, atmospheric, and
gory as hell. The James boys would have
loved it. Terrific score by Ry Cooder.

The Lost Boys

Warner Brothers, 1987; Color; 98
   minutes
Director: Joel Schumacher
Producer: Harvey Bernhard
Writers: Janice Fischer, James
   Jeremias, Jeffrey Boam
With: Corey Feldman, Jason Patric,
   Corey Haim, Dianne Wiest, Kiefer

Sutherland, Edward Herrmann, Barnard Hughes

Though its title is taken from *Peter Pan*, *The Lost Boys* is a hip, contemporary vampire tale (with almost the same plot as *Near Dark*, another hip, contemporary vampire tale made the same year). Patric and Haim move to sleepy Santa Clara, California, with their divorced mom (Wiest) and encounter a group of motorcycle punks who happen to be vampires. When Patric becomes an undead (or semi-undead), little brother Haim enlists the aid of *Friday the 13th* alumnus Feldman (doing a very funny turn as a prepubescent Sylvester Stallone) in destroying the vampires and returning Patric to normal. Shot like a music video, *The Lost Boys* is terrific to look at. But director Schumacher's all-too-frequent use of tight close-ups during the FX sequences dull their impact. The film is also a bit too flip to generate many scares. It's funny, though, with a lot of witty dialogue. Crackpot grandpa Hughes's closing line is especially priceless.

Lunch Meat

Monogram Entertainment Group and Tapeworm Productions, 1987; Color; 86 minutes
Director: Kirk Alex
Producer: Mark Flynn
Writer: Kirk Alex
With: Kim McKamy, Chuck Ellis, Elroy Wiese, Joseph Ricciardella, Robert Oland

Unabashed rip-off of *The Texas Chainsaw Massacre*, about a family of cannibals that kills people, sells the bulk of the carcasses to a local burger joint, and eats the leftovers. Spotting some vacationing teens, they detour them into the woods and begin hacking away at them with machetes, meat cleavers, pickaxes and shovels. At the conclusion, one of the teens—a girl—manages to find her way to the highway and escape with the overweight junior member of the meat-loving clan in whirling pursuit. The gore FX of people having their throats torn out and eaten, their heads severed, and their feet impaled with a pickaxe are plentiful and fairly well executed despite the project's distinctly poverty row origins. The film's so cheap you can even hear the camera noise in the background, and the editing, which allows you to see the splices most of the time, seems to have been done with one of the prop meat cleavers.

Macabro

Distributor unknown, 1980; Color; 91 minutes
Director: Lamberto Bava
Producers: Gianni Minervi, Antonio Avati
Writers: Lamberto Bava, Pupi Avati, Roberto Gandus
With: Bernice Stegers, Roberto Posse, Stanko Molnar

This feature film debut by the son of Mario Bava reveals the heavy shadow of Bava *père* (for whom Bava *fils* worked many years as an assistant)—but with an equally heavy dash of Roman Polanski and Michael Powell tossed in for good measure. Stegers is a sexually bizarre young woman who keeps the severed head of her former lover on hand—and in bed with her—for, well, who *knows* what for! A nosy neighbor (Posse), who's blind, becomes obsessed with the girl but winds up killing her instead. This doesn't sit too well with the head in the bed, which proceeds to chomp the blind man to death in retribution. The film was not released theatrically in the United States. Coscenarist Pupi Avati later wrote and directed the intriguing *Revenge of the Dead*.

The Mad Butcher

Ellman Films, 1972; Color; 85 minutes
Director: Guido Zurli
Producer: Harry Hope
Writer: Charles Ross
With: Victor Buono, Karen Field, Brad
   Harris, John Ireland

Buono does away with his victims' bodies
by grinding them up into sausages and
selling them to the police. Yet another
variation on the story of Sweeney Todd.

Madhouse

Distributor unknown, 1981; Color; 90
   minutes
Director: Ovidio G. Assonitis
Producer: Ovidio G. Assonitis
Writers: Ovidio G. Assonitis, Stephen
   Blakely, Peter Shepherd, Robert
   Gandus
With: Trish Everley, Michael MaCrea,
   Dennis Robertson

Good sister/bad (i.e., nutso) sister psychofilm in the mold of Brian De Palma's
Sisters. Everley's deranged and deformed
twin escapes from the madhouse where
Everley had her committed. With the help
of a vicious trained dog, bad sis sets out
to terrorize good sis to death by killing
everyone around her. The film includes
lots of rotting corpses plus that old standby
of the 1980s splatter film scene, "the power
drill through the head" bit. There's also
a twist ending.

Madman

Distributor unknown, 1981; Color; 88
   minutes
Director: Joe Giannone
Producer: Gary Sales
Writer: Joe Giannone
With: Alexis Dubin, Harriet Bass, Seth
   Jones, Tony Fish

Another *Friday the 13th* clone about a
summer camp—closed years before when
a mass-murdering lunatic sliced and diced
most of the counselors—that reopens,
thus encouraging the lunatic's return. Like
Jason, the knife-wielding crazy of the title
(here named Madman Marz) is virtually
a supernatural creature who seemingly
can't be stopped. Typical of the mad slasher
subgenre, the splatter murders—here executed by Jo Hansen—are graphic and
convincing.

The Majorettes

Major Films, 1987; Color; 93 minutes
Director: Bill Hinzman
Producer: John Russo
Writer: John Russo
With: Kevin Kindlin, Terrie Godfrey,
   Mark V. Jevicky, Sueanne
   Seamens, Denise Holt, Carl
   Hetrick, Russ Streiner

This reunion of some of the old *Night of
the Living Dead* gang—including NOLD
cowriter Russo (who also has a cameo as
a coroner), NOLD coproducer and actor
Streiner (who plays a Baptist minister) and
NOLD graveyard ghoul Hinzman (who, in
addition to directing, has a cameo as a
cop)—yields very disappointing results. A
mad slasher is killing high school majorettes, one of whom has also been targeted
by her infirm grandmother's German nurse
(who's out to get the girl's inheritance). A
devil-cult biker gang is also mixed into the
boiling pot. Lots of graphic throat slashings
and other fun stuff (well executed by FX
chief Gerald Gergely) and leering shots of
the nubile majorettes removing their bras.
But the pace is interminable.

Make Them Die Slowly

Distributor unknown, 1981; Color; 93
   minutes
Director: Umberto Lenzi

Producer: Antonio Crescenzi
Writers: Umberto Lenzi
With: Lorraine de Selle, Bryan
    Redford, John Morghen, Zora
    Kerova

Young anthropologists visiting Colombia in search of cannibals run into something worse—drug dealers who torture their native slaves when they fail to produce the goods fast enough. The natives turn on their dope-dealing masters, as well as the young anthropologists, torturing them and making them die slowly—thus the title. In one particularly gruesome scene, one of the female anthropologists is strung up by her breasts and left to die screaming as the others watch. It is aka *Cannibal Ferox.*

Maniac

Analysis Films, 1981; Color; 91
    minutes
Director: William Lustig
Producers: Andrew Garroni, William
    Lustig
Writers: Z. A. Rosenberg, Joe Spinell
With: Joe Spinell, Caroline Munro

Spinell is a psycho who murders girls in all sorts of horrible ways, scalps them, then uses their scalps to adorn the heads of female department store mannequins that he keeps for sex at home. A roller coaster ride of pathology and splatter that gives new meaning to the word *sleaze.* Effects by Tom Savini, who has since disavowed the film. Splatter fans tend to hate it also for being too ugly and depressing. It is certainly both.

The Man with Two Heads

Mishkin Films, 1972; Color; 80
    minutes
Director: Andy Milligan

Producer: William Mishkin
Writer: Andy Milligan
With: Denis DeMarne, Julia Stratton,
    Berwick Kaler, Jacqueline
    Lawrence

Umpteenth retelling of the R. L. Stevenson tale of Dr. Jekyll and his murderous alter ego. What sets this one apart is that it was made for about a dollar and a half. In this version, Dr. Jekyll downs his infamous potion and turns into the appropriately named Mr. Blood. Made in England. It is aka *Dr. Jekyll and Mr. Blood.*

Mark of the Devil

Hallmark Releasing, 1970; Color; 97
    minutes
Director: Michael Armstrong
Producer: Adrian Hovan
Writer: Sergio Cassner
With: Herbert Lom, Udo Keir, Reggie
    Nalder, Adrian Hovan

The first U.S. film to be heavily promoted with the fictitious V for Violence rating. And to show that the distributors knew what they were talking about, squeamish patrons were supplied free "vomit bags" at the door. (Why not? The airlines do it.) Lom plays a sadistic nineteenth-century witch-finder who uses all manner of torture to make women (usually naked) confess that they are in league with the devil. His methods, sad to say, are all based on fact. But *Mark* is not intended as a history lesson. It's a splatter show—plotless but stomach-churningly effective—with lots of graphic depictions of dismemberments, amputations, hangings, burnings, and so on. Oh, and sex too, of course.

Mark of the Devil Part 2

Hallmark Releasing, 1972; Color; 90
    minutes
Director: Adrian Hovan

Producer: Adrian Hovan
Writer: Adrian Hovan
With: Anton Diffring, Jean-Pierre
  Zola, Erica Blanc, Reggie Nalder

Hovan, who produced and played a part in *Mark of the Devil,* here takes the route of the triple-threat *auteur*—he also plays another small part, but uses a pseudonym (Percy Parker), so as not to appear overly credit-conscious. This time around, Diffring plays the witch-finder in search of nubile victims to maim and mutilate. He's also after the fortune of a count (whom he killed) that has fallen into the hands of the count's voluptuous widow. What better way to separate widow from cash than to have her declared a witch? Nalder is his leering assistant and together they have a high old time subjecting the widow (and others) to the rack and the lash. Hallmark again advertised the film as rated V for Violence, but dispensed with the "vomit bag" gimmick.

Martin

A Libra Films Release, 1978; Color
  and B&W; 95 minutes
Director: George A. Romero
Producer: Richard P. Rubinstein
Writer: George A. Romero
With: John Amplas, Lincoln Maazel,
  Christine Forrest, Elyane Nadeau,
  Tom Savini

Loner teen Martin (Amplas) goes to live with his superstitious cousin (Maazel), who is convinced the boy is a vampire. Whether vampire or garden-variety psychopath, Martin is definitely one screwed-up kid. Slashing his victims with a razor, he drinks their blood—then discusses his escapades on a late-night radio talk show. All of this takes place in a decaying Pennsylvania town called Braddock, where even the church has decided to move on—

leaving the place spiritually defenseless and therefore easy prey for Nosferatu-psycho Martin. More cerebral and suspenseful than gory—though Martin's murders and demise will not disappoint Romero fans. Romero has a delightful cameo as a priest whose favorite film is *The Exorcist.* The film marked Tom Savini's debut as Romero's special-effects chief.

Mausoleum

Western International Pictures, 1983;
  Color; 96 minutes
Director: Michael Dugan
Producers: Robert Barich, Robert
  Madero
Writers: Robert Barich, Robert
  Madero
With: Marjoe Gortner, Bobbie Bresee,
  Norman Burton, La Wanda Page,
  Maurice Sherbanee, Julie Christy
  Murray

A young girl (Murray) fleeing from her mother's funeral is drawn to a sinister mausoleum, where she is possessed by a demon because of a seventeenth-century curse. Her family name is Nomed. Get it? As an adult (Bresee), she murders a masher, her aunt, and a delivery boy by telekinesis, while preferring to dispatch the gardener and her husband (Gortner) by more old-fashioned means, such as slashing with a garden implement and a body-bursting bear hug. Her appearance while possessed ranges mindlessly from glowing green eyes, through heavy makeup, to early John Buechler prosthetics. She is eventually exorcised with a crown of thorns by her psychiatrist uncle. The gore scenes are short, poorly conceived and edited, and never register with any emotional force. The only original touch is the demon's breasts, which transform into miniature replicas of its own head.—D. K.

She-Devils on Wheels—1968
(Copyright © 1968 Mayflower Pictures, Inc.)

Silent Night, Bloody Night—1973
(Courtesy, Cinemabilia)

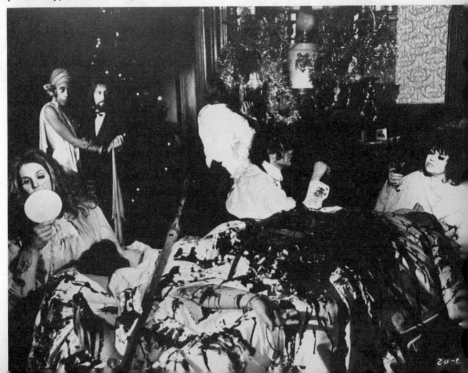

The Sender—1982
(Copyright © 1982
Kingsmere Properties Ltd.)

The Texas Chainsaw Massacre
—1974 (Courtesy, Edwin Neal)

The Baby—1974
(Copyright © 1973 Quintet
Films/Courtesy, Daniel Krogh)

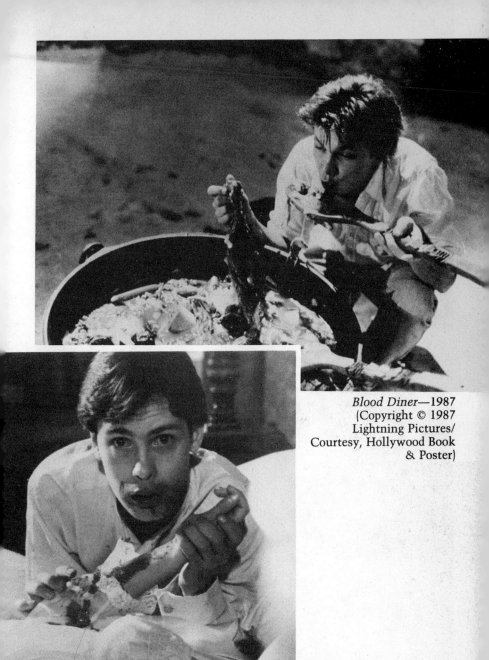

Blood Diner—1987
(Copyright © 1987
Lightning Pictures/
Courtesy, Hollywood Book
& Poster)

Martin—1978
(Copyright © 1977 Braddock
Associates/Courtesy,
Hollywood Book & Poster)

Island of the Alive—1986
(Copyright © 1986 Larco Productions/Courtesy, Hollywood Book
& Poster)

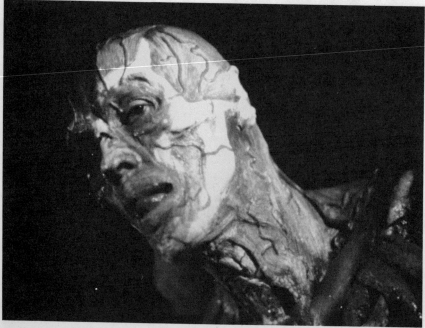

Hellraiser—1987
(Copyright © 1987 New World Pictures/Courtesy, Hollywood
Book & Poster)

The Flesh and Blood Show—
1973 (Copyright © 1973
Entertainment Ventures, Inc./
Courtesy, Hollywood Book
& Poster)

*The Fly—*1986
(Copyright © 1986 Twentieth
Century-Fox/Courtesy,
Hollywood Book & Poster)

Rawhead Rex—1986
(Copyright © 1986 Alpine Pictures/
Courtesy, Hollywood Book & Poster)

Don't Look in the Basement—1973
(Copyright © 1973 Hallmark Releasing
Corp./Courtesy, Hollywood Book &
Poster)

The Beast Within—1982
(Copyright © 1982 United Artists
Corp./Courtesy, Hollywood Book
& Poster)

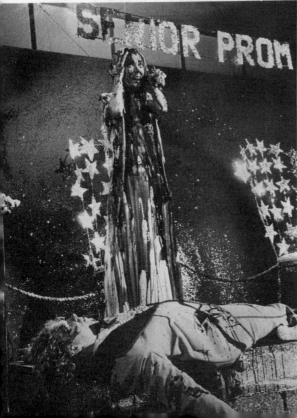

The Bird with the Crystal Plumage
—1969 (Courtesy, Cinemabilia)

The Brood—1979
(Copyright © 1979
New World Pictures)

Andy Warhol's Frankenstein—
1974 (Copyright © 1974
Bryanston Pictures)

Maximum Overdrive

De Laurentiis Entertainment Group,
    1986; Color; 98 minutes
Director: Stephen King
Producer: Martha Schumacher
Writer: Stephen King
With: Emilio Estevez, Laura
    Harrington, Pat Hingle, John
    Short

When earth passes through the tail of a comet, all the machines on the planet turn against man. Most of the film's action is set at a truck stop, where the mechanical beasts outside circle the trapped humans inside like bloodthirsty Indians in an old Western. (Director King pays more than a few nods in the film not only to the Western but to pal George Romero's *Dead* films and, especially, Hitchcock's *The Birds*.) The film opens well with a spectacular pileup on a malfunctioning bridge. After that, the splatter is applied quite thickly as trucks and lawnmowers, you name it, start wiping out humans. Presumably some violent scenes were cut to avoid an X rating. King calls his directorial debut ". . . the cinematic equivalent of a Big Mac and fries." Wait! I've heard that one before; he says the same thing about his books. Unlike his books, however, there isn't an ounce of suspense or characterization in this interminable mess.

Microwave Massacre

Distributor unknown, 1979; Color; 76
    minutes
Director: Wayne Berwick
Producers: Thomas Singer, Craig
    Muckler
Writers: Thomas Singer, Craig
    Muckler
With: Jackie Vernon, Loren Schein, Al
    Troupe

That electronic, fast-food wonder, the microwave oven, becomes an instrument of death at the hands of late comedian Jackie Vernon when he discovers how good his wife tastes at the sound of the chime. Borrowing liberally from Roger Corman's classic black comedy, *The Little Shop of Horrors*, this pointed satire on the rising tide of splatter isn't as funny as it might have been, but Vernon's deadpan style is a comic plus; his character of an entrepreneur who hooks the neighborhood on eating human flesh looks forward to the Blands (Paul Bartel and Mary Woronov) in *Eating Raoul*, which has a similar plot.

Midnight

Distributor unknown, 1981; Color; 91
    minutes
Director: John A. Russo
Producer: Donald Redinger
Writer: John A. Russo
With: Lawrence Tierney, Melanie
    Verliin, John Hall, Charles
    Jackson, John Amplas

Gross and overbearing cop Tierney tries to seduce stepdaughter Verliin. She runs away from home and winds up the prisoner of a religious cult that plans to sacrifice her at, you guessed it, *midnight*. A made-in-Pennsylvania independent by *Night of the Living Dead* cocreator Russo, who adapted the screenplay from his own novel (which, frankly, I found a lot *more* horrifying than the film version). The basic problem with *Midnight* is that there isn't a likable character in it; there's no one with whom to really identify, as there was in *Night of the Living Dead*. Tom Savini handled the special effects, which are very good.

Mixed Blood

Sara Films, 1984; Color; 97 minutes
Director: Paul Morrissey
Producers: Antoine Gannage, Steven
    Fierberg
Writer: Paul Morrissey
With: Marilia Pera, Richard Ulacia,
    Linda Kerridge, Marcelino Rivera

If Paul Morrissey had filmed *West Side
Story*, it might have looked a lot like *Mixed
Blood* (and been a lot more fun in the
process). Extremely and graphically violent, *Mixed Blood* nevertheless manages
to be more quirkily amusing than appal-
ling, not in the least due to the typically
wigged-out Morrissey cast. Impossible
though it may seem, Morrissey managed
to find a Brazilian Joe Dallesandro in
Richard Ulacia, who plays the brain-damaged Thiago, son of Rita La Punta (Marilia
Pera), the Carmen Miranda-fixated head
of a motley assortment of Brazilian drug
dealers in New York. Pera, who lords over
her little band from a rickety throne en-
shrined with Christmas lights and sheet
music from Carmen Miranda pictures, is
even better at capturing Morrissey's
strange nonacting style. The plot is something of a shambles but scarcely matters
in view of the vastly entertaining tangents
into which Morrissey continually drifts,
including a visit to a store that sells nothing but Menudo souvenirs and clothing
that must be seen to be believed. Linda
Kerridge is on hand as a bleached blonde,
vaguely English-accented Debbie Harry
clone who falls for Thiago and is shot
through the head for her pains ("I must
look like hell," she comments before expiring). The lunatic spirit of the whole
thing, though, is best summed up when
Marcelino Rivera asks Pera just why Miranda "never stop smiling." "Why should
she?" Pera glowers, explaining, "She was
the Abraham Lincoln of Brazil—*and she
knew it*!" And Lincoln never sang "The

Lady in the Tutti Fruiti Hat," so perhaps Carmen was one up on him.
—K. H.

Mondo Trasho

New Line Cinema, 1969; B&W; 95
    minutes
Director: John Waters
Producer: John Waters
Writer: John Waters
With: Mary Vivian Pearce, Divine,
    David Lochary, Mink Stole

Waters's first feature (made for $2,000!)
follows Pearce's exploits through Baltimore's underbelly. Along the way, she
meets a foot fetishist, gets run over by a
Jayne Mansfield look-alike (Divine), gets
committed to an insane asylum, gets
wounded in a knife fight, and winds up
dying in a pigpen. A self-described "gutter
film."

Monkey Shines

Orion Pictures, 1988; Color; 112
    minutes
Director: George A. Romero
Producer: Charles Evans
Writer: George A. Romero
With: Jason Beghe, John Pankow,
    Kate McNeil, Joyce Van Patten,
    Christine Forrest

Romero's first film since splitting with
longtime producer Richard Rubinstein—
and his first with major studio backing
—is contrived and unconvincing. It's also
quite bland. Romero eschews ultra-gory
FX to the point of self-consciousness, but
substitutes little else in return. Aspiring
athlete Beghe becomes a quadriplegic after being hit by a bus. Pal Pankow, a research scientist, gives him a bright little
capuchin monkey named Ella to lend a
helping hand. Ella turns out to be very
bright indeed. Through some undefined

mind-link process, she picks up on Beghe's anger and resentment toward others and becomes a nocturnal avenger. When he finds out and tries to stop her, she turns on him—hell hath no fury like a monkey spurned, I guess. The movie is like a dozen other man versus beast (the hero is even named "Mann"), science/nature gone wrong, monster from the id potboilers. It even includes a gory cliché shock epilogue that was apparently imposed upon Romero to give the film some badly needed zip. Ella and the other actors are good, but the characters and their motivations are paper-thin. A real disappointment.

Monty Python and the Holy Grail

Cinema 5, 1975; Color; 86 minutes
Directors: Terry Gilliam, Terry Jones
Producers: Michael White, John Goldstone
Writers: Terry Gilliam, Terry Jones, and the rest of the Python troupe
With: Graham Chapman, Eric Idle, Michael Palin, Terry Jones, John Cleese, Terry Gilliam

Lunatic retelling of the legend of King Arthur, his knights (pronounced ka-*nig*-its), and their search for the Holy Grail by England's most-celebrated band of comic crazies since Spike Milligan and his Goons. Death-dealing rabbits, oversized knights who get bloodily whittled down to size, catapulted horses, and liberal dousings of *merde* converge in this full-scale splatter comedy. Uneven but frequently hilarious. And visually quite sumptuous.

Monty Python's Meaning of Life

Universal, 1983; Color; 103 minutes
Director: Terry Jones
Producer: John Goldstone

Writers: The Monty Python gang
With: Eric Idle, Michael Palin, Terry Jones, Graham Chapman, John Cleese, Terry Gilliam, Carol Cleveland

More gross-out comedy in the vein of *Monty Python and the Holy Grail*, minus the gallons of blood. The funniest scene —perhaps because it *is* the grossest— features Terry Jones as a hugely obese diner at a restaurant, who keeps puking all over everyone so that he can make room for more food. A mixed bag.

Moonshine Mountain

Herschell Gordon Lewis Productions, 1964; Color; 90 minutes
Director: Herschell Gordon Lewis
Producer: Herschell Gordon Lewis
Writer: Charles Glore
With: Chuck Scott, Adam Sorg, Jeffrey Allen, Bonnie Hinson

Country-western singer Scott goes back home to the Carolina hills to recharge his creative batteries and gets involved in a battle between some moonshiners and "The Revenooers." Typically tongue-in-cheek as well as over-the-top gore epic from splatter pioneer H. G. Lewis (his directorial credit reads: "Directed by Herschell Gordon Lewis, who ought to know better, but don't"). In addition to all his other duties, Lewis also photographed the film and even composed the score. Lots of nasty murders and cornball "good ole boy" humor. Filmed in "Lightnin' Color" in the "Beautiful Carolinas."

Motel Hell

United Artists, 1980; Color; 102 minutes
Director: Kevin Connor
Producers: Robert and Steven-Charles Jaffe

Writers: Robert and Steven-Charles
   Jaffe
With: Rory Calhoun, Nancy Parsons,
   Paul Linke, Nina Axelrod,
   Wolfman Jack

Yet another *Texas Chainsaw Massacre*-inspired "meat movie," though one that strives more for laughs—at least until the gore-filled conclusion where the deranged Calhoun dons a pig mask for a chain-saw duel with the heroine. Calhoun plays a backwoods motel owner (his place is called Motel Hello, but the *o* is always on the blink) and farmer specializing in specially cured meats. The special curing process involves waylaying travelers, slicing their vocal chords, and burying them up to their necks in his garden—making his products homegrown, as it were. His motto: "It takes all kinds o' critters to make Farmer Vincent fritters!" Overlong and, though pointedly satiric, not all that funny, either. The chain-saw duel is good, though.

Mother's Day

United Film Distribution, 1980; Color;
   98 minutes
Director: Charles Kaufman
Producers: Charles Kaufman, Michael
   Kravits
Writers: Charles Kaufman, Warren
   Leight
With: Nancy Hendrickson, Deborah
   Luce, Rose Ross, Tania Pierce

A trio of vacationing ex-college girls are captured and tortured by two perverted hillbillies and their even more demented mother (Ross). When one of the girls dies after being repeatedly raped and beaten, the other two pool their resources and strike back. Though conventionally gruesome and bloody, this is also an unconventional satire. Mad mom and her boys are consummate media junkies. Every-

thing they do is motivated by the tube, which chatters away from its shrine-like position in the living room. When one of the hillbillies is crowned with an unused set at the splattery finish, he enters his TV world for real, his head twitching and sparks flying. A clever and unjustly maligned splatter movie; its major failing is one of those terrible shock epilogues.

Mountaintop Motel Massacre

New World Pictures, 1983; Color; 95
   minutes
Director: Jim McCullough, Sr.
Producers: Jim McCullough, Sr., Jim
   McCullough, Jr.
Writer: Jim McCullough, Jr.
With: Bill Thurman, Anna Chappell,
   Will Mitchell

Mental case Chappell is released from a home and goes back to run the decaying Mountaintop Motel (a place that makes the Bates Motel look positively high class) with her equally unstable daughter. When she catches the daughter performing some kind of weird ritual, she flips out and accidentally kills the girl with a hand scythe. A blinding rainstorm à la *Psycho* results in an influx of customers—some newlyweds, an itinerant mechanic, an adman and two nubile hitchhikers he picked up. Chappell releases snakes, rats, and cockroaches into their cabins via trapdoors. When that doesn't drive the guests away, she goes after them with her trusty hand scythe. The splatter murders are predictably graphic but nothing special—except for Chappell's demise, in which a nice touch of irony is coupled with the blood. The low-key acting ranges from mediocre to okay. And there's a supernatural undercurrent to the proceedings that doesn't really work. All that said, however, there is a compelling atmosphere and creepiness about the film that can't be denied.

Ms. 45

Rochelle Films, 1981; Color; 84
   minutes
Director: Abel Ferrara
Producer: Rochelle Weisberg
Writer: Nicholas St. John
With: Zoe Tamerlis, Steve Singer,
   Peter Yellen, Jack Thibeau, Albert
   Sinkys

A Polanski-inspired psychodrama. Tamerlis plays Thana, a mute garment worker
who is raped twice in a single afternoon.
She manages to kill her second assailant,
chops up the body, and disposes of the
various parts around town. Having armed
herself with the dead man's gun, she blows
away another potential assailant, then
mounts an all-out war on the city's hus-
tlers, pimps, street gangs, and other mi-
sogynists. Invited to a costume party by
her chauvinistic boss (Sinkys), who puts
the move on her, Thana, dressed as a nun,
starts blasting away at everybody until she
is fatally stabbed by a female friend. Kinetic feminist exploitation film directed
with real style by Ferrara, who also appears in the film (under his pseudonym
Jimmy Laine) as one of Thana's would-
be assailants. Tamerlis claims an attempt
was actually made on her life because of
the female-avenger image she created in
the film. It is aka *Angel of Vengeance.*

Multiple Maniacs

New Line Cinema, 1970; B&W; 90
   minutes
Director: John Waters
Producer: John Waters
Writer: John Waters
With: Divine, David Lochary, Mary
   Vivian Pearce, Mink Stole, Edith
   Massey

Baltimore's redoubtable John Waters
concocted this picaresque tale of a trav-
eling freak show called the Cavalcade of

Perversion. Run by the psychotic Divine,
the show serves as a front for a gang of
drug-crazed killers who bear a striking
resemblance to the Manson family. Film's
climax has Divine raped by a giant lobster.

Murder by Mail

See Schizoid

The Murder Clinic

Europix, 1966; Color; 86 minutes
Director: Elio Scardmaglia
Producer: Elio Scardmaglia
Writers: Ernesto Gastaldi, Luciano
   Martino
With: William Berger, Francoise
   Prevost, Mary Young, Barbara
   Wilson

Surgeon attempts to restore the face of a
deformed woman. The locale of the operation is an out-of-the-way clinic for the
incurably eccentric. As the doc works on
the face, a hooded killer with a knife roams
the corridors in search of someone to stick
it in. Based on the novel *The Knife in the
Body* by Robert Williams. It is aka *The
Blade in the Body, Night of Terrors, The
Murder Society,* and *Revenge of the Living Dead.* Italian title: *La Lama Nel Corpo.*

The Murder Society

See The Murder Clinic

Mutant

New World Pictures, 1982; Color; 86
   minutes
Director: Allan Holzman
Producer: Roger Corman
Writer: Tim Curran
With: Jesse Vint, Dawn Dunlap,
   Linden Chiles, June Chadwick

Now here's a unique plot line. Wonder where they came up with it? An alien creature invades a spaceship and grows larger and more vicious each time it chows down on one of the unsuspecting crew. Instead of blasting it into outer space, however, the quick-thinking survivors kill it with poison—by operating on a terminally ill crew member and feeding his cancerous organs to the impudent beast. It is aka *Forbidden World*.

My Bloody Valentine

Paramount Pictures, 1981; Color; 91 minutes
Director: George Mihalka
Producers: John Dunning, Andre Link, Stephen Miller
Writer: John Beaird
With: Paul Kelman, Lori Hallier, Neil Affleck, Don Francks, Keith Knight

A psychotic miner terrorizes the Canadian town of Valentine Bluffs on guess what day? His motive: revenge for a mining disaster that took place twenty years earlier. Intense but typical slasher film that was heavily scissored of its gore prior to release.

Nail Gun Massacre

A Terry Lofton/Futuristic Films Production, 1985; Color; 90 minutes
Directors: Bill Leslie, Terry Lofton
Producer: Terry Lofton
Writer: Terry Lofton
With: Rocky Patterson, Michelle Meyer, Ron Queen, Beau Leland

A woman is raped by the workers on a construction site. Soon, it's open season on construction workers and others as they are stalked by a killer wearing camouflage clothes and a visored crash helmet, who wields a pneumatic nail gun and drives a hearse. This film should be big with body-count buffs because it delivers fifteen bloody murders in less than ninety minutes. They start, imaginatively enough, with a man's hand being nailed to his forehead as he shields his face. Another man is nailed in the groin after accidentally urinating on the killer's boots. A third has his clasped hands nailed together as he pleads for his life; and others are nailed to trees and walls. After the first half-dozen, however, the filmmakers just start piling up bodies. Although the killer's voice is disguised to sound like a poor man's Darth Vader, you'll know him by what he says when he first appears unmasked. The doctor hero and the sheriff eventually get wise too, and the killer falls to his death from an elevated ore conveyor. Most elements of this production are merely competent, but the music rises above the rest to generate some tension and suspense, even though the climax still peters out in the end.—D. K.

Near Dark

De Laurentiis Entertainment Group, 1987; Color; 94 minutes
Director: Kathryn Bigelow
Producer: Steven-Charles Jaffe
Writers: Eric Red, Kathryn Bigelow
With: Adrian Pasdar, Jenny Wright, Lance Henricksen, Bill Paxton

A vampire road movie, or *Bonnie and Clyde* meets *The Lost Boys*. Oklahoma farmboy Pasdar encounters otherworldly Wright one night outside a cowboy honky-tonk and she puts the bite on him, turning him into a neophyte vampire. She takes him to her home—a stolen van with duct tape and aluminum on the windows to keep the daylight out—where she lives with an undead wild bunch armed to the teeth with knives and guns. They balk at having Pasdar join their cross-country bloodletting party and he proves too squeamish to become one of them. His veterinarian pop gives him a transfusion, returning him to normalcy but incurring the wrath of the bloodsuckers. There's a wild barroom brawl in which the cowboy vampires slice people with knives and spurs to get at their blood, and an even wilder motel shootout where the bullet holes in the walls send shafts of daylight (à la *Blood Simple*) streaming into the trapped vampires' lair. There are also lots of good lines, as when one of the undead sets fire to a van and the blaze reminds him of "that fire we started in Chicago." Apparently Mrs. O'Leary's cow wasn't guilty after all. Gordon Smith's FX of the vampires smoldering and exploding into flame in the sunlight are also top-notch.

Necropolis

Empire Pictures, 1987; Color; 77 minutes
Director: Bruce Hickey
Producers: Cynthia DePaula, Tim Kincaid
Writer: Bruce Hickey
With: LeeAnne Baker, Jacquie Fitz, Michael Conte, William K. Reed

Dreadful satanist/reincarnation flick that introduces a kinky new twist to splatter movie sexuality—soul sucking. The film begins with an 1868 prologue (set to the anachronistic beat of eighties disco music) where satanist Baker claims virgin bride Fitz just as she is being wed to Conte. Flash forward to 1986. Baker, all decked out in black leather, is prowling the streets of New York City in search of Fitz's reincarnation so that she can sacrifice her once more. To help out, she raises her dead disciples by sucking the souls out of various druggies and prostitutes and feeding the gooey substance (didn't know souls were gooey, did you?) to the rotting corpses to give them a pick-me-up. Conte, reincarnated as a Stallone-like cop, tries to save Fitz with the help of a black reverend

who knows how to throw a mean cross. The effects by Ed French are okay but nothing new.

A New Beginning

See Friday the 13th—Part V: A New Beginning

The New Blood

See Friday the 13th—Part VII: The New Blood

New Year's Evil

Cannon Films, 1980; Color; 85 minutes
Director: Emmett Alston
Producers: Menahem Golan, Yoram Globus
Writers: Emmett Alston, Leon Neubauer
With: Roz Kelly, Kip Niven, Grant Cramer, Chris Wallace, Louisa Moritz

Psychopathic killer goes on a cross-country murder spree, timing each of his orgies of bloodletting to occur at midnight so that they coincide with local coverage of a coast-to-coast New Year's Eve TV special. Kelly, the host of the special, was once a regular on TV's "Happy Days" during happier days.

The New York Ripper

Distributor unknown, 1982; Color; 92 minutes
Director: Lucio Fulci
Producer: Abrizio de Angeli
Writers: Lucio Fulci, Gianfranco Clerici, Dardano Sacchetti, Vincenzo Mannino
With: Jack Hedley, Almanta Keller, Howard Ross, Andrew Painter

Gore galore! If real hard-core splatter is your cup of blood—er, tea—you've come to the right place. No implied blood and guts here. No discreet cutting away at the point of action—Lucio Fulci delivers the real thing! The psycho killer drags a blade across the face of a young woman, leaving a trail of blood. When he reaches her eye, he simply continues cutting while the camera records every grisly detail. The poor woman even manages to roll her eyeball as it is being cut—a detail that lends an unnerving and realistic touch. There are several other violent deaths during the course of the film. Unfortunate victims being repeatedly stabbed and sliced with very convincing effects work. The rest of the film? Oh, yeah. Well, it's a pretty routine story about a hard-boiled New York City detective tracking down a psycho/slasher who turns out to be a character you'd never suspect.—J. B.

The Night Andy Came Home

See Deathdream

Nightmare

21st Century Pictures, 1981; Color; 97 minutes
Director: Romano Scavolini
Producers: John L. Watkins, William Milling
Writers: Romano Scavolini, William Milling
With: Baird Stafford, Sharon Smith, C. J. Cooke, Mik Cribben

Sexual psychopath Stafford is given drugs to curb his appetite for violence. Pronounced cured, he is released from a mental hospital, but he quickly reverts and begins stalking a young woman and her children on a southbound journey from New York to Florida. The film's ads trum-

peted Tom Savini as the effects maestro even though he scarcely worked on the film. Lurid and gross.

Nightmare Hotel

Distributor unknown, 1973; Color; 92 minutes
Director: Eugenio Martin
Producer: José Lopex Moreno
Writers: Eugenio Martin, Antonio Fos
With: Judy Geeson, Aurora Batista, Victor Alcazar, Lone Fleming

A made-in-Spain meat movie that bears more than a passing resemblance to *Psycho*. Sexually repressed hotel owner/restaurateur Batista (taking her cue from Norman Bates) carves up any and all female guests who exhibit signs of a healthy libido and stores their raw meat in the food cellar (no, not the *fruit* cellar) to be served up later to unsuspecting guests. Pert British tourist Geeson, whose sister stopped by the hotel and was quickly dispatched to the meat locker, catches on and in the tradition of *Psycho*'s enterprising Sam Loomis and Lila Crane decides to smoke out the psycho sicko on her own. At least director Martin avoids all those endless close-ups of eyes that made his cult favorite *Horror Express* such an unintentional howler.

A Nightmare on Elm Street

New Line Cinema, 1984; Color; 91 minutes
Director: Wes Craven
Producer: Robert Shaye
Writer: Wes Craven
With: John Saxon, Ronee Blakley, Heather Langenkamp, Amanda Weiss

The dreams of sleeping teens are haunted by the specter of a murderous child molester named Freddy Krueger whom their parents vengefully had put to death years before. One by one the teens are knocked off until heroine Langenkamp forces herself to go to sleep so that she can track down and destroy Freddy in her dreams. Though not *The Hills Have Eyes* by a long shot, *Nightmare* is one of Craven's better splatter efforts. It boasts an interesting concept (the seamless interweaving of dream states and waking states) plus a number of truly spectacular splatter set pieces. It's also got one of those annoying post-*Carrie* shock epilogues that, in this case, destroys the film's precariously balanced sense of logic. Followed by three sequels.

A Nightmare on Elm Street Part 2: Freddy's Revenge

New Line Cinema, 1985; Color; 84 minutes
Director: Jack Sholder
Producer: Robert Shaye
Writer: David Chaskin
With: Mark Patton, Kim Myers, Clu Gulager, Hope Lange, Robert Englund

The further adventures of Freddy Krueger, everybody's favorite killer sandman. Patton and his folks (Gulager and Lange) move into the Elm Street house where most of Freddy's dream antics took place last time—and he immediately becomes possessed by the spirit of the steel-fingered one. In a climax pilfered from *Altered States*, Freddy is driven out and Patton is returned to normalcy by the purifying love of his high school sweetheart (Myers, who looks like a teenage Meryl Streep). The meaningless shock epilogue returns the film to the sequence that opened it, as a high school bus is shanghaied by the unstoppable Freddy. Good effects, though not as many as in the first film.

A Nightmare on Elm Street Part 3: The Dream Warriors

New Line Cinema, 1987; Color; 96 minutes
Director: Chuck Russell
Producer: Robert Shaye
Writers: Wes Craven, Bruce Wagner, Chuck Russell, Frank Darabont
With: Heather Langenkamp, Craig Wasson, Patricia Arquette, Robert Englund, John Saxon

The last surviving kids from the old Elm Street neighborhood, all of them still suffering from dreams about Freddy, have been locked away in a local institution. A now grown-up Langenkamp returns as a therapist specializing in "pattern dreaming." With the help of the kids—whom no one but she, of course, will believe, she finishes off Freddy seemingly, though doubtfully, for good. This entry in the *Elm Street* saga throws in every conceivable kind of special effect possible—from splatter to stop-motion animation. The ending where Wasson and Saxon are attacked by Freddy's sword-wielding skeleton looks like something out of a Ray Harryhausen fantasy.

A Nightmare on Elm Street Part 4: The Dream Master

New Line Cinema, 1988; Color; 93 minutes
Director: Renny Harlin
Producers: Robert Shaye, Rachel Talalay
Writers: Brian Helgeland, Scott Pierce
With: Robert Englund, Brooke Bundy

Though Part 4 boasts some of the wildest FX sequences in the series, it also ranks with Part 2 as the dullest and most preposterous installment. It begins with Freddy's resurrection by the three remaining Elm Street kids (progeny of the vengeful adults who killed Freddy years before), who thought they'd dispatched him for good in Part 3. He kills them off, but the last one brings another school friend into her dream shortly before expiring and, presto, Freddy has another whole slew of teens to slay—the implication being that Part 4 will not be the last of the series. The most creative death occurs to a body-building teen whom Freddy turns into a bug so that he can squash her like same. The "Freddy Rap" composed expressly for the film and "sung" over the closing credits is a real groaner. Story by William Kotzwinkle (who should know better) and Brian Helgeland.

Night of Terrors

See The Murder Clinic

Night of the Creeps

Tri-Star Pictures, 1986; Color; 90 minutes
Director: Fred Dekker
Producer: Charles Gordon
Writer: Fred Dekker
With: Jason Lively, Steve Marshall, Jill Whitlow, Tom Atkins, Dick Miller

The teaser sequence takes place in outer space and the credits roll over black and white images circa 1959, but the body of this well-conceived SF/Horror/Splatter hybrid takes place on a college campus in the mid-eighties. Chris (Lively) and his paraplegic buddy J. C. (Marshall) are students pledging a fraternity, so Chris can win the love of Cynthia (Whitlow), his dream girl. Instructed by their brothers to steal a body from the medical lab, Chris and J. C. end up liberating a zombie from the past with a brainful of alien parasites. Soon, the parasite-infested zombies are multiplying, and a neurotic police detective (Atkins) with a dark secret in his past has entered the case. In the end, the de-

tective, Cynthia, and Chris battle an army of Chris's zombie frat brothers with a pistol, shotgun, and flamethrower. Director Dekker draws the diverse elements of his story together and neatly pays off on plot points made earlier in order to reach a climax with enough exploding heads, slimy parasites, blood, and burned flesh to satisfy the gore fans. Dick Miller makes a cameo appearance as a cop.—D. K.

Night of the Living Dead

Continental/Image Ten, 1968; B&W; 96 minutes
Director: George A. Romero
Producers: Russell Streiner, Karl Hardman
Writer: John A. Russo
With: Duane Jones, Judith O'Dea, Karl Hardman, Russell Streiner, Judith Ridley, Keith Wayne, Marilyn Eastman

Produced on a shoestring over a long series of weekends by a crew of filmmaking unknowns, this ghoulishly clever splatter movie became a minor cause célèbre on its initial release. Much of that furor has since died down and the film is now considered to be a classic. Its plot is very straightforward: All manner of corpses come back from the dead due to a freakish and undefined outer-space accident and begin to feed upon the living. Despite some imperfections, this low-budget shocker really delivers the goods. That's writer Russo who gets a tire iron yanked out of his forehead and director Romero as a Washington, D. C., reporter. Followed by *Dawn of the Dead* (1979) and *Day of the Dead* (1985).

Night School

Lorimar, 1981; Color; 89 minutes
Director: Kenneth Hughes
Producers: Larry Babb, Ruth Avergon

Writer: Ruth Avergon
With: Leonard Mann, Rachel Ward, Drew Snyder, Joseph R. Sicari

Produced with all the polish and expertise of a big studio production, this film emerges as more of a traditional thriller than a gritty splatter movie. A shame, too, because all the elements are present for a real gorefest. A psycho slasher wearing an ominous black motorcycle helmet and visor and wielding a wicked-looking knife tracks down attractive young women and decapitates them. Pretty gruesome stuff but director Kenneth Hughes somehow manages to make it all rather subtle and tasteful. The script isn't too bad, but there aren't enough suspects to keep the real killer's identity secret for very long and Rachel Ward simply has too much class and sophistication to be believable in the part she is asked to play. Not enough suspense to succeed as a conventional whodunit and not enough guts (literally and figuratively) to work as a splatter movie.—J. B.

Nurse Sherri

Independent International Pictures, 1977; Color; 88 minutes
Director: Al Adamson
Producer: Mark Sherwood
Writers: Michael Bockman, Gregg Tittinger
With: Jill Jacobson, Geoffrey Land, Marilyn Joi, Prentiss Moulden

A religious zealot with a bad ticker is spirited to the hospital but protests being operated on—maybe he's a Christian Scientist. His mistrust of medical science proves well founded, however, when he dies on the operating table. You can't keep a bad man down, though—at the exact moment of his passing, his vengeful spirit takes possession of one of the attendant nurses, Nurse Sherri (Jacobson). She robotically carries out his murderous revenge on the doctors who killed him, using all manner of sharp hospital instruments at his/her command—such as a pitchfork? Not as bad as Adamson's The *AstroZombies*, which has got to be one of the ten worst movies ever made.

Of Unknown Origin

Warner Brothers, 1983; Color; 90 minutes
Director: George Pan Cosmatos
Producer: Claude Heroux
Writer: Brian Taggart
With: Peter Weller, Jennifer Dale, Lawrence Dane, Shannon Tweed

Canadian executive Weller appears to be suffering a mid-life crisis due to a sterile job that doesn't challenge him anymore. When his wife (Tweed) goes out of town for the weekend, he finds his challenge in the form of a superrat that has invaded his apartment. He and the rat virtually destroy the apartment in a duel to the death. Many friends of mine felt this orgy of rat-man violence to be a clever "sleeper." I thought it was inane—even more inane after a second viewing. The rat may be clever, but its initial triumphs over "man" are due mostly to Weller's stupidity—he is surely one of the dumbest "heroes" to ever grace a splatter movie (hard to believe he became Robocop)! Tweed is a former model and Playmate of the Year.

The Omen

Twentieth Century-Fox, 1976; Color; 111 minutes
Director: Richard Donner
Producer: Harvey Bernhard
Writer: David Seltzer
With: Gregory Peck, Lee Remick, David Warner, Billie Whitelaw, Harvey Stephens, Leo McKern, Patrick Troughton

Peck is the U. S. Ambassador to the Court of St. James, whose newborn son is switched at birth by a group of satanists and replaced by the offspring of the devil. Little Damien grows into a very nasty toddler indeed, causing murder and mayhem wherever he goes. Mom Remick takes a header from a skyscraper hospital into a parked ambulance (director Donner must like this type of "creative death" a lot because he repeats it in his 1987 hit *Lethal Weapon*); priest Troughton gets skewered with a spear; Warner gets decapitated. And so it goes. Followed by *Damien—Omen II* (1978) and *The Final Conflict* (1981).

Omen II

See Damien—Omen II

Omen III

See The Final Conflict

Once Upon a Frightmare

See Frightmare

Orca

Paramount Pictures, 1977; Color; 92 minutes
Director: Michael Anderson
Producer: Luciano Vincenzoni
Writers: Luciano Vincenzoni, Sergio Donati
With: Richard Harris, Charlotte Rampling, Will Sampson, Keenan Wynn, Bo Derek

Whaler Harris catches a pregnant killer whale that proceeds to give birth on the deck of his boat. Both mama whale and her baby die, however, and papa, who has been watching from nearby, "flippers" out and decides to get revenge on Harris and company. A totally absurd mock *Jaws* from Dino De Laurentiis. Derek, one of the victims of Orca's wrath, sheds one of her legs instead of her clothes this time around.

The Other Side

See Poltergeist II—The Other Side

The Outing

The Movie Store, 1986; Color; 87 minutes
Director: Tom Daley
Producer: Warren Chaney
Writer: Warren Chaney
With: Deborah Winters, James Huston, Danny D. Daniels, Andrea St. Ivanyi

Some punks bent on robbery break into an old woman's house and find an ancient Aladdin-type lamp. When they kill the old woman, the lamp releases the spirit of a genie, who proceeds to splatter the disagreeable punks in high style. The lamp is turned over to a local museum. The curator's daughter persuades some of her high school chums to sneak in after hours for some merriment among the mummies, rubs the lamp, and unleashes the genie. The genie is suitably grotesque and spiteful as he goes about his business of killing the teens and others by such inventive means as decapitation by ceiling fan, impalement by ancient javelin, a revivified snake, an iron mask with interior spikes, and so on. The trouble is, the film's almost half over before it gets to all this "good stuff." An opera-singing guard who gets offed by the javelin but returns after the closing credits to take a final bow gives the film a definite lift.

Outland

Warner Brothers, 1981; Color; 109
   minutes
Director: Peter Hyams
Producer: Richard A. Roth
Writer: Peter Hyams
With: Sean Connery, Peter Boyle,
   Frances Sternhagen, Kika
   Markham

Connery is the newly installed federal
marshal of a mining colony on one of
Jupiter's moons, a forbidding place where
overworked miners are developing acute
cases of the crazies. He learns that they're
being given lethal drugs that step up their
productivity but drive them insane. Determined to stop the carnage, he finds
himself alone. His final showdown against
a trio of gunmen hired by company man
Boyle rips off *High Noon* (1952). Lots
of explosions and bleeding inside space
helmets.

Outlaw Force

Trans World Entertainment, 1988;
   Color; 95 minutes
Director: David Heavener
Producers: David Heavener, Ronnie
   Hadar
Writer: David Heavener
With: David Heavener, Paul Smith,
   Frank Stallone, Robert Bjorklund

Who does Heavener think he is, Clint
Eastwood or Charles Bronson? The answer is: *both*. In this absurdly derivative
vengeance melodrama, Heavener plays a
put-upon do-gooder who saves a gas station attendant from some violent, no-good
"good ole boy" rednecks. The rednecks
don't take too kindly to his interference
and decide to get even by raping and killing Heavener's wife, then kidnapping his
daughter. When the police prove to be
little help in bringing the culprits to jus-

tice and returning his daughter home,
Heavener decides he must do the job himself Eastwood/Bronson style. Low budget
and bad.

Parasite

Embassy Pictures, 1982; Color; 85
   minutes
Director: Charles Band
Producer: Charles Band
Writers: Alan J. Adler, Michael
   Shoob, Frank Levering
With: Robert Glaudini, Demi Moore,
   Luca Bercovici, Vivian Blaine,
   Cherie Currie

Another spawn of *Alien* (1979), featuring
malevolent sluglike creatures that rip their
way through people's bodies. The setting
is earth following "The Big One" where,
as if the parasites aren't enough, civi-
lization is also locked in combat with
splatter-punk gangs and right-wing paramilitary groups. Filmed in 3-D.

The Parasite Murders

See They Came from Within

People Who Own the Dark

Newcal Trefilms, 1975; Color; 86
   minutes
Director: Leon Klimovsky
Producer: Salvatore Romero
Writers: Vicente Aranda, Harry
   Narunsky
With: Maria Perschy, Tony Kendall,
   Paul Naschy, A. de Mendoza, T.
   Gimpera

Spanish postnuclear holocaust drama in
which the survivors, followers of the Marquis de Sade, find the chaos that envelops
them very much to their liking. They get
their comeuppance, though, when a de-

contamination team finds them, puts them to sleep, then buries them alive. Strives for significance but is just unpleasant. Spanish title: *Planeta Ciego*.

Phantasm

Avco Embassy, 1978; Color; 90
  minutes
Director: Don Coscarelli
Producers: Don Coscarelli, Paul
  Pepperman
Writer: Don Coscarelli
With: Michael Baldwin, Bill
  Thornsberry, Reggie Bannister,
  Angus Scrimm, Kathy Lester

Two brothers investigate a mysterious house where a friend was recently murdered and they encounter some very strange goings-on indeed. For example, a bizarre undertaker called The Tall Man (Scrimm), a proliferation of limb-tearing ghouls, and a flying silver disc that, when hurled at its victims, sprouts a sharp blade for quick impalement. Definitely original but it makes little narrative sense. Some gore effects were removed prior to release. Followed ten years later by a sequel—*Phantasm II* ("This summer . . . the ball is back!")—that's a lot gorier and more high-tech than the first film (a bigger studio, Universal, was behind the sequel) but not substantially different. Coscarelli again wrote and directed and Scrimm reappeared as The Tall Man.

Pink Flamingos

New Line Cinema, 1972; Color; 93
  minutes
Director: John Waters
Producer: John Waters
Writer: John Waters
With: Divine, David Lochary, Mary
  Vivian Pearce, Mink Stole, Edith
  Massey

Two groups of outcasts compete for the title of "The Filthiest People Alive" in this self-billed exercise in poor taste by the Baltimore director who could have written a book on the subject—in fact, he did. There are some raunchily funny moments (such as the furniture-licking scene), but overall, it's just plain disgusting—as it was meant to be. Divine's parting shot, which wins her the title, is especially nauseating. A genuinely rancid movie.

Piranha

New World Pictures, 1978; Color; 92
  minutes
Director: Joe Dante
Producers: Jon Davidson, Chako Van
  Leeuwen
Writer: John Sayles
With: Bradford Dillman, Kevin
  McCarthy, Heather Menzies,
  Keenan Wynn, Barbara Steele,
  Dick Miller

Wacko scientist McCarthy unleashes a strain of supercharged—and superhungry —experimental piranha into the waters of a nearby holiday resort run by Dick Miller, who, in the best Murray Hamilton tradition, refuses to warn the summer trade and risk losing profits during the busiest season of the year. Not so much a rip-off of *Jaws* as a parody of it—with lots of underwater blood and gore.

Planeta Ciego

See People Who Own the Dark

Poltergeist

MGM/UA, 1982; Color; 114 minutes
Director: Tobe Hooper
Producers: Steven Spielberg, Frank
  Marshall

Writers: Steven Spielberg, Michael
Grais, Mark Victor
With: JoBeth Williams, Craig T.
Nelson, Beatrice Straight, Heather
O'Rourke

Suburban home is beseiged by evil spirits
emanating from the family TV set. The
uninvited houseguests snatch the family's youngest daughter, then subject
everyone to a reign of supernatural terror. Mom and dad bring in parapsychol-
ogy researchers and an eccentric
spiritualist to help reclaim their stolen
tot. Turns out that a greedy land devel-
oper (James Karen) built their house on
land that was once a cemetery but didn't
bother to relocate the dead. Nice combination of humor, horror, and splatter
that suffers a bit from an overabundance
of technical razzle-dazzle. Though Hooper
is credited as director, the film bears the
unmistakable and, in this case, not wholly
desirable "Spielberg touch." Followed by
Poltergeist II (1986).

Poltergeist II—The Other Side

MGM/UA, 1986; Color; 91 minutes
Director: Brian Gibson
Producers: Michael Grais, Mark
Victor
Writers: Michael Grais, Mark Victor
With: Craig T. Nelson, JoBeth
Williams, Heather O'Rourke,
Oliver Robins, Will Sampson,
Julian Beck

This sequel to *Poltergeist* makes no sense
whatsoever. In the first film, the Freel-
ings were attacked by creatures from "the
other side" because their house had been
built over an Indian cemetery. In this film,
they've moved yet are plagued again! Why?
Because that's what happens in sequels,
that's why! The late Will Sampson plays
an Indian who uses tribal medicine to
ward off the avenging spirits. Beck is creepy

as a black-garbed whatever whom people
can walk through—and who can disap-
pear at will. The special effects are high-
tech and spectacular. When drunken Nelson regurgitates a tequila worm that's over
a foot long, you'll swear off the sauce for
life.

Possession

Distributor unknown, 1982; Color;
127 minutes
Director: Andrzej Zulawski
Producer: Marie-Laure Reyre
Writer: Andrzej Zulawski
With: Isabelle Adjani, Sam Neill,
Heinz Bennent

Menage à quatre splatter movie in which
the delectable Adjani finds herself torn
between three lovers, one of whom resembles the creature in *Alien* and may or
may not be a product of her confused
mind—like Catherine Deneuve's phantom lover in *Repulsion*. At any rate, their
frequent love scenes together are graphic
and erotic—not to mention slimy. She
gets pregnant but loses the baby in a
gruesome miscarriage scene that, for sheer
revulsion and audaciousness, almost
eclipses the scene where Samantha Eggar
gives birth to an id creature in David Cronenberg's similar-themed *The Brood.*
Adding to the fun of *Possession,* the jealous alien gobbles up everyone who threat-
ens his/its domestic bliss. One gets the
feeling that there's some kind of psychosexual, or, perhaps, political (the film
was shot in the divided city of Berlin),
undercurrent to all of this. But your guess
is as good as mine. The video version, cut
to ninety minutes, resolves even fewer
questions.

The Possession

See Amityville II: The Possession

Predator

Twentieth Century-Fox, 1987; Color;
107 minutes
Director: James McTiernan
Producers: Lawrence Gordon, Joel
Silver, John Davis
Writers: Jim and John Davis
With: Arnold Schwarzenegger, Carl
Weathers, Bill Duke, Jesse
Ventura

Space-age variation on Richard Connell's oft-filmed story *The Most Dangerous Game*—mixed with elements from *Alien, The Lost Patrol,* and half a dozen other movies. CIA man Weathers lures special agent Arnold and his muscle-bound band into the Central American jungles to rescue some diplomats who've been taken hostage by hostile guerillas. Once there, they find themselves up against a far more terrifying enemy—a chameleon space creature that hunts them down, kills them, and strips them of their flesh. Tough guy Arnold proves a resourceful opponent, however, and the mortally wounded creature finally nukes itself to death. McTiernan's direction is fast-paced, but the plot is oddly unsuspenseful. The effects (by Stan Winston and others) are top-notch, though. Watch for the scene where Weathers has his arm blown off while he's firing at the creature—and the severed limb keeps on firing. Gross stuff but inventive. Kevin Peter Hall plays the oversized interstellar sportsman with the scorpionlike face and mean laugh.

Prince of Darkness

Universal, 1987; Color; 102 minutes
Director: John Carpenter
Producer: Larry Franco
Writer: Martin Quatermass (John
Carpenter)
With: Donald Pleasence, Victor

Wong, Jameson Parker, Lisa
Blount, Alice Cooper

Seems that somewhere around seven million years ago (carbon-dating time), Satan—or maybe Son o' Satan—was imprisoned in the world's first lava lamp, but rather than swirl atop someone's TV set, he ended up perched on a secret altar guarded by a Catholic sect so mysterious even the Vatican hierarchy is unaware of its existence. Alas, this liquid Lucifer wants out so he can drag his even nastier father back from the "Dark Side" and start the millenium. Carpenter's entry in the Apocalyptic Claptrap Sweepstakes contains large doses of *The Exorcist, The Sentinel,* and *Evilspeak* to name a few of its more obvious sources. It's almost stately for about two-thirds of its length, then launches into the expected gooey horrors. The most unsettling aspect of the film is the obnoxious idea that the devil can control "lower life forms"—including worms, ants, beetles, and, shockingly, street people!—K. H.

Prison

Empire Pictures, 1988; Color; 101
minutes
Director: Renny Harlin
Producer: Irwin Yablans
Writer: C. Courtney Joyner
With: Lane Smith, Viggo Mortensen,
Chelsea Field, Lincoln Kilpatrick,
Tom Everett, Ivan Lane

Warden Sharpe (Smith), who suffers from nightmares about a prisoner executed for a crime the warden himself committed, is put in charge of the newly reopened, but rundown, Wyoming penitentiary where the execution took place. Among the busload of arriving inmates is the ghost of the dead prisoner (Mortensen). Sharpe inexplicably orders the walled-up execution chamber unsealed, unleashing a ma-

levolent light beam. A guard is strangled with barbed wire, a prisoner is burned to death, another prisoner is impaled with an iron bar, the inmates riot in fear for their lives, and Warden Sharpe gets his. The old, abandoned prison provides an interesting setting for this variation on standard haunted house themes. The FX are good and the direction stylish. But the script is such a jumbled mess and the characters' motivations so unclear that by the time you figure out even the rudiments of what's happening, you've long ceased caring.

Programmed to Kill

Trans World Entertainment, 1986; Color; 91 minutes
Director: Allan Holzman
Producers: Don Stern, Allan Holzman
Writer: Robert Short
With: Robert Ginty, Sandahl Bergman, Louise Caire Clark, James Booth

Mideast terrorists attack a marketplace in Greece and take two American children hostage. Ex-*Exterminator* Ginty, here playing a maverick CIA operative, puts aside his blowtorch for an Uzi, rescues the kids, and captures terrorist Bergman. Back in the U.S.A., the terminally wounded Bergman undergoes a special operation and is turned into a cyborg killing machine—the new "action Barbi" as one character calls her. She's sent back to the Middle East to terminate her former colleagues, but after she does, her memory circuits click in (as in *Robocop*) and she returns Stateside to get even with her programmers. She's superstrong and nearly unstoppable; she rips one guy's arm off, but when she loses a hand, she simply glues it back on. But Ginty gets her in the end, cutting her in half with a bulldozer as she tries to put him away with a bazooka.

Prom Night

Avco Embassy, 1980; Color; 91 minutes
Director: Paul Lynch
Producer: Peter Simpson
Writer: William Gray
With: Jamie Lee Curtis, Leslie Nielsen, Robert Silverman, Antoinette Bower, Casey Stevens

A masked killer stalks a group of high schoolers on the night of their senior prom, as revenge for an accidental death (fall from a window) caused by some of the teens six years earlier. Predictable *Halloween* (1978) clone, but with a little more stab and drip added.

Prom Night II

See Hello Mary Lou—Prom Night II

Prophecy

Paramount Pictures, 1979; Color, 95 minutes
Director: John Frankenheimer
Producer: Robert L. Rosen
Writer: David Seltzer
With: Robert Foxworth, Talia Shire, Armand Assante, Victoria Racimo

Anti-rape-the-landscape, pro-Indian, environmentalist monster movie in which doctor Foxworth and pregnant wife Shire travel to backwoods Maine to investigate the effects of pollution from a local lumber mill on the area's flora and fauna. What they discover is a race of toxic mutants that resemble a cross between Godzilla and a pizza with all the trimmings. After a genuinely scary opening where a pack of hunting dogs and their masters are pulled to their doom by who knows what, the film descends into ludicrousness and cheap thrills.

The Prowler

Sandhurst, 1981; Color; 91 minutes
Director: Joseph Zito
Producers: Joseph Zito, David Streit
Writer: Glenn Leopold
With: Vicki Dawson, Christopher
Goutman, Cindy Weintraub,
Laurence Tierney, Farley Granger

Ex-Jason Zito stepped behind the camera for this revenge shocker in the *Friday the 13th* (1980) mold about couples who are systematically butchered by a pitchfork-wielding maniac at a graduation dance, a reprise of similar events that occurred thirty-five years earlier at another graduation dance. Nothing new here except for Tom Savini's potent gore effects. It is aka *The Graduation*.

Psycho from Texas

Showcase Entertainment, Inc., 1981;
Color; 90 minutes
Director: Jim Feazell
Producer: Jim Feazell
Writer: Jim Feazell
With: John King III, Herschel Mays,
Tommy Lamey, Candy Dee, Janel
King, Joanne Bruno, Reed
Johnson

There's a lot of local Texas color in this movie, but very little of it is blood-red. The psycho of the title, Wheeler (King III), likes to degrade, beat up, and sometimes kill women because he saw his mommy turnin' a trick when he was just a young'un. Wheeler's in town to participate in a kidnapping scheme masterminded by a mysterious Mr. Big with his local henchman Slick (Lamey). The victim is oil man Bill Philips (Mays), whose daughter Connie (Dee) is about to marry her beau, Steve Foster. Philips escapes from Slick and they engage in a foot chase as long and boring as an Olympic marathon. Meanwhile, Wheeler rapes and/or kills Connie's best friend Ellen (King). We glimpse her bruised and bloody body as it falls out of a closet. Philips finally stabs Slick dead in the neck with a gaff (look it up). Steve, who turns out to be Mr. Big, is shot by the police after another seemingly endless foot chase (Can't these guys afford gas?). Wheeler meets a similar fate on his way out of town.—D. K.

Psychos in Love

Wizard Video/Generic Films, Inc.,
1986; Color; 88 minutes
Director: Gorman Bechard
Producer: Gorman Bechard
Writers: Gorman Bechard, Carmine
Capobianco
With: Carmine Capobianco, Debi
Thibeault, Frank Stewart, Cecilia
Wilde, Donna Davidge

It's cheap, crude, sleazy, sick, and funny, and I liked it! This neat little black comedy tells the story of Joe (Capobianco), a bartender, and Kate (Thibeault), a manicurist, who have two things in common: They both murder members of the opposite sex and they both hate grapes. Falling in love, they continue their murderous ways, at first separately, in an open relationship without jealousy or suspicion. When Kate does get jealous of one of Joe's victims, they decide to collaborate on their next killing for the sake of togetherness. This leads to a scene in which their victim, a stripper from Joe's bar who's like "The Shape" in *Halloween,* refuses to expire again and again. When the magic goes out of their murders, they turn to slasher videos, but then return to the real thing. Our loving psychos finally marry, but can they survive a cannibalistic killer plumber? This film's contrasting of domestic bliss and bickering with its many bloody murders is hilarious. It works because the victims are portrayed as despicable individuals who deserve to be offed,

and the film uses distancing devices—such as asides to the camera, having the microphone dip into the frame, and even showing the effects crew—to remind us that it's only a movie. The gore effects are crude but effective.—D. K.

Psycho II

Universal, 1983; Color; 113 minutes
Director: Richard Franklin
Producer: Hilton A. Green
Writer: Tom Holland
With: Anthony Perkins, Vera Miles, Robert Loggia, Meg Tilly, Dennis Franz

Twenty-two years after the fact, Norman Bates (Perkins) is judged "restored to sanity" and thrust back into society, much to the irritation of another *Psycho* veteran, Lila Loomis (Vera Miles). Yes, Lila appears to have married her late sister's lover, but since John Gavin, who played Sam Loomis, entered big-time acting as Ambassador to Mexico, he has conveniently expired in the meantime according to the script. Of course, it isn't long before the violins start screeching and the knife starts slashing; but is Norman responsible, or is Lila doing it all in an excessive attempt to prove him insane, or is there someone else? Okay, so it ain't Hitchcock, but for three-quarters of its length, *Psycho II* is a surprisingly good film—due almost entirely to Perkins's brilliant performance, in which he makes us as much afraid *for* Norman as of him. The film is slickly made, handsome, and director Franklin shows a lot of style—mostly other people's (Hitchcock, James Whale, Charles Laughton). It all degenerates into a thoroughly enjoyable, utterly absurd bloodbath and a gimmick ending that just doesn't work. Still, there's Perkins, plus lots of places in the Bates house we didn't get to see the first time, and, oh, it could have been so much worse.—K. H.

Psycho III

Universal, 1986; Color; 96 minutes
Director: Anthony Perkins
Producer: Hilton A. Green
Writer: Charles Edward Pogue
With: Anthony Perkins, Diana Scarwid, Jeff Fahey, Roberta Maxwell, Hugh Gillin

Having been directed during his career by two of the most brilliant of all filmmakers, Alfred Hitchcock and Ken Russell, Anthony Perkins takes over the directorial reins himself for the third installment in the *Psycho* series, and proves he learned much from his teachers. Sure, there are echoes of both Hitch and Russell throughout the film, but Perkins uses them to good effect (many of the Hitchcock evocations are obviously intended to be recognized to make a point), and the approach is bolder and more effective than *Psycho II*'s Richard Franklin achieved by bending over backward (and falling) *not* to emulate the original. This time the mystery element is missing (we know all along who's in that ugly dress and those sensible shoes) and the story concentrates on Norman's inner struggle with his alter ego when he falls in love with a suicidal ex-nun (Scarwid, who resembles Janet Leigh) who has lost her faith. (When she slashes her wrists in the Bates Motel at precisely the same moment Mother Bates comes calling, the confused girl's mind transforms her would-be attacker into a vision of the Virgin, and the shock jolts Norman back to himself.) Perkins doesn't flinch at graphic splatter effects, but the story is mostly an examination of two disaffected characters who *might* have been each other's salvation. The film is witty enough that it can easily be read as either an intensely serious Catholic meditation on guilt and redemption, or as a harsh parody of it. The motel setting (embodiment of the American Dream gone bad) takes precedence this time, giving the film an added depth. Hitchcock might well have been pleased.—K. H.

Q—The Winged Serpent

United Film Distribution, 1982; Color; 92 minutes
Director: Larry Cohen
Producer: Larry Cohen
Writer: Larry Cohen
With: Michael Moriarty, Candy Clark, Richard Roundtree

A pterodactyl (actually the revivified Quetzalcoatl of Mexican folklore) builds a nest in New York City's high-rise Chrysler Building, where, coincidentally, some stolen loot has also been stashed by petty thief Moriarty. As New York's finest pursue Moriarty and his stash, Q gobbles up anyone who comes near. Amusing monster movie parody laced with gore. Moriarty is very funny as the seemingly dim-witted thief/hero, a performance he would reprise in Cohen's *The Stuff*.

Rabid

New World Pictures, 1977; Color; 90 minutes
Director: David Cronenberg
Producer: John Dunning
Writer: David Cronenberg
With: Marilyn Chambers, Joe Silver, Howard Ryshpan, Patricia Gage, Susan Roman, Frank Moore

Porn queen Chambers plays an accident victim who undergoes a skin-grafting experiment that results in her turning into a rabies-spreading vampire. Instead of biting her victims in the neck, she lets her armpit do the work. Writer-director Cronenberg has proven himself capable of much better things than this frothy but decidedly mediocre reprise of *Night of the Living Dead* (1968). It is aka *Rage*.

Rage

See Rabid

Raiders of the Lost Ark

Paramount Pictures, 1981; Color; 115 minutes
Director: Steven Spielberg
Producer: Frank Marshall
Writer: Lawrence Kasdan
With: Harrison Ford, Karen Allen, John Rhys-Davies, Denholm Elliott, Ronald Lacey, Paul Freeman

Exec producer George Lucas and director Spielberg's fast-moving tribute to old-time serials is full of freewheeling action, but it also boasts a substantial *yechhh* factor, which makes it a splatter movie—one of the most spectacular and, to date, the most financially successful one ever made. The plot centers on hero Indiana Jones's (Ford) search for the Ark of the Covenant, which holds the tablets bearing the Ten Commandments (or what's left of them) —and the efforts of the Nazis to steal the Ark first. Its epic snake scene is guaranteed to make the tightest of skins crawl —and the denouement full of melting faces and exploding heads is rousing indeed. Followed in 1984 by a prequel, *Indiana Jones and the Temple of Doom*.

The Rats Are Coming! The Werewolves Are Here!

Mishkin Films, 1972; Color; 92 minutes
Director: Andy Milligan
Producer: William Mishkin
Writer: Andy Milligan
With: Hope Stansbury, Jacqueline Skarvellis, Berwick Kaler, Noel Collins

Another bargain-basement splatter bonanza from Andy Milligan—shot on location in his beloved England and Staten Island. Apocalyptic nightmare (With a title like that, what *else* could it be?) about a family of werewolves and a deranged girl who raises man-eating rats. Terrible, but the title ranks right up there with *I Dismember Mama* as one of the splatter genre's best. To promote the film, Milligan suggested that theater owners conduct drawings, with the winner collecting a live rat to feed to his/her mother-in-law!

Rawhead Rex

Alpine Pictures, 1986; Color; 89
    minutes
Director: George Pavlou
Producers: Kevin Attew, Don Hawkins
Writer: Clive Barker
With: David Dukes, Kelly Piper, Niall
    Tobin, Ronan Wilmot, Heinrich
    von Schellendorf

Lightning knocks over an Irish totem, releasing an eight-foot-tall flesh-eating devil creature buried there centuries ago following a legendary battle between good and evil. The supernatural creature is known as King Rawhead (or Rawhead *Rex*). In order to destroy the religious weapon that once defeated him (it's hidden in a church), Rawhead possesses a local cleric. He also spends some time decimating a nearby trailer park. A visiting American historian (Dukes), whose son was gobbled up by the creature, locates the weapon and with the help of his Irish-American wife (Piper) sends Rawhead back where he belongs in a protracted light show reminiscent of the climax of *Raiders of the Lost Ark*. This first feature written by horror-fiction superstar Clive Barker is stupefyingly awful. The special effects are cheap and unconvincing. The script, acting, and direction are even worse. A real bomb.

Raw Meat

American-International, 1973; Color;
    87 minutes
Director: Gary Sherman
Producer: Paul Maslansky
Writer: Ceri Jones
With: Donald Pleasence, Christopher
    Lee, Norman Rossington, David
    Ladd, Sharon Gurney, Hugh
    Armstrong

Men and women trapped when a London underground station collapsed upon them back in 1892 survive over the years by feasting on their dead and mating with each other. When their food runs out, they surface, kidnapping derelicts and commuters to restock their larder. When the cannibal leader's wife expires, he's compelled to go upstairs again and seek out a new bride (Gurney) to keep the race going. Her husband (Ladd) doesn't take too kindly to being cuckolded by a cannibal, however, and follows beauty and the beast to the subterranean lair. Pleasence and Lee are police inspectors in search of all those missing persons. Lee is on-screen for only a few minutes, however. A vivid, atmospheric, well-done little horror tale with plenty of raw meat to satisfy splatter fans. It is aka *Death Line*.

Razorback

Distributor unknown, 1984; Color; 95
    minutes
Director: Russell Mulcahy
Producer: Hal McElroy
Writer: Everett de Roche
With: Gregory Harrison, Arkie
    Whitely, Bill Kerr, Judy Morris

A savage wild boar called a "razorback" that's about the size of a VW bus goes on the rampage in the Australian outback. American Harrison and Aussie Morris join in the hunt, which climaxes at the farm of a pair of murderous brothers who illegally slaughter kangaroos for their meat. They get their comeuppance, though, courtesy of "Raze"'s lethal tusks. Flashy and violent variation on the familiar *Jaws* theme that lacks any real suspense due to a lack of empathy for any of the characters. Not released theatrically in the United States, though it is available on video.

Re-Animator

Empire Pictures, 1985; Color; 87 minutes
Director: Stuart Gordon
Producer: Brian Yuzna
Writers: Dennis Paoli, William J. Norris, Stuart Gordon
With: Jeffrey Combs, Bruce Abbott, Barbara Crampton, Robert Sampson

"Herbert, this has got to *stop!*" cries the stalwart hero (Bruce Abbott) of *Re-Animator* upon learning that Herbert (Jeffrey Combs) has just decapitated arch-villain Dr. Hill (Robert Sampson) with a shovel and then "re-animated" both his head and body. That off-the-wall lunacy pretty well sums up the approach of the film and helps explain why it marks one of the most audacious directorial debuts in many moons. No question that this is splatter with a vengeance (the film boasts no MPAA seal, but undoubtedly would have been awarded the dreaded X), yet it is what might be called "fun splatter," done with loads of style, energy, wit, and delirious bad taste. H. P. Lovecraft, from whose early "Herbert West—Re-Animator" stories the film is adapted, might well revolve in his sepulcher could he see the outrageous antics of Gordon and his top-notch ensemble cast. The less reverent among us are more apt to be delighted by such unseemly displays as exploding

eyeballs and two grown men trying to appear to be pursuing an obviously absent re-animated cat around a cellar with a baseball bat! This may well be your only chance this lifetime to see a body hold its decapitated head in its hands while attempting to orally arouse an understandably recalcitrant heroine. Not to be missed.—K. H.

The Rebel Nun

See Flavia Priestess of Violence

The Redeemer

Dimension Pictures, 1978; Color; 83 minutes
Director: Constantine S. Gochis
Producer: Sheldom Tromberg
Writer: John Michael Seymer
With: Michael Hollingsworth, Damien Knight, Gyr Patterson, T. G. Finkbinder, Nikki Barthen

Six ex-students attend a class reunion and find they're the only ones who showed up—except for a disfigured master of ceremonies who proceeds to murder them for various "sins" they've committed since graduation. Such as not getting a job? It is aka *The Redeemer . . . Son of Satan.*

The Redeemer . . . Son of Satan

See The Redeemer

The Red Sign of Madness

See Hatchet for a Honeymoon

Rest in Pieces

Calepas International, Inc., 1987;
    Color; 90 minutes
Director: Joseph Braunstein
Producer: José Frade
Writer: Santiago Moncada
With: Scott Thompson Baker, Lorin
    Jean Vail, Dorothy Malone, Jack
    Taylor, Patty Shepard

Wealthy Aunt Carol (Malone, who's aged into a Carol Channing look-alike) commits suicide on home video. Vail inherits Malone's subdivided estate (called 8 Manors), where a number of weird characters have been living for years rent-free. Vail's ambitious husband (Baker) learns there's a fortune buried somewhere and sets out to find it even though his wife is being terrified by apparitions of dead Aunt Carol and wants to move out. Turns out that all the residents are dead—also suicide victims. They're awaiting Aunt Carol's return and want Vail to slit her wrists and join them. The title suggests some all-out splatter, which is not delivered—though an occasional decapitation, amputation, and "hypodermic needle through the eye" scene is sprinkled throughout. One thing you'll definitely come away remembering about this film is the name of Vail's husband (Bob), which she screams endlessly as she's being terrified. A tedious, unrewarding, and unremarkable U.S.–Spanish coproduction.

Return of the Living Dead

Orion Pictures, 1985; Color; 91
    minutes
Director: Dan O'Bannon
Producers: Tom Fox, Graham
    Henderson
Writer: Dan O'Bannon

With: Clu Gulager, James Karen,
    Linnea Quigley, Don Calfa, Brian
    Peck

Unofficial sequel to *Night of the Living Dead*, based on a script by John Russo. Metal drums containing the deadly virus that caused the dead to rise in the earlier film have been secreted away by the army. They're discovered, opened, and, presto, the dead rise once more. In this film, they do more than grunt and groan, however. They actually speak, expressing their wants and needs with a recurring cry of "I want to eat your brains!" Whereas Romero's zombie films possess a satiric undercurrent, this one strives for outright laughs—and gets them. A good example of splatter slapstick—or *splatstick*, as it were.

Return of the Living Dead II

Lorimar, 1988; Color; 89 minutes
Director: Ken Wiederhorn
Producer: Tom Fox
Writer: Ken Wiederhorn
With: James Karen, Thom Mathews,
    Dana Ashbrook, Marsha Dietlein

This should have been titled *Abbott and Costello Meet the Living Dead*. The only thing missing is Abbott and Costello, but the humor is on the same level and the flesh-eating zombies are given a send-up in much the same way that the comedy team used to send up the old Universal monsters. Perhaps filmmakers have gotten all the mileage out of the Romero-style zombies that they're going to get and it may be time to bury the unfortunate creatures once and for all. Not as awful as many fans think—in fact, there are even a few chuckles—but if you're hoping to see a suitable follow-up to Dan O'Bannon's highly effective *Return of the Living Dead*, you won't find it here.—J. B.

Revenge of the Dead

A Motion Picture Marketing Release,
1984; Color; 100 minutes
Director: Pupi Avati
Producers: Gianni Minervini, Antonio
Avati
Writers: Pupi Avati, Maurizio
Costanzo, Antonio Avati
With: Gabriele Lavia, Anne Conovas,
Paolo Tanziana, Cesare Barbetti

An aspiring writer is given an electric
typewriter by his wife as an anniversary
present. On the used ribbon, he discovers
an account of a pseudoscientific project
aimed at bringing the dead to life. The
letters discuss K-zones, places where time
doesn't exist and where the dead can
reenter the land of the living. He decides
this would be a good subject for his next
novel and, assuming the role of amateur
sleuth to learn all he can about the project, runs headlong into a deadly conspir-
acy. Though this film was packaged and
promoted to appear similar to one of
Romero's zombie films, it really has more
in common with the work of Jacques
Tourneur, whose style was the antithesis
of splatter. The film even includes a
swimming pool scene inspired by Tourneur's *Cat People.* The scientific experiment that succeeds in raising the armies
of the dead is also quite similar to an
unfilmed Tourneur project called *Whis-
pering in Distant Chambers.* Though occasionally disjointed, this is an effective
supernatural thriller with infrequent but
suitably gross interludes of mayhem.

Revenge of the Living Dead

See The Murder Clinic

The Ripper

United Entertainment Pictures, 1986;
Color; 100 minutes
Director: Christopher Lewis

Producer: Linda Lewis
Writer: Bill Groves
With: Tom Schreier, Mona Van
Pernis, Wade Tower, Tom Savini

A made for home video release, this tale
of the revivified spirit of Jack the Ripper
was shot on location in Tulsa, Oklahoma.
A college professor who teaches a course
in crime cinema finds Jack the Ripper's
ring in an antique shop, puts it on, and
takes up where Jack left off. Though Savini gets star billing, he only appears for
a couple of minutes at the end, where he
has his fingers cut off. David Powell and
Robert Brewer handled the gore effects,
which are convincing and genuinely disgusting. Christopher Lewis is the son of
actress Loretta Young.

Road Games

Avco Embassy, 1981; Color; 100
minutes
Director: Richard Franklin
Producers: Richard Franklin, Barbi
Taylor
Writer: Everett De Roche
With: Stacy Keach, Jamie Lee Curtis,
Marion Edward, Grant Page, Bill
Stacey

Stylistic clone of *Psycho* about a maniacal
trucker who makes occasional pit stops
to wield his bloody knife. Keach is another trucker hot on the killer's trail;
Curtis is an American hitchhiking through
Australia who gets picked up by Keach
and decides to help him out. Filled with
nods to the late, great master of suspense
by devotee Franklin, who studied film at
USC and later got the job to direct *Psycho
II* on the basis of his Hitchcockian flour-
ishes in *Road Games.* He's no Hitchcock,
though. Minimal gore but nice scenery.

Robocop

Orion Pictures, 1987; Color; 103
minutes
Director: Paul Verhoeven

Producer: Arne Schmidt
Writers: Edward Neumeir, Michael
    Miner
With: Peter Weller, Nancy Allen,
    Daniel O'Herlihy, Ronny Cox,
    Kurtwood Smith, Miguel Ferrer

This American film debut by the Dutch director of the spellbinding *Fourth Man* is as slam-bang a piece of action/splatter filmmaking as you're likely to see. Weller is a cop in futuristic Old Detroit, where a multinational corporation runs the police department. The company wants to tear down the old city and build a high-rise, high-tech paradise in its place, but first it has to rid the streets of crime. When Weller is literally blown to pieces by a sadistic gang of drug dealers, executive Ferrer (the look-alike son of actor José Ferrer) has him reconstructed as a cybernetic Dirty Harry called Robocop. Trouble is, Weller's human memory circuits haven't been completely erased and he goes after the bad guys who blew him away. The trail leads all the way up the corporate ladder to villainous number-two man Ronny Cox. The cardboard, comic-book plot is little more than a setup for a potential (and possibly more interesting) series of Robocop adventures. But the pace is relentless and the firepower and gore (courtesy of Rob Bottin) are truly spectacular.

The Running Man

Tri-Star Pictures, 1987; Color; 101
    minutes
Director: Paul Michael Glaser
Producers: Tim Zenneman, George
    Linder
Writer: Steven de Souza
With: Arnold Schwarzenegger, Maria
    Conchita Alonso, Yaphet Kotto,
    Jesse Ventura, Richard Dawson

Fly-boy policeman Arnold is unjustly sent to prison for slaughtering a bunch of Bakersfield civilians. He escapes (one of his fellow escapees isn't so lucky; his head is blown up by an electronic booby trap) and is given a chance to clear himself on a nationally televised game show called *The Running Man.* Contestants are given a head start, then mercilessly tracked by chain-saw and spiked hockey-stick-wielding "stalkers." The show boasts some successful past contestants, but this proves a ruse, for no one has ever successfully run the gauntlet. Arnold discovers the sham, kills his foes by blowing off their heads and turning them into sopranos with a buzz saw. Then he goes after the obnoxious game-show host (played impeccably by the obnoxious Richard Dawson), whose other worries include a ratings battle with a rising sitcom called *The Hate Boat.* Arnold's delivery of his Bondian one-liners makes Roger Moore look like Cary Grant. Based on a novel by Richard Bachman (Stephen King).

The Satanic Rites of Dracula

Warner Brothers, 1973; Color; 97
    minutes
Director: Alan Gibson
Producer: Roy Skeggs
Writer: Don Houghton
With: Christopher Lee, Peter Cushing,
    William Franklyn, Michael Coles,
    Joanna Lumley, Freddie Jones

No longer a caped predator putting the bite on his victims one by one, Dracula (Lee) has become a reclusive and powerful Howard Hughes figure whose mysterious "company" is blackmailing scientists into developing a deadly new virus aimed at killing every living creature on earth—except for Van Helsing's (Cushing) daughter, whom Drac intends to make his eternal bride. Hammer had long run out of plots for its Dracula series by this time (though Houghton's script for this last entry does add a few new wrinkles) and compensated with increasing doses of gore. This is by far the splatteriest of the series—full of bullet hits, stakings, the gamut, plus a sequence involving a nest of female vampires that's almost worthy of George Romero. Due to the box-office failure of Hammer's previous *Dracula A.D. 1972*, the film was not theatrically released in the United States. (It is shown on television, though, often uncut). It is aka *Dracula Is Dead and Well and Living in London*.

Saturn 3

Associated Films, 1980; Color; 88 minutes
Director: Stanley Donen
Producer: Stanley Donen
Writer: Martin Amis
With: Kirk Douglas, Farrah Fawcett, Harvey Keitel

Douglas and Fawcett are a husband and wife team of outer-space botanists who create an artificial Garden of Eden for research purposes—into which barge Keitel and a shiny death-dealing robot. Fawcett loses her clothes while the others lose various body parts.

Savage Weekend

Upstate Murder Company, 1976; Color; 83 minutes
Director: David Paulsen
Producers: David Paulsen, John Mason Kirby
Writer: David Paulsen
With: Christopher Allport, James Doerr, Marilyn Hamlin, Kathleen Heaney, David Gale

That old splatter movie standby, the masked killer, is loose again, this time using cars, fishhooks, chain saws, and

bench saws to dispatch his victims. Director Paulsen has since become a writer and producer on TV's "Dallas." It is aka *The Upstate Murders* and *The Killer Behind the Mask*.

Scanners

Avco Embassy, 1981; Color; 102 minutes
Director: David Cronenberg
Producer: Claude Heroux
Writer: David Cronenberg
With: Patrick McGoohan, Stephen Lack, Jennifer O'Neill, Michael Ironside

An underground society of telepaths ("scanners") whose abilities are the result of an experimental drug unleashed on their mothers during pregnancy by scientist McGoohan must conceal themselves from those who wish them ill will—and from those within their own ranks who wish to use the group's powers as a weapon. A provocative script marred by some truly terrible acting (by Lack, who has the lead!). O'Neill's part is a throwaway. McGoohan is good, though—as are the effects by Dick Smith, who was called in to salvage the finale, a splattery duel between good scanner Lack and bad scanner Ironside.

Scarecrows

Manson International, 1988; Color; 88 minutes
Director: William Wesley
Producers: Cami Winikoff, William Wesley
Writers: Richard Jefferies, William Wesley
With: Ted Vernon, Michael Simms, Victoria Christian, B. J. Turner

Paramilitary types heist $3 million from Camp Pendleton, then hijack a plane to escape. One of the thieves absconds with

the loot by parachuting into a graveyard protected by huge scarecrows. The others go in after him and one-by-one all the thieves are snuffed out by the malevolent, antitrespassing scarecrows, who take possession of the interlopers' bodies, turning them into zombie killers that bleed when their throats are cut and their heads are chopped off, yet ooze straw when they're disemboweled. The pilot's daughter manages to get away in the hijacked aircraft, but a dog on board scarfs up the remains of one of the zombie killers, gets zombified itself and gives everyone back at the airport an unpleasant greeting. Good FX by Norman Cabrera, but the film itself is plodding and relentlessly predictable.

Schizo

Niles International, 1977; Color; 109 minutes
Director: Pete Walker
Producer: Pete Walker
Writer: David McGillivray
With: Lynn Frederick, John Leyton, Stephanie Beacham, John Fraser, Jack Watson

Splattery whodunit in which the the heroine (Frederick—wife of the late Peter Sellers) and the knife-wielding psychopath stalking her are revealed at fadeout to be one and the same person—not that the film's title is any kind of a tip-off.

Schizoid

Cannon Films, 1980; Color; 91 minutes
Director: David Paulsen
Producers: Menahem Golan, Yoram Globus
Writer: David Paulsen
With: Klaus Kinski, Marianna Hill, Craig Wasson, Donna Wilkes

Someone is knocking off therapist Kinski's patients. Could it be he? Or is that

axe in his hand really a red herring? One of his patients, an "advice to the lovelorn" columnist (Hill), receives letters threatening her life and, fearing she'll be next, he sets out to track the killer down. Standard mad-slasher stuff with a twist ending. It is aka *Murder by Mail*.

Scream Baby Scream

A Westbury Films Production, 1969; Color; 80 minutes
Director: Joseph Adler
Producer: Joseph Adler
Writer: Laurence Robert Cohen
With: Ross Harris, Eugenie Wingate, Chris Martel, Suzanne Stuart, Larry Swanson

This is not a gore movie but a disfigurement movie. Jason Grant (Harris) and Janet Wells (Wingate) and their friends Scotty and Marika (Martel and Stuart) are young art students who fall under the sinister influence of Charles Butler (Swanson), an inverted, romantic, mad artist who glorifies the ugly. Chris Martel, the idiot son from Herschell Gordon Lewis's *The Gruesome Twosome*, turns his friends on to sugar-cube acid in a cup of coffee and sings psychedelic rock songs with the group Odessey. Butler himself is a victim of Dr. Garrison's flesh-melting injections because he once coveted Garrison's daughter. Now, Butler uses the same serum to disfigure the models for his grotesque paintings. Ironically, even though Janet smashes a glass vase over the mad artist's head (the heaviest gore in the film), both Jason and Janet end up as grotesque facial freaks who were just made for each other.—D. K.

Scream Bloody Murder

Indepix, 1972; Color; 85 minutes
Director: Robert J. Emery
Producer: Robert J. Emery

Writer: Robert J. Emery
With: Fred Holbert, Leigh Mitchell,
    Robert Knox, Suzette Hamilton

A young boy grinds up his dad with the family tractor (hope it was paid for) but mangles his hand in the bargain. Outfitted with your basic, all-purpose, steel-claw prosthetic, he goes on a murder spree, making his mom, stepdad, and others "cry uncle." You've seen it all before—and since.

Scream for Help

Lorimar, 1984; Color; 94 minutes
Director: Michael Winner
Producer: Michael Winner
Writer: Tom Holland
With: Rachael Kelly, David Brooks,
    Marie Masters, Rocco Sisto, Lolita
    Lorre

Embarrasingly bad splatter/thriller with most of the gore set pieces occurring in the almost howlingly funny last half hour. Kelly discovers that her stepfather (Brooks) is trying to kill her mother (Masters) in order to get at the family fortune. She tries to blow the whistle on him, but nobody will believe her. Lorre and Sisto are Brooks's partners in crime—and a more incompetent trio you've never seen. You won't believe a single scene in this contrived mess. John Paul Jones's atrocious musical score, which seems to belong to another movie, rounds out the awfulness. There's a good deal of diverting nudity, though.

Screams of a Winter Night

Dimension Pictures, 1979; Color; 92 minutes
Director: James L. Wilson
Producers: Richard Wadsack, James
    L. Wilson
Writer: Richard Wadsack
With: Gill Glasgow, Mary Cox, Robin
    Bradley, Matt Borel, Patrick Byers

Anthology film in which kids camping at a remote mountain lake spin ghost stories to terrify one another. The stories deal with a Big Foot–type monster, a sexually repressed girl who carves up people who are overly libidinous, and a demon Indian. Originally shot in 16mm, then blown up to 35mm for theatrical distribution—of which it got little.

The Secret of Dr. Alucard

See A Taste of Blood

The Seduction

Embassy Pictures, 1983; Color; 104 minutes
Director: David Schmoeller
Producers: Irwin Yablans, Bruce Cohn
    Curtis
Writer: David Schmoeller
With: Morgan Fairchild, Michael
    Sarrazin, Andrew Stevens, Vince
    Edwards

More mad slasher nonsense from producer Irwin Yablans, who hasn't been able to make anything else since his successful connection with *Halloween.* Stevens plays a crazy fan of L.A. TV reporter Fairchild. Living just up the hill from her multi-windowed home allows him ample opportunity to see her take nude swims, fanning his desire. The next logical step is to make her his, but first he has to knock off her boyfriend (Sarrazin), whom he knifes in her hot tub. Cop Edwards can do nothing, of course, so Fairchild must get out the family shotgun and settle things herself.

The Sender

Paramount Pictures, 1982; Color; 91 minutes
Director: Roger Christian

Producer: Edward S. Feldman
Writer: Thomas Baum
With: Kathryn Harrold, Zeljko Ivanek,
    Shirley Knight, Paul Freeman

A troubled young man (Ivanek) tries to commit suicide by drowning but winds up with amnesia instead. He is put under the care of compassionate psychiatrist Harrold. Her curative powers are severely put to the test, however, when Ivanek starts sending her gruesome telepathic images from his nightmarish dream-sleep. Low-key but deservedly R-rated psychological shocker made in England.

The Sentinel

Universal, 1976; Color; 93 minutes
Director: Michael Winner
Producers: Michael Winner, Jeffrey
    Konvitz
Writers: Michael Winner, Jeffrey
    Konvitz
With: Chris Sarandon, Cristina Raines,
    Martin Balsam, Burgess Meredith,
    John Carradine, José Ferrer, Ava
    Gardner, Arthur Kennedy, Sylvia
    Miles, Deborah Raffin, Eli
    Wallach, Jerry Orbach

Michael Winner's superbly stylish spook and splatter show is perhaps the only one of his post-1960s films to reflect the brilliance he showed in the previous decade with films such as *I'll Never Forget What's 'is Name* and *The Jokers* (both 1967). Unfortunately, the film has always been badly misunderstood, misinterpreted, and maligned, not in the least because Winner (who has always liked to squirt a little blood) really delivers the gore goods. His graphic nastiness is unflinching in a way not generally seen in a decently budgeted mainstream film. In the process of damning the film's excesses, nearly everyone missed the fact that, while it's somewhat illogical, the film is one of the creepiest

demonic-possession thrillers ever to lurch across the screen. If the viewer can accept the basic premise that the entrance to hell (guarded by the Sentinel of the title) is in Brooklyn Heights, Winner's film affords many an effective shudder, in part because one is disoriented by the fact that the good guys (a lunatic branch of the Catholic Church) are as weird a lot as the demons. As a bonus, there are a series of wonderfully ripe performances by Burgess Meredith, John Carradine, Ava Gardner, and Sylvia Miles. Beware the TV print, which is not only severely cut but is littered with substitute footage (removing all references to the Catholic Church), making the film even more illogical.
    — K. H.

The Serpent and the Rainbow

Universal, 1988; Color; 89 minutes
Director: Wes Craven
Producers: David Ladd, Doug
    Claybourne
Writers: Richard Maxwell, A. R.
    Simoun
With: Bill Pullman, Cathy Tyson, Zakes
    Mokae, Paul Winfield

Based on the book of the same name by Wade Davis, which in turn was based on Davis's real life experiences, *The Serpent and the Rainbow* funnels factual information related to voodoo practices into a fictional story. This gives the film a ring of truth—we believe that what is happening is possible and consequently it becomes more frightening. Director Wes Craven knows a good script. He builds the plot slowly. As the protagonist, Dennis Alan (Bill Pullman), we are led progressively deeper into the more bizarre elements of the story. In a scene where he is buried alive, we experience the horror with him as the point-of-view shots literally place us in his position. Sure, it's been done before, but it's still chilling. Not much excess gore, but there is one unnerving scene when the villain tortures the hero in a way that will have at least the male viewers wincing. Toward the end, Craven gets carried away with too much visual razzle-dazzle not in keeping with the rest of the film, but, for the most part, *The Serpent and the Rainbow* effectively combines traditional atmospheric horror with contemporary shocks and thrills.

—J. B.

The Severed Arm

Media Cinema/Media Trend, 1973; Color; 92 minutes
Director: Thomas S. Alderman
Producer: Gary Adelman
Writers: Thomas S. Alderman, Darrel Presnell, Larry Alexander, Marc B. Rand
With: Deborah Walley, Paul Carr, Roy Dennis, Marvin Kaplan, David G. Cannon, John Crawford

Trapped by a landslide, spelunkers turn to cannibalism to survive—drawing lots and eating the loser's arm. After they're saved, the loser who surrendered his limb goes after the rest to get even.

Sharkey's Machine

Orion Pictures, 1981; Color; 120 minutes
Director: Burt Reynolds
Producer: Hank Moonjean
Writer: Gerald Di Pego
With: Burt Reynolds, Vittorio Gassman, Brian Keith, Rachel Ward, Charles Durning, Henry Silva

Special vice squad unit headed by Reynolds sets out to bring down sleazeball mobster Gassman's call girl empire by spying on one of his $1,000-a-night hook-ers (Ward). Reynolds becomes fixated on the girl instead. When she gets a face-lift courtesy of hitman Silva's shotgun, love-sick Reynolds goes on a bloody rampage. Turns out she's not dead, however; it was someone else who got blown away. Surprise, surprise—unless, of course, you've seen Otto Preminger's *Laura,* which this film borrows from quite liberally. John Boorman was originally set to direct but suggested that Reynolds do it himself. Wise decision, John. Bad advice, Burt.

She-Devils on Wheels

A Mayflower Pictures Release, 1968; Color; 83 minutes
Director: Herschell Gordon Lewis
Producer: Herschell Gordon Lewis
Writer: Allison Louise Downe
With: Betty Connell, Pat Poston, Nancy Lee Noble, Christie Wagner

After *Blood Feast,* this tale of a free-spirited all-girl gang of motorcyclists who call themselves The Maneaters was H. G. Lewis's most financially successful splatter pic. To lend authenticity to the film, Lewis employed real female bikers. The plot centers around the conflict between The Maneaters and a rival gang of male bikers, who do them dirt. When Noble is beaten to a raw and bloody pulp by one of the males, the girls mount their "Harley Hogs" and peel out to get even. In one scene, they string a wire across the highway, decapitating Joe-Boy, the rival gang leader, as he unwittingly roars by. Another of the boys is dragged along the road until he's a bloody mess. Grisly and funny, the film boasts such memorable lines as: "Go fumigate yourself, craphead!"

Shivers

See They Came from Within

Shock

See Beyond the Door II

Shogun Assassin

Distributor unknown, 1981; Color; 84
   minutes
Directors: Kenji Misumi, Robert
   Houston
Producers: Shintaro Katsu, Hisaharu
   Matsubara, David Weisman
Writers: Kazuo Koike, Robert
   Houston, David Weisman
With: Tomisaburo Wakayama,
   Masahiro Tomikawa, Kayo
   Matsuo

When his wife is killed by the warriors of
a villainous shogun, a samurai takes his
young son (who provides the voice-over
narration so that we know what's going
on) on a cross-country blood spree of medieval Japan, hacking off his enemies'
limbs, cutting their throats, severing their
hands, you name it, to get even. Ultraviolent Japanese "Western" that is also
quite funny—intentionally so. The little
boy has a wonderfully dry wit.

Shriek of the Mutilated

American Films, 1974; Color; 92
   minutes
Director: Michael Findlay
Producer: Ed Adlum
Writers: Ed Adlum, Ed Kelleher
With: Alan Brock, Jennifer Stock,
   Tawn Ellis, Darcy Brown

Cannibal-cult "meat movie" from the
producer-director of *Invasion of the Blood
Farmers* and the codirector of *Snuff*. An
anthropology professor enlists the aid of
some of his students in searching out a
Big Foot–type creature reportedly seen
on a remote island. There they meet up
with the island's population of two—another doctor and his faithful Indian
companion—who give the group some
tips. Predictably, the students start getting offed by the mysterious bearlike creature, but then—surprise, surprise—one
of the brighter students picks up on the
fact that there's no Big Foot at all. It's
really a ruse, cooked up by the two doctors and some other locals, all members
of a cannibal cult in need of nubile human
vitals as vittles for their annual banquet.
The students are ceremoniously hacked
up with an electric carving knife and
summarily eaten.

Silent Night, Bloody Night

Cannon Films, 1973; Color; 88
   minutes
Director: Theodore Gershuny
Producers: Jeffrey Konvitz, Ami Artzi
Writer: Theodore Gershuny, Jeffrey
   Konvitz
With: Patrick O'Neal, James
   Patterson, Mary Woronov, Walter
   Abel, John Carradine

This film is clearly low budget; the photography is grainy and murky, and sometimes the image is too dark to see what
is going on. In spite of these problems,
the filmmakers appear to have believed
in what they were doing. The film boasts
an incredibly complicated plot, but we are
pulled in slowly so that as layer after layer
of the story is peeled away, we become
intrigued as to just how far things are
going to go. There's an almost surrealistic
quality to the story—a kind of illogical
logic, as if the film exists in its own
dreamlike world. The sepia-toned flashbacks are moody and evocative and the
period details are convincing enough to
lend some credibility to the more farfetched plot developments. The acting,
while sometimes amateurish, works because the cast is sincere and approaches
the material with conviction. There are

some gruesome bits of business, although the gore is suggested more through editing than Savini-like special effects. Problems? Yes, to be sure. But there is an overriding ambience here—a dark and somber mood that draws one in and somehow makes it all work.—J. B.

Silent Night, Deadly Night

Manson International, 1984; Color;
    85 minutes
Director: Charles E. Sellier, Jr.
Producer: Ira Richard Barmak
Writer: Michael Hickey
With: Lilyan Chauvan, Gilmer
    McCormick, Robert Brian Wilson,
    Linnea Quigley

Little Billy's nutso grandpa scares the kid into believing that Santa Claus punishes those who are naughty and gives to those who are nice. Shortly after, Billy's parents are murdered by a psycho dressed in a Santa suit. Billy and his brother are spirited to a Catholic orphanage, where the Mother Superior (Chauvan) reinforces the punishment message. The disturbed boy grows up and gets a job in (where else?) a toy store, where, come Christmas, his employer enlists him to play Santa Claus. Billy dons the suit, flips out, and, axe in hand, sets off in pursuit of naughty folks to chop up. Bottom-of-the-barrel, madslasher fare that unabashedly strives to include every cliché of the genre—Quigley's impalement on some moose antlers strikes the only original note. Billy gets his, of course, but the implication is that his little brother will don the killer Santa suit in a future installment. The film caused somewhat of a stir when its distributors decided to release it during the Christmas season—a tasteless decision that resulted in some initially brisk business at the box office, but the controversy prompted them to pull it from release and reopen it in the spring. Original title: *Slayride.*

Silent Night, Deadly Night—Part II

Manson International, 1986; Color;
    88 minutes
Director: Lee Harry
Producer: Lawrence Appelbaum
Writers: Lee Harry, Joseph H. Earle
With: Eric Freeman, James L.
    Newman, Elizabeth Cayton, Jean
    Miller

Little Ricky (not of "I Love Lucy" fame) takes up where older brother Billy left off in this lame sequel that incorporates an astonishing twenty-five minutes (a third of its running time!) of flashback footage from the first film. So many scenes from the first film are used that the closing credit roll lists complete casts and credits for *both* films. The advantage, of course, is that you can catch the sequel and see the first film all at once, thus saving time. Part II is more lighthearted as Eric Freeman (as Ricky) goes around imitating Jack Nicholson from *The Shining,* shouting "NAUGHTY!" as he dispatches victims with an axe, a gun, and a set of battery charger cables. The ending, where Ricky is blown away but survives, paves the way for a Part III—which, if equal quantities of flashback footage from the two earlier films are used, might make for a spirited short subject.

Silent Scream

American Cinema Releasing, 1980;
    Color; 87 minutes
Director: Denny Harris
Producers: Denny and Joan Harris
Writers: Ken and Jim Wheat, Wallace
    E. Bennett
With: Rebecca Balding, Cameron
    Mitchell, Avery Schreiber,
    Barbara Steele, Yvonne De Carlo

Young lodgers in a rooming house run by De Carlo are knocked off by a secret

*Frankenstein and the
Monster from Hell*—1974
(Copyright © 1973
Hammer Film
Productions Ltd.)

Vampire Circus—1971
(Copyright © 1971
Hammer Film Productions
Ltd./Courtesy, Hollywood
Book & Poster)

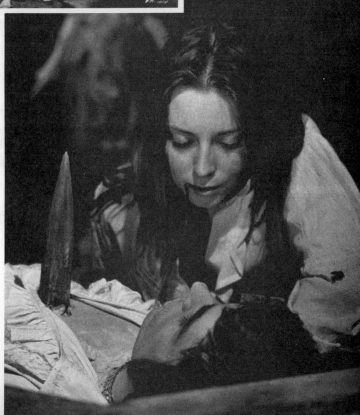

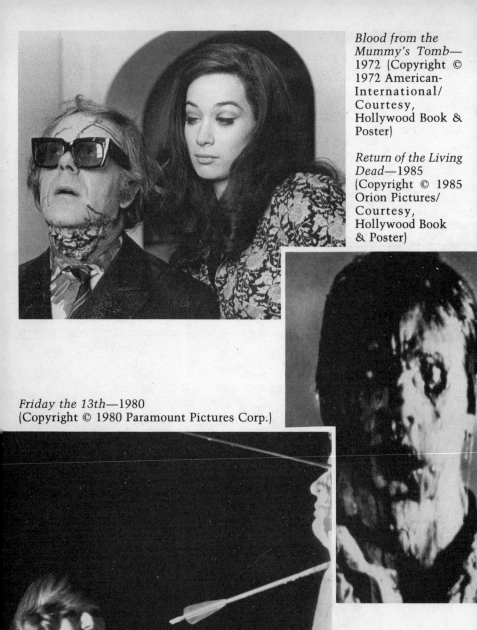

Blood from the Mummy's Tomb—1972 (Copyright © 1972 American-International/Courtesy, Hollywood Book & Poster)

Return of the Living Dead—1985 (Copyright © 1985 Orion Pictures/Courtesy, Hollywood Book & Poster)

Friday the 13th—1980 (Copyright © 1980 Paramount Pictures Corp.)

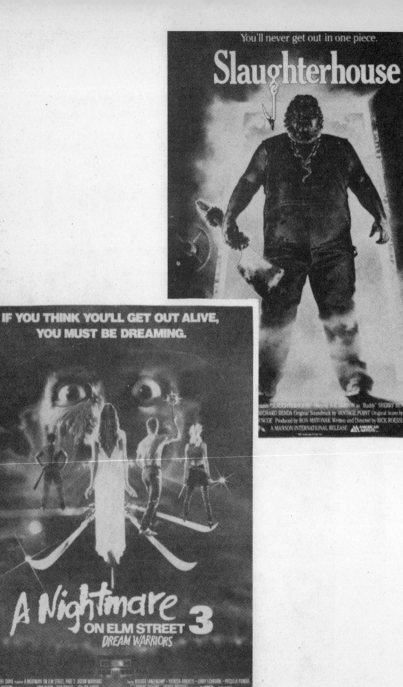

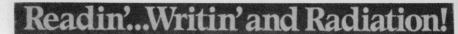

Readin'...Writin' and Radiation!

A LLOYD KAUFMAN/MICHAEL HERZ PRODUCTION

CLASS OF NUKE'EM HIGH

Starring
JANELLE BRADY · GILBERT BRENTON · ROBERT PRICHARD · R.L. RYAN · JAMES NUGENT VERNON · BRAD DUNKER
GARY SCHNEIDER · THÉO COHAN · Screenplay by RICHARD W. HAINES, MARK RUDNITSKY, LLOYD KAUFMAN,
STUART STRUTIN · Special Effects and Special Effects Make-up SCOTT COULTER AND BRIAN QUINN
Special Matte Effects and Matte Photography THÉO PINGARELLI · Edited by RICHARD W. HAINES
Associate Producer STUART STRUTIN · Executive Producer JAMES TREADWELL
Produced by LLOYD KAUFMAN AND MICHAEL HERZ · Directed by RICHARD W. HAINES AND SAMUEL WEIL
 Released by TROMA, INC. © TNT CO/TROMA, INC. MCMLXXXVI | Original Songs by CLIVE BURR, DAVID BARRETO, DAVID BEHENNAH

SILENT NIGHT, DEADLY NIGHT PART 2

The nightmare
is about to begin...Again

SILENT NIGHT RELEASING CORP. Presents
A LAWRENCE APPELBAUM Production "SILENT NIGHT, DEADL
Starring ERIC FREEMAN · JAMES L. NEWMAN · ELIZABETH CA
Director of Photography HARVEY GENKINS Music by MICHAEL
Screenplay by LEE HARRY & JOSEPH H. EARL
Produced by LAWRENCE APPELBAUM Edited & Directed by
©1987 Silent Night Releasing Corp. 〳〵 A MANSON INTERNA

DON'T CLOSE
YOUR EYES...

THE
NEIGHBORS
ARE
RESTLESS.

REST IN PIECES

CALEPAS INTERNATIONAL INC. PRESENTS
"REST IN PIECES"
SCOTT THOMPSON BAKER · LORIN JEAN and DOROTHY MALONE
JACK TAYLOR · PATTY SHEPARD
EDITOR BRYAN SMEDLY-ASTON EXECUTIVE IN CHARGE OF PRODUCTION ALFRED WARD DIRECTOR OF PHOTOGRAPHY JHON THARP
PRODUCED BY JOSE FRADE DIRECTED BY JOSEPH BRAUNSTEIN

Her Power Goes Beyond Life... His Rage Survives Even Death.

ZOMBIE
NIGHTMARE

GOLD-GEMS Presents ZOMBIE NIGHTMARE
AM WEST, JON MIKL THOR, TIA CARRERE, FRANK DIETZ, LINDA SINGE
ROGET RACINE JOHN M. FASANO SHELDON GOLDSTEIN
ELEANOR HILOWITZ ANTHONY C. BUA JACK BRAVMAN

IT IS WRITTEN EVIL WILL INHERIT THE EAR
AND LAUGHTER WILL ECHO THROUGHOU
THE UNIVERSE...

Spookies

SAFIR FILMS LTD. PRESENT A TWISTED SOULS INC. PRODUCTION
FELIX WARD DAN SCOTT ALEC NEMSER
FRANK M. FAREL THOMAS DORAN BRENDAN FAULKNER

boarder—De Carlo's deranged daughter (Steele), who has a thing for knives. Mitchell and Schreiber are the cops assigned to the case; their scenes together are (unintentionally?) quite funny. Director Harris capitalizes sensationally on the "sex leads to death" controversy by intercutting a bloody murder with a couple reaching orgasm. One wonders. Was he making a moral statement?

Simon—King of the Witches

The Fanfare Corporation, 1971; Color; 91 minutes
Director: Bruce Kessler
Producer: David Hammond
Writer: Robert Phippeny
With: Andrew Prine, Brenda Scott, Ultra Violet

Psychedelic potboiler about a warlock (Prine) and his predilection for human sacrifices—especially those involving nude young women. Ultra Violet was one of the late Andy Warhol's campy superstars; haven't seen her in too many films since. Maybe if she changed her name to Ultra Violence, she'd get more work.

Sisters

American-International, 1973; Color; 93 minutes
Director: Brian De Palma
Producer: Edward Pressman
Writers: Brian De Palma, Louisa Rose
With: Margot Kidder, Jennifer Salt, Bill Finley, Charles Durning, Lisle Wilson

Kidder is one half of a deadly Siamese twin sister act; she's a model; her sister's a deranged murderess. Finley is the creepy doctor who separated the two. De Palma's first and best Hitchcock pastiche boasts some really nasty murders. Film's scary atmosphere is aided immeasurably by Bernard Herrmann's riveting score, one of his last and best.

Sisters of Satan

A Dallas Laser Leasing III Presentation, 1975; Color; 77 minutes
Director: Juan Lopez Moctezuma
Producers: Eduardo Moreno, Max Guefen
Writers: Juan Lopez and Yolanda L. Moctezuma, Alexis T. Arroxo
With: Claudio Brook, David Silva, Tina Romero, Susana Kamini

There are two films with this title; this one is much better than the other, which stars Anne Heywood and Ornella Muti and has only minimal gore. In 1865, Alucarda (Romero) and Justine (Kamini), two fifteen-year-old orphan convent girls, are seduced into demonic possession by a satyrlike gypsy devil. The gore starts subtly with a blood-sister ritual in which the girls lick blood from small cuts on each other's breasts. It builds through a bloody long-distance psychic battle for the girls' souls between Sister Angelica and a gypsy witch, to an orgy of flagellation by the nuns when the girls' possession is discovered. Justine is killed in an exorcism attempt when her belly is repeatedly pierced by a large needle, the head priest decapitates a possessed nun with a spurt of blood and then picks her severed head up off the floor, and Justine rises naked from a literal bloodbath in a coffin to slash Sister Angelica with her nails and take a killing bite out of her neck. Justine is destroyed by holy water that burns her like acid, while Alucarda plays "Carrie" in the convent by burning the place up along with half its occupants. Good gore, frenzied acting, hallucinogenic images and editing, and a lot of nudity make this film a must see! It is aka *Alucarda* and *Innocents from Hell.*—D. K.

The Slaughter

See Snuff

Slaughter High

Vestron Pictures, 1987; Color; 95
  minutes
Directors: George Dugdale, Mark
  Ezra, Peter Litten
Producers: Steve Minasian, Dick
  Randall
Writers: George Dugdale, Mark Ezra,
  Peter Litten
With: Caroline Munro, Simon
  Scuddamore, Kelly Baker, Billy
  Hartman

Nerdy chemistry major Marty (Scuddamore) is tormented by his fellow classmates on April Fool's Day. One of the
pranks results in an explosion in the chem
lab and Marty's permanent disfigurement. The plot skips forward five years as
the classmates are invited to a special April
Fool's Day reunion at the now closed high
school. Would you go? Me, neither. Anyway, one by one, Marty's former tormentors are impaled, reduced to bones in an
acid bath, disemboweled with a lawn mower
blade, and electrocuted. Come on, it
couldn't *really* be Marty who's behind all
this, could it? Oh yes, it could. There is
an attempt at a surprise twist, but it's
dumb and doesn't work. It does, however,
provide the filmmakers with the opportunity to throw in one last splatter
murder—in this case a hypodermic needle
thrust in somebody's eye. Trite *Friday the
13th* clone with cloned score by *F13th*
alumnus Harry Manfredini.

Slaughter Hotel

Hallmark Releasing, 1973; Color; 97
  minutes
Director: Fernando Di Leo

Producers: Armando Novelli, Tizio
  Longo
Writers: Fernando Di Leo, Nino
  Latino
With: Klaus Kinski, Margeret Lee,
  Monica Strebel, John Karlson

Another "V for Violence" opus—from the
friendly folks who brought us *Last House
on the Left* and *Mark of the Devil*, parts
1 and 2. "Carved out of today's head-
lines," Hallmark attempted to exploit the
notoriety surrounding the Richard Speck
murder case, in which the deranged Speck
("Born to Kill") had brutally slain several
Chicago nurses ("See the slashing massacre of 8 innocent nurses!" the ads
screamed). Alas, twenty years after the
fact, this come-on doesn't mean much—
especially when you consider how many
nurses have been dispatched in splatter
movies since then. Besides, the film really
has nothing to do with Speck—nor does
it take place in a hotel. The setting is
actually an up-scale clinic for the men-
tally disturbed run by nutso doctor Kinski. There, not just nurses but many of
the residents seeking treatment are tortured, maimed, carved up, and beheaded
by a masked killer on the loose. Typical,
badly dubbed Italian-made murder melodrama.

Slaughterhouse

American Artists, 1987; Color; 85
  minutes
Director: Rick Roessler
Producer: Ron Matonak
Writer: Rick Roessler
With: Sherry Bendorf, Don Barrett,
  William Houck, Joe Barton, Eric
  Schwartz, Jane Higginson, Jeff
  Grossi

Beware! This movie may turn you into a
vegetarian. The credits sequence graphically depicts a pig's real last mile on the

way to our dinner tables. Lester Bacon (Barrett) and his demented giant of a son, Buddy (Barton), live in their deserted slaughterhouse, which was put out of business by the new mechanized packing plant. The plant owner, a lawyer, and the sheriff conspire to steal the Bacons's home. Liz Borden (Bendorf), the sheriff's daughter, and her teen friends use the slaughterhouse to make out, shoot a home music video, and play pranks. But they, the conspirators, and others start disappearing when Buddy grabs his butcher's axe. This fine film delivers nearly a dozen bloody murders and doesn't take its time about it. Great gore moments include a deputy covered by his own gun while it's still clutched in his severed hand, and Lizzie's lesson from Lester that the smallest cut can be the most painful.—D. K.

Slave of the Cannibal God

New Line Cinema, 1978; Color; 86 minutes
Director: Sergio Martino
Producer: Luciano Martino
Writers: Sergio Martino, Cesare Frugoni
With: Stacy Keach, Ursula Andress, Claudio Cassinelli

Andress hires guide Keach to take her into the jungle in search of her missing husband, and both are taken captive by a cult of hungry cannibals. Replay of *King Solomon's Mines*, but with trendy nudity and gore.

Slayride

See Silent Night, Deadly Night

Sleepaway Camp

American Eagle Film Corp., 1983; Color; 88 minutes
Director: Robert Hiltzik

Producers: Michele Tatosian, Jerry Silva
Writer: Robert Hiltzik
With: Mike Kellin, Katherine Kamhi, Paul DeAngelo, Jonathan Tierston, Robert Earl Jones

This very perverse little psycho-splatter movie starts out similar to a *Friday the 13th* clone. A divorced man (he's gay) and his two children are victims of a freak boating accident. The surviving child is sent to live with a man-hating aunt and her young son, Ricky. The movie skips forward eight years. Ricky and his stepsister, Angela, are sent away to camp for the summer. Shy and retiring Angela, who's terrified to go swimming because of what happened years before, becomes the victim of a nasty cook, who makes sexual advances, and some of the other kids. Soon, her various tormentors start turning up dead—one is scalded with boiling water, another is knifed, a third is stung to death by wasps. There's very little mystery as to who done it. And about halfway through, one begins to suspect that the reason why Angela won't go swimming or even shower with the other girls is that she's been brought up by her twisted aunt to act like a girl, when, in fact, she's really a boy. The ending still comes as a shock, though—due mostly to Ed French's grotesque makeup of the girl/boy when she finally reveals herself. There's also a perverse love song played over the film's closing credits. Director Hiltzik dedicated his film: "In fond memory of mom, a doer." One can only wonder what *that* means!

Slumber Party Massacre

New World Pictures, 1982; Color; 84 minutes
Director: Amy Jones
Producer: Amy Jones

Writer: Rita Mae Brown
With: Michele Michaels, Michael Villela, Robin Stille, Debra DeLiso

Girls having a slumber party are visited by a maniac (Villela) brandishing an outsized power drill (get the phallic symbolism?). He kills most of them plus a couple of their boyfriends before being set upon by one of the survivors (Michaels), a friend of hers, and the friend's younger sister. They beat him with baseball bats and finally carve him up with an electric saw. Is there a feminist message lurking about here? Doubt it. Despite the participation of feminist author Rita Mae Brown (whose script, I understand, was considerably altered), this is just another exploitative slasher flick in which female director Amy Jones piles on the gore with the same skill and gusto as her male counterparts in the field.

Slumber Party Massacre II

Concorde Pictures, 1987; Color; 90 minutes
Director: Deborah Brock
Producers; Deborah Brock, Don Daniel
Writer: Deborah Brock
With: Crystal Bernard, Kimberly McArthur, Juliette Cummins, Patrick Lowe

The younger sister (Bernard) who helped to kill the drill-wielding psycho in the first film has now grown up. Her sister is recuperating in an asylum and she herself is still plagued by nightmares about what happened. An aspiring rock singer, she joins some other members of her all-female band for another slumber party at an expensive condo—and the psycho, whom she apparently conjures up from her nightmares, returns. This time, however, he assumes the form of a satanic guitar player, whose guitar handle doubles as an even longer, more lethal (and more phallic) power drill. Repetitive, uninspired sequel.

Snuff

Monarch Releasing Corp., 1974; Color; 82 minutes
Directors: Michael and Roberta Findlay
Producers: Michael Findlay, Allan Schackleton
Writers: Michael and Roberta Findlay
With: Credits unavailable

Almost plotless gore-fest set in South America about a south-of-the-border Manson family that mutilates an actress and some of her friends. As a splatter movie, it's really no worse than many, but its advertising campaign, which encouraged audiences to believe that one of the killings was real, succeeded in packing 'em in. The claim was a hoax (fortunately!). Director Michael Findlay was later killed in a freak helicopter accident, but his wife, Roberta, is still making splatter pics. It is aka *The Slaughter*.

The Soldier

Avco Embassy, 1982; Color; 96 minutes
Director: James Glickenhaus
Producer: James Glickenhaus
Writer: James Glickenhaus
With: Ken Wahl, Klaus Kinski, William Prince

Globe-trotting spy yarn in which somnolent, uncharismatic CIA operative Wahl (it rhymes with wall, which is a fairly accurate description of the actor's emotional range) tries to avert a Russian plot to blow up an Arabian oil field, thereby throwing the oil-dependent West into political and economic chaos. Short on suspense and logic but long on chase scenes, violent set pieces, and wild stunts.

Soldier Blue

Avco Embassy, 1970; Color; 112 minutes
Director: Ralph Nelson
Producers: Harold Loeb, Gabriel Katzka
Writer: John Gay
With: Peter Strauss, Candice Bergen, Donald Pleasence, John Anderson

Cavalry officer Strauss and settler Bergen are thrown together after an Indian attack that wipes out his entire company. Their journey to survival climaxes at Sand Creek, where more boys in blue led by the murderous Colonel Chivington (Anderson) get even by raiding an Indian village and slaughtering every Indian in sight, man, woman, or child. Another revisionist Western made in the wake of the stunning impact of Sam Peckinpah's *The Wild Bunch.* The film was made, according to its producers and director, to offer a statement about the genocide of the American Indian. Come on, guys—you just wanted to do a massacre scene bloodier than Peckinpah's. Admit it! See soldier boys chop off the breasts of protesting Indian maidens! See brave Indian warriors get disemboweled! See Indian children shot in the head! See sensitive, guilt-ridden soldier blue Strauss toss up his cookies at the bloody spectacle! See Candice Bergen looking as if she just stepped out of Bloomingdale's! In this splatter Western, disguised as an "important movie," you'll see all that and less.

Sorority House Massacre

Concorde Pictures, 1986; Color; 74 minutes
Director: Carol Frank
Producer: Ron Diamond
Writer: Carol Frank
With: Angela O'Neill, Wendy Martel, Pamela Ross, Nicole Rio, John C. Russell

What a waste! There's really some talent here. The first fifteen or twenty minutes of the film contain promise, but things go downhill from there. The scenes where Beth, the main character, arrives at the sorority house are intercut not only with her memories, dreams, and hallucinations but also with the real and out-of-body experiences of a patient at a local mental hospital. This is strong visual stuff, and it is to the credit of director Carol Frank that it never gets confusing. A repeated viewing of these early scenes reveals just how adroit Frank really is with this footage. There are other pleasures as well during these early sequences: Blood slowly drips onto an immaculately set dinner table until the china, silver, candles, and linen become spotted—a haunting and ironic image. The inmate at the hospital turns his head at the exact moment he turns his head in Beth's hallucination, and Frank cuts while the turn is in progress, suggesting that the psycho is really in both places at the same time. Unfortunately, this highly cinematic beginning is not sustained; the film becomes progressively more routine and predictable.—J. B.

Southern Comfort

Embassy Pictures, 1981; Color; 106 minutes
Director: Walter Hill
Producer: David Giler
Writers: Michael Kane, Walter Hill, David Giler
With: Keith Carradine, Powers Boothe, Fred Ward, Franklyn Seales, Peter Coyote

National Guardsmen on weekend maneuvers in the Lousiana swamps mess with the local Cajuns and die to regret it. Hill's Vietnam allegory is really a composite (polite word for rip-off) of *Deliverance* and John Ford's *The Lost Patrol*. Most of the characters are so overdrawn—and bone-headed to boot—that one doesn't care whether they get killed or not. The "creative deaths" are suitably spectacular and bloody. Tense but stupid. Andrew Laszlo's photography and Ry Cooder's score are terrific, though.

Spasms

Distributor unknown, 1983; Color; 87 minutes
Director: William Fruet
Producers: John G. Pozhke, Maurice Smith
Writer: Don Enright
With: Peter Fonda, Oliver Reed, Kerrie Keanue, Al Waxman

Canadian-made giant-serpent movie in which financier Reed finds himself in telepathic contact with a lethal South American snake that killed his explorer brother. When it's captured, he buys it and hires scientist Fonda to come up with an explanation for the bizarre mind link. A group of snake worshipers, believing the reptile to be a god, let it loose by heating up its cage. The hothouse effect causes the snake to grow to the size of an elephant. The venomous creature busts loose and bites Reed and several others before being destroyed by Fonda. The oversized mechanical snake head created for the film is okay, though it doesn't do much except bite people, causing them to drool a lot and develop a case of what looks like the mumps. The real snake is a lot scarier.

Splatter University

A Troma Team Release, 1984; Color; 78 minutes
Director: Richard W. Haines
Producers: Richard W. Haines, John Michaels
Writer: Richard W. Haines
With: Francine Forbes, Cathy Lacommare, Dick Biel, Denise Texeria

Splatter University's low budget and lack of resources is evident from the beginning, but what is really amazing about the production is the total lack of talent on the part of the cast and crew. Every aspect of the production is amateurish and lacking inspiration. The story is a whodunit, but the murderer is so obvious from the start that any chance for suspense is lost (kindly priests with short tempers who are confined to wheelchairs and who spend a great deal of time spying on people are often suspicious characters!). Even the potential for an ironic ending is missed. The nominal hero could easily have been framed for the murders, leaving the imposter priest free to resume his demented deeds and the filmmakers with a natural sequel. Perhaps it's just as well the film ended as it did. The last thing we need is *Splatter University II*!
—J. B.

Spookies

Miggles Corporation, 1985; Color; 85 minutes
Directors: Eugenie Joseph, Thomas Doran, Brendan Faulkner
Producers: Eugenie Joseph, Thomas Doran, Brendan Faulkner, Frank M. Farel
Writers: Frank M. Farel, Thomas Doran, Brendan Faulkner
With: Felix Ward, Dan Scott, Alec Nemser, Maria Pechukas

Young people in search of a place to party get trapped inside a mansion owned by a codger who looks a bit like John Zacherly and speaks with a Yiddish accent. He plans

to kill the partygoers in order to revivify his long-dead bride—who actually committed suicide because she couldn't stand him! One by one, the young folks are splattered down to size by all sorts of slimy, graphically decaying creatures; my favorite are the "Muck Men" who continually break wind as they descend upon their victims. Various graveyard zombies and a flesh-ripping lizard creature round out the cast of "spookies." The film has good FX, but its threadbare (and largely incomprehensible) plot and ludicrously bad acting work against it.

Squirm

American-International, 1976; Color; 92 minutes
Director: Jeff Lieberman
Producers: Edgar Lansbury, Joseph Beruh
Writer: Jeff Lieberman
With: John Scardino, Patricia Pearcy, R. A. Dow, Peter MacLean

A freak electrical storm launches an attack of night crawlers on a sleepy southern town. The film takes some time to get started, but once the worms take over, you won't be disappointed. Includes scenes of worms burrowing into (and out of) people's faces; worms oozing out of faucets; worms hiding out in plates of spaghetti. Not recommended for wormophobes.

Stanley

Crown International Pictures, 1972; Color; 96 minutes
Director: William Grefe
Producer: William Grefe
Writer: Gary Crutcher
With: Chris Robinson, Alex Rocco, Steve Alaimo, Susan Carroll

Seminole Indian and returned Vietnam vet Robinson uses his pet rattlesnake to drive poachers off his happy hunting ground. Creepy—especially if you have an aversion to snakes—with a few moments of grisly gristle thrown in, such as one scene where a character bites the head off a snake. Yechhh!

Starlight Slaughters

See Eaten Alive

Steel Justice

Atlantic Releasing, 1987; Color; 95 minutes
Director: Robert Boris
Producer: John Strong
Writer: Robert Boris
With: Martin Kove, Sela Ward, Ronny Cox, Bernie Casey

Vietnam vet Kove goes back home to Los Angeles only to find that a corrupt expatriate South Vietnamese general has set up shop as a drug kingpin. For awhile it's "let sleeping dogs lie," but when an expatriate Vietnamese pal of Kove's (and the pal's whole family) is slaughtered by the drug lord's son and chief executioner, Kove goes into action, sidestepping the inept and inefficient police (aren't they always in vigilante dramas like these?) to topple the drug thugs and bring them to justice. Lots of bodies and blood but not much suspense, as the film is shot like an extended music video.

A Stranger Is Watching

MGM/UA, 1982; Color; 92 minutes
Director: Sean S. Cunningham
Producer: Sidney Beckerman
Writers: Earl MacRauch, Victor Miller
With: Kate Mulgrew, Rip Torn

On the strength of the box-office receipts of his *Friday the 13th* (1980), low-budget filmmaker Cunningham finally got his shot at the big time with this adaptation of Mary Higgins Clark's best-seller. Torn kidnaps TV reporter Mulgrew and the daughter of a prominent politician and conceals them in a special hideaway beneath Grand Central Station. Ludicrous over-the-top thriller (Torn chews up the scenery). The slow-motion beheading finale is straight out of—you guessed it— *Friday the 13th.*

Student Bodies

Paramount Pictures, 1981; Color; 80 minutes
Director: Mickey Rose
Producer: Allen Smithee
Writer: Mickey Rose
With: Kristen Riter, Matt Goldsby, Richard Brando, Mimi Weddell

Parody of mad-slasher movies in which crazed masked killer Brando, nicknamed The Breather on account of how he sounds behind his mask, wipes out school kids with such ingenious weapons as paper clips and erasers. Frequently very funny, but its absurdities often fail to outdo the real thing. Smithee is a favorite Hollywood pseudonym used to protect the guilty.

The Stuff

New World Pictures, 1985; Color; 93 minutes
Director: Larry Cohen
Producer: Paul Kurta
Writer: Larry Cohen
With: Michael Moriarty, Andrea Marcovicci, Paul Sorvino, Garrett Morris, Patrick O'Neal

Corporate bigwigs hire deceptively moronic industrial spy Moriarty to steal the secret formula behind America's fastest-selling junk-food dessert—The Stuff, a creamy yogurtlike concoction that scrambles people's brains. Turns out The Stuff bubbles up out of the earth, like The Blob of yore. Moriarty gets help from survivalist millionaire Sorvino by convincing him The Stuff is the stuff of a communist plot. Moderately funny satire on junk-food fads, with good stop motion and gore effects by David Allen, Jim Danforth, Ed French, and others. The Ramboesque Sorvino has the film's best line when he machine-guns a whipped cream–oozing "Stuffie" and says, "I kinda like blood, but *this* is disgusting!" Look for cameos by Tammy Grimes, Brooke Adams, and the late Clara Peller ("Where's the Stuff?").

The Supernaturals

Republic Entertainment International, 1985; Color; 85 minutes
Director: Armand Mastroianni
Producers: Joel Soisson, Michael S. Murphey
Writers: Joel Soisson, Michael S. Murphey
With: Maxwell Caulfield, Talia Balsam, Bradford Bancroft, LeVar Burton, Bobby DiCicco, Nichelle Nichols

Return with us now to *2000 Maniacs* territory (with a dash of *Southern Comfort* thrown in). Yankee soldiers use Rebs as guinea pigs to test a mine field. Several of them are killed, including the mother of a little boy named Jeremy, who has supernatural healing powers and returns her to life. A century or so later, the modern equivalent of the same Yankee regiment is on tactical maneuvers in the same spot; fog creeps in and the dead Rebs rise up as zombies, led by the boy's mother, to exact revenge. One by one the greenhorn lost patrolers are mutilated, maimed, and knocked off until the resurrected mother is sent back to her grave by her

100-plus-year-old mummy of a son. This short movie seems to take forever to get going—and the wait isn't worth it. Truly pitiful.

Surf Nazis Must Die

A Troma Team Release, 1986; Color; 83 minutes
Director: Peter George
Producer: Robert Tinnell
Writer: Jon Ayre
With: Barry Brennan, Gail Neely, Dawn Wildsmith, Michael Sonye, Bobbie Bresee

The Big Quake hits L. A., killing 80,000 people. The overburdened police department becomes ineffectual as youth gangs run wild, fighting for control of Power Beach, a surfer's paradise. The worst of the bunch are the Surf Nazis, a group that includes surfer Adolf, Eva, Mengele, and some other surf troopers, including one wearing a hook. The competing gangs—the Samurai Surfers, Designer Waves, and the Pipelines—seem impotent in the face of this Führer of the New Beach. But Adolf and his gang are finally brought down by a gun-and-grenade-toting black mama (Neely) whose son was murdered by the Surf Nazis. The film might have been an action-filled, outrageous splatter satire—except that there's little action, the splatter is reduced to a minimum, and there aren't any laughs. There's lots of pretty but tedious surfing footage, though, suggesting that the project started out as something else. The best thing about *Surf Nazis Must Die* is the title.

Suspiria

Twentieth Century-Fox, 1976; Color; 99 minutes
Director: Dario Argento
Producer: Claudio Argento
Writers: Dario Argento, Daria Nicolodi
With: Jessica Harper, Joan Bennett, Alida Valli, Udo Keir, Stefania Casini

American ballet student Harper arrives in Rome to take up studies at a ballet school run by Bennett and Valli and finds herself up to her ears in maggots (which rain from the ceiling) and a coven of witches. Yet another exercise in pure style by Mario Bava protégé Dario Argento, who includes his usual generous helping of murders and whatnot. The protracted deaths of two of the ballet students in the film's opening scene—one crashes through a skylight with a rope around her neck, while the other is skewered by all the broken glass—is guaranteed to grab your attention. So will the flamboyant color scheme—Argento piles on the red with Antonioniesque glee. Though most of his fans tend to like *Deep Red* more, this is probably Argento's best film—it is certainly his wildest. The pounding score is again by The Goblins.

The Sword and the Sorcerer

Bedford Films, 1982; Color; 100 minutes
Director: Albert Pyun
Producers: Brandon and Marianne Chase
Writer: Tom Karnowsky
With: Lee Horsley, Kathleen Beller, Simon MacCorkindale, George Maharis, Richard Lynch

Horsley's family is murdered by evil sorcerer Lynch, so when the lad grows up, he naturally vows revenge and commits himself Conan-style to toppling the powerful magician from his throne. Empty-headed but fast-moving debut feature by Pyun in the Robert E. Howard tradition, with some very good (and gruesome) special effects. Definitely a B movie, but it doesn't look like one.

Tales from the Crypt

Cinerama Releasing, 1972; Color; 92 minutes
Director: Freddie Francis
Producers: Max J. Rosenberg, Milton Subotsky
Writer: Milton Subotsky
With: Ralph Richardson, Joan Collins, Ian Hendry, Peter Cushing, Richard Greene, Nigel Patrick

George Romero's *Night of the Living Dead* had already introduced the grisly spirit of EC horror comics to the screen. This anthology film, based on one of EC's most popular horror comics, *Tales from the Crypt*, draws its stories from the pages of the comic book itself. Ralph Richardson is the "Crypt Keeper," who spins the tales, all of them centering on the theme of revenge. The episode featuring Cushing as a victimized widower who literally claims his tormentor's heart, is the most emotionally affecting; the segment in which victimizer Patrick must make his way in the dark through a corridor lined with razor blades as a savage dog pursues him is undeniably the grisliest. Gruesome good fun.

A Taste of Blood

Creative Film Enterprises, 1967; Color; 120 minutes
Director: Herschell Gordon Lewis
Producer: Herschell Gordon Lewis
Writer: Donald Stanford
With: Bill Rogers, Elizabeth Wilkinson, Thomas Wood, Otto Schlesinger, Sheldon Seymour (Lewis)

After drinking Slivovitz that has been spiked with who knows what, Rogers discovers he's a descendant of Count Dracula, turns into a vampire, and sets out to kill the ancestors of those who did in his infamous relative. But Schlesinger, the ancestor of good old Dr. Van Helsing, puts the stake to him first. This is probably Lewis's best-*looking* film. It's also his longest—almost a gore epic. It's awfully talky, though. Lewis appears in a cameo at the beginning of the film as a mustachioed longshoreman. It is aka *The Secret of Dr. Alucard.*

Tenebrae

Distributor unknown, 1982; Color; 110 minutes
Director: Dario Argento
Producer: Claudio Argento
Writers: Dario Argento, George Kemp
With: Anthony Franciosa, John Saxon, Daria Nicolodi, Guiliano Gemma

After making two splatter movies with supernatural overtones, Argento returned to the whodunit theme that characterized his early *giallo* thrillers—most notably *The Bird with the Crystal Plumage*, which this film resembles in many ways. Franciosa is an American detective-story writer visiting Italy to promote his latest book. He gets some unwanted publicity when a psychopath starts murdering women, using methods borrowed from the book. Without giving the ending away, the old Hitchcock "transference of guilt" theme plays an important part in the final twist. The film was not released theatrically in the United States and is not, as of this writing, available on video.

10 to Midnight

MGM/UA, 1983; Color; 100 minutes
Director: J. Lee Thompson
Producers: Pancho Kohner, Lance Hool

Writer: William Roberts
With: Charles Bronson, Andrew Stevens, Lisa Eilbacher, Gene Davis

Bronson trades in his persona as an avenger working outside the law for that of an avenger working inside the law—well, almost. He's an L.A. cop on the trail of a nasty serial killer/rapist who cavorts about the city carrying out his nefarious deeds in the nude. Charlie gets the goods on the nudist nutso, but as the goods aren't sufficient to stand up in court, he falsifies the evidence to make it more convincing. His straight-arrow junior partner (Stevens) can't abide this constitutional rape and turns Charlie in; Charlie then gets thrown off the force. This minor setback only makes Charlie more determined than ever to get his quarry—especially since the killer is now stalking Bronson's own daughter. And, of course, get the killer he does—by shooting him down stark naked in the street. Typically liberal-minded Bronson fare.

The Terminator

Orion Pictures, 1984; Color; 107 minutes
Director: James Cameron
Producer: Gale Ann Hurd
Writers: James Cameron, Gale Ann Hurd
With: Arnold Schwarzenegger, Linda Hamilton, Michael Biehn, Paul Winfield, Lance Henriksen, Dick Miller

Cameron was chosen to direct the sequel to *Alien* on the basis of this futuristic blood and thunder *Alien* clone. Schwarzenegger isn't an alien; he's a robot killing machine sent back in time to assassinate the mother (Hamilton) of a future political messiah. Biehn is one of the messiah's revolutionary followers who journeys back in time to prevent the as-

sassination from occurring. The ending where lone survivor Hamilton must fight the relentless cyborg on her own by setting it on fire, then crunching it in a punch press is unquestionably exciting. Probably Schwarzenegger's best movie (because he doesn't speak much).

Terror Circus

See Barn of the Naked Dead

Terror House

See Folks at the Red Wolf Inn

The Texas Chainsaw Massacre

Bryanston Pictures, New Line Cinema, 1974; Color; 86 minutes
Director: Tobe Hooper
Producers: Tobe Hooper, Kim Henkel
Writers: Tobe Hooper, Kim Henkel
With: Marilyn Burns, Paul A. Partain, Edwin Neal, Jim Siedow, Gunnar Hansen

Young people on vacation run out of gas and seek help at a farmhouse inhabited by a family of crazed cannibal-killers, who proceed to stalk them, kill them, and turn them into prime ribs. Most viewers (and critics) perceive this film as being much gorier than it actually is, and this is Hooper's cleverest ploy: The title alone has you cringing before you even sit down. Rather than gobs of graphic gore, it's the pervading *atmosphere* of violence and depravity in this film that makes it seem so relentless. That and the infernal *whirr* of Leatherface's chain saw. Undeniably one of the scariest of all splatter movies, *Chainsaw* was based (loosely) on the Ed Gein case, the same true crime that inspired Hitchcock's *Psycho*! Followed in

1986 by a sequel also directed by Hooper, which is everything this film has often been accused of being but is not.

The Texas Chainsaw Massacre 2

Cannon Films, 1986; Color; 101 minutes
Director: Tobe Hooper
Producers: Menahem Golan, Yoram Globus, Tobe Hooper
Writer: L. M. Kit Carson
With: Dennis Hopper, Caroline Williams, Jim Siedow, Bill Moseley, Bill Johnson

After a series of interesting but generally disappointing films, Tobe Hooper returns to the fertile ground that first made his name and comes up a winner with this amazingly vicious and "sick" sequel, which offers a brutal slap-in-the-face satire of the Reaganic Traditional Family Unit to rival David Lynch's more famous *Blue Velvet*. This time the demented (but undeniably solid) Sawyer clan have moved their nefarious trade to the Dallas area, where they've made a name for themselves with their prize-winning chili ("The secret's in the meat," enthuses ringleader Jim Siedow, whose dialogue is mostly made up of American Success Ethic clichés). Unfortunately for them, ex–Texas Ranger Dennis Hopper (whose nephew was massacred in the first film) has spent years tracking them to their new lair, an abandoned amusement park (which one of their number wants to turn into "what the public want—'Nam Land!"). Hopper himself is quite insane (naturally) and winds up having a chain-saw duel with Leatherface in a sequence that must be seen to be believed. Astoundingly, Grandpa is still with us—just as unable to wield (or even hold) a sledgehammer as ever, and just as absurdly revered by his family. Frequently very funny (in an unwhole-

some fashion), often disturbing, always good to look at (the subterranean set is a stunner), the film's only real failing is that it may go too far—even for hard-core splatter fans.—K. H.

Theatre of Blood

United Artists, 1973; Color; 104 minutes
Director: Douglas Hickox
Producers: John Kohn, Stanley Mann
Writer: Anthony Greville-Bell
With: Vincent Price, Diana Rigg, Harry Andrews, Robert Morley, Ian Hendry, Jack Hawkins

Hammy Shakespearean actor Price commits suicide after being ridiculed one too many times by the critics. His death is a ruse, however. With the help of daughter Rigg (who's disguised as a bewigged, mustachioed hippie), he rises like the phoenix to murder each of his tart-tongued adversaries, modeling their deaths after violent set pieces created by the Bard himself. Reminiscent of Price's *Dr. Phibes* films, but a lot more gruesome—and a lot funnier, too. Price has a field day in his role as the death-dealing thespian. The rest of the impressive cast matches him every step of the way—especially Morley as a gluttonous gourmet critic who overindulges himself to the grave after feasting on his precious French poodles.

They Came from Within

A Trans-America Release, 1976; Color; 87 minutes
Director: David Cronenberg
Producer: Ivan Reitman
Writer: David Cronenberg
With: Paul Hampton, Joe Silver, Lynn Lowry, Allan Migicovsky, Barbara Steele

Residents of the Starliner Towers, a completely self-contained, up-scale apartment complex that even boasts its own medical clinic, are infected by a parasite that turns them into sexual crazies. Reserved doctor Hampton, who refuses to get turned on even when his nurse strips in front of him, is the last to succumb. When it's not imitating *Night of the Living Dead*, Cronenberg's debut feature is quite good, generating some real tension and nasty shocks as the parasites ooze out of people's mouths, latch on to people's faces, and have to be pulled off with pliers—courtesy of some excellent special effects by Joe Blasco. The film clearly seems to come down on the side of the free-loving maniacs as they spread their libidinous contagion from one body to the next—a cathartic viewpoint that isn't nearly so easy to accept now that we know about AIDS. It is aka *Shivers, Frissons,* and *The Parasite Murders.*

They Live

Universal, 1988; Color; 94 minutes
Director: John Carpenter
Producer: Larry Franco
Writer: Frank Armitage
With: Roddy Piper, Meg Foster, Keith David, Raymond St. Jacques

Who *is* that behind those Foster Grant's? Why it's wrestler turned actor Rowdy Roddy Piper giving one of the worst debut performances in recent screen history. Piper plays an out-of-work construction worker who catches on to the fact that the earth has been taken over by aliens who dominate the human race by feeding on human greed and apathy. Thanks to special sunglasses developed by revolutionaries who run a shelter for the homeless, he's able to see who's an alien and who isn't. Charged with patriotic fervor, he takes up arms and sets out to "Kick some ass and chew bubblegum." The movie does the same thing. Once again, Carpenter rifles the work of Nigel Kneale (in this case Kneale's *Quartermass II*) for

an interesting concept which he then proceeds to do absolutely nothing with. At one point in the film, an alien talk show host discussing media violence chides Carpenter for going "too far" in his movies. The truth though is that Carpenter, a B filmmaker here masquerading as a Z one, never goes far enough—especially with his plots.

The Thing

Universal, 1982; Color; 109 minutes
Director: John Carpenter
Producers: David Foster, Lawrence Turman
Writer: Bill Lancaster
With: Kurt Russell, Richard Dysart, Richard Masur, A. Wilford Brimley, Donald Moffat, David Clennon, T. K. Carter

Carpenter's remake of Howard Hawks's 1951 classic *The Thing* has a lot of things going for it and they're all spelled Rob Bottin. Makeup wiz Bottin's astounding, splattery special effects of *Thing-ness* are the real stars—in fact, they're the only stars. Bill Lancaster's (Burt's son) script harks back to the original John Campbell story upon which Hawks's film was also (loosely) based, but it leaves out any sense of characterization. One simply doesn't care whether this Arctic team gets *Thinged* or not. *But oh, those effects!*

The Thirsty Dead

International Amusement, 1974; Color; 96 minutes
Director: Terry Becker
Producer: Wesley E. Depue
Writer: Charles Dennis
With: John Considine, Jennifer Billingsley, Tani Gutherie, Judith McDonnell

Blood-drinking vampire corpses rise from the dead to deliver nubile virgins to their satanist lord of the jungle—Considine, not Tarzan. Bottom-of-the-barrel shocker, made in the Philippines, that will *not* leave you thirsting for more. It is aka *Blood Cult of Shangri-La.*

This Stuff'll Kill Ya!

An Ultima Productions, Inc. Release, 1971; Color; 100 minutes
Director: Herschell Gordon Lewis
Producer: Herschell Gordon Lewis
Writer: Herschell Gordon Lewis
With: Tim Holt, Jeffrey Allen, Gloria King, Ray Sager, Erich Bradley

Bloody companion piece to Lewis's earlier hillbilly splatter epic, *Moonshine Mountain,* featuring B-Western star Tim Holt in his last screen role. (Holt had costarred in Orson Welles's *The Magnificent Ambersons* and John Huston's *The Treasure of the Sierra Madre,* then he'd fallen on hard times.) Allen is a moonshiner posing as a preacher. Holt is one of the "revenooers" determined to put him out of business. The moonshiners are a tough bunch. Those who threaten to blow the whistle on them are stoned to death, burned alive, blown away, or crucified. Lewis, using his Sheldon Seymour pseudonym, composed the country and western songs that lace the sound track. It is aka *The Devil Wears Clodhoppers.*

Thou Shalt Not Kill . . . Except

Film World Distributors, 1985; Color; 84 minutes
Director: Josh Becker
Producer: Scott Spiegel
Writers: Josh Becker, Scott Spiegel
With: Brian Schulz, Robert Rickman, John Manfredi, Tim Quill, Sam Raimi

A platoon led by Lt. Miller and Sgt. Stryker is almost decimated trying to take a Vietnamese village. Stateside, a Manson-like cult wipes out a family, then retires to the K.I.A. (Killed In Action?) campground to snare and torture vacationers. Back home, the wounded Stryker, who lives in a cabin nearby, is reunited with three of his Nam pals. When the vets discover what the cult is up to, they arm themselves and go after them. The result: ultragore. In Nam, a Marine is shot in the head and his buddy is drenched with the man's brains. Back home, the cult members are shotgunned, skewered with knives and hedge clippers, and impaled on trees. Sound serious? Well, it starts out that way, but the over-the-top mayhem, punctuated by sardonic dialogue, quickly reminds you of *The Evil Dead.* That's no accident. The film was made in Detroit by associates of *Dead* director Sam Raimi, who plays the wild-eyed Manson-like cult leader. The spirit of the film is summed up by one of the vets after the carnage is over: "Let's get the hell out of here, man, and get somethin' to eat!" Worth a look.

Three on a Meathook

Studio One, 1973; Color; 79 minutes
Director: William Girdler
Producers: John Ashman, Lee Jones
Writer: William Girdler
With: Charles Kissinger, James Pickert, Carolyn Thompson

Another backwoods slasher film—from the director of *Grizzly, The Manitou,* and even more undistinguished fare. This one, loosely based on the infamous Ed Gein Case, is again about a psycho who kills nubile young women, eats parts of their bodies, and wears their skins as souvenirs as he dallies around his ramshackle farmhouse. As with *The Texas Chainsaw Massacre,* which was also loosely based on the Gein case and which this film preceded by one year, it's laced with absurd situations and dialogue. It's a whole lot

gorier than *Chainsaw*, though, but not as good. Still, it's a must-see for Ed Gein–inspired "meat movie" completists.

Tombs of the Blind Dead

Hallmark Releasing, 1973; Color; 86 minutes
Director: Amando De Ossorio
Producer: Salvadore Romero
Writer: Amando De Ossorio
With: Lone Fleming, Cesar Burner, Joseph Thelman, Rufino Ingles

First of three popular (in Europe, anyway) Spanish-made zombie/ghoul—or "blind dead"—movies all helmed by Ossorio. Executed for crimes against humanity and buried in unmarked graves, the vicious medieval sect known as the Knights Templar magically spring to life and rise from their tombs seven centuries later to revenge themselves on modern-day man and, especially, woman—whom they proceed to maim, mutilate, and drain of blood. These living dead creatures are, for the most part, in worse physical shape than George Romero's zombies—their eyes, as well as their flesh, have long since rotted away, making it a bit difficult for them to spot victims. Nature—and illogical splatter-movie scripting—has compensated, however, giving the "blind dead" supersensitive hearing that allows them to locate victims from the slightest sound and chow down.

The Toolbox Murders

Cal-Am, 1977; Color; 95 minutes
Director: Dennis Donnelly
Producer: Tony Didio
Writers: Neva Friedenn, Robert Easter, Ann Kindberg
With: Cameron Mitchell, Pamelyn Ferdin, Wesley Eure, Tim Donnelly, Aneta Corseault

Police are stymied by a series of suburban psycho murders where the crazed killer (Mitchell) wipes out his victims with power drills, screwdrivers, hammers, and nail-guns. Brutal stuff—but also fairly dull. One of the few splatter movies to have been discussed at length on the Donahue show—where the nail-gun murder was shown and greeted by groans of horror and dismay from the studio audience.

The Tormented

See The Eerie Midnight Horror Show

Torso

Joseph Brenner, 1974; Color; 89 minutes
Director: Sergio Martino
Producer: Antonio Cervi
Writers: Sergio Martino, Ernesto Castaldi
With: Suzy Kendall, Tina Aumont, Carla Brait, John Richardson

It appears that the Italian filmmakers behind this production were attempting to create an American-style thriller. They failed. The major problem seems to be that they're not quite sure exactly what type of American film they want to emulate. A whodunit with no real mystery or suspense, a splatter movie with minimal gore (choppy editing indicates that some footage may have been cut), and a soft-core porn film with very little sex (a lot of bare breasts and one mild lesbian scene) leaves the viewer feeling that he really hasn't seen much of anything. There is some suspense toward the end of the film when an American girl is trapped in an upstairs bedroom while the killer saws up her dead girlfriends downstairs, but this scene simply doesn't justify sitting through a pretty tepid eighty-nine minutes. Bad dubbing and an indifferent, often inappropriate, score further alienate the viewer.—J. B.

Torture Dungeon

Mishkin Films, 1970; Color; 80
    minutes
Director: Andy Milligan
Producer: William Mishkin
Writers: Andy Milligan, John Borske
With: Jeremy Brooks, Susan Cassidy

Arguable plot deals with a brutal noble-man who tortures, kills, and dismembers any and all pretenders to the throne of England—which, naturally, he covets for himself. Lots of splatter murders—including one by pitchfork. Staten Island locales stand in for England—but, hey, a dungeon is a dungeon, after all.

Tourist Trap

Compass International Pictures, 1979;
    Color; 85 minutes
Director: David Schmoeller
Producer: J. Larry Carroll
Writers: David Schmoeller, J. Larry
    Carroll
With: Chuck Connors, Joe Van Ness,
    Jocelyn Jones, Robin Sherwood,
    Tanya Roberts, Keith McDermott

Yet another "vacationing teenagers in peril" flick. On a trip through the desert (where else?), they run into car trouble and seek help at a gas station run by wacko Connors. In addition to pumping gas, Connors also has a museum on his property; when the teens go in to take a look, the mannequins on exhibit come dangerously to life and start knocking the teens off one by one. Some suspenseful moments and the gore is fairly low-key. But like *Phantasm* (1978), which it somewhat resembles, the film doesn't make a great deal of sense.

Tower of Evil

Independent International Pictures,
    1972; Color; 89 minutes
Director: Jim O'Connelly
Producer: Richard Gordon
Writer: Jim O'Connelly
With: Bryant Halliday, Jill Haworth,
    Anna Palk, Jack Watson, George
    Coulouris, Dennis Price

American Haworth is suspected of murdering her companions with an ancient spear discovered at a scenic vacation spot called Snape Island. She claims she's innocent, so Scotland Yard and a team of archaeologists, who believe the spear may point the way to a long-lost Phoenician treasure, go back to the island with her to investigate. And once again, the corpses start piling up. Boasting some good effects, this film is really a murder mystery with a hint of *Psycho* (1960) lurking about. It is aka *Horror on Snape Island.*

Transmutations

Distributor unknown, 1985; Color;
    103 minutes
Director: George Pavoul
Producers: Don Hawkins, Kevin
    Attew, Graham Ford
Writers: Clive Barker, James Caplin
With: Denholm Elliott, Steven Berkoff,
    Larry Lamb, Nicola Cowper,
    Miranda Richardson

Virginal beauty Cowper is kidnapped from the high-class brothel where she works by a band of grotesquely misshapen subterranean beasts. Her former bodyguard and lover (Lamb) is lured out of "retirement" by gangster Berkoff to find her. The trail leads to a villainous doctor (Elliott) who's invented a powerful hallucinogenic drug that induces extreme euphoria. It also has an unfortunate side effect,

causing the faces of the doctor's human guinea pigs to swell up and rot, which is why they're hiding underground away from the eyes of society. Convoluted and excruciatingly dull variation on the beauty and the beast theme, with most of the FX relegated to the film's conclusion—Elliott's face, for example, rots and then explodes in flame and various people get shot and/or punctured with needles.

Trick or Treat

De Laurentiis Entertainment Group, 1986; Color; 97 minutes
Director: Charles Martin Smith
Producers: Michael S. Murphey, Joel Soisson
Writers: Michael S. Murphey, Joel Soisson, Rhet Topham
With: Marc Price, Tony Fields, Lisa Orgolini, Doug Savant

Trick or Treat takes an interesting premise—a dead rock star using hidden messages in his recordings to influence the living—and tries to build a horror film around it. Unfortunately, director Charles Martin Smith makes two fundamental mistakes. First, he refuses to take his horror seriously. Humor can be a vital part of a horror film, but respect must be maintained for the basic horror elements; the director must know where to draw the line. Smith doesn't. The second problem is that too much happens too quickly and the story loses credibility. A good horror film pulls us in a bit at a time. The director carefully builds the story so that by the time the more outrageous plot developments occur, we have surrendered to the dramatic momentum and accept the events as plausible. Smith piles on too much too soon; we simply can't buy it. A promising premise worked on by some talented people goes astray.—J. B.

Twilight of the Dead

See Gates of Hell

Twilight People

New World Pictures, 1972; Color; 84 minutes
Director: Eddie Romero
Producers: Eddie Romero, John Ashley
Writers: Eddie Romero, Jerome Small
With: John Ashley, Pat Woodell, Pam Grier, Eddie Garcia, Jan Merlin

Return with us once more to *The Island of Dr. Moreau* (uncredited, of course) on which a mad scientist is busy experimenting with genetic engineering, turning animals—and even trees—into grotesque-looking humans. The humanimal makeups are passable, the gore murders effective, but the script is ridiculous and the direction even worse. Romero must have a fixation with Wells's classic tale, for he produced another uncredited (and loosely adapted) version in 1959 called *Terror Is a Man.* Frankly, that film was a lot better, though it eschewed the splatter of the later film. Made in the Philippines. It is aka *Island of the Twilight People.*

Twitch of the Death Nerve

Hallmark Releasing, 1973; Color; 90 minutes
Director: Mario Bava
Producer: Giuseppe Zaccariello
Writers: Mario Bava, Joseph McLee
With: Claudine Auger, Claudio Volante, Luigi Pistilli, Leopoldo Trieste

Splattery parody—at least it could be interpreted that way—of Agatha Christie's

And Then There Were None. Except that there's not one murderer herein; *everybody*'s the killer. Greedy to grab on to some valuable—and scenic—property, a host of prospective buyers, rather than attempt to outbid one another, opt to bump each other off, using spears, knives, axes, meat cleavers, whatever's handy. The mayhem eventually gets so out of hand that at the ironic conclusion the surviving land grabbers are unexpectedly slain by their own kids, who've come to believe that this is the way the world works. Shot on a shoestring, this isn't one of Bava's better films, but it is one of his bloodiest—maybe even *the* bloodiest. It is aka *The Ecology of a Crime.*

2000 Maniacs

Box Office Spectaculars, 1964; Color; 88 minutes
Director: Herschell Gordon Lewis
Producer: David Friedman
Writer: Herschell Gordon Lewis
With: Connie Mason, Thomas Wood, Jeffrey Allen, Ben Moore

A southern town (actually St. Cloud, Florida) magically reappears *Brigadoon*-style 100 years after its devastation by Yankee troops during the Civil War. As a group of northern tourists (led by former *Playboy* playmate Mason) pass through, the revenge-hungry townsfolk of the title take them captive, torture and murder them in a variety of ingenious and graphically horrible ways—including a very pointed variation on the old theme of "Roll Out the Barrel." Colorfully photographed (by Lewis) hackwork and the personal favorite of its director, who, due to budget constraints, couldn't deliver the sizable cast of crazies the film's title promises (he falls short by about 1,980). But who's counting?

The Undertaker and His Pals

Howco, 1967; Color; 60 minutes
Director: David C. Graham
Producer: David C. Graham
Writer: T. L. P. (Tom) Swicegood
With: Robert Lowry, W. Ott, Rad Fulton, Ray Dennis

Meat movie laced with black humor about of a couple of Burke and Harestyle bikers who kill and mutilate women to help out their undertaker pal's not-so-thriving business. Prior to the help of his friends, he'd been forced to cut rates and even give out trading stamps. The enterprising fiends sell the uninterred body parts in a restaurant. They don't kill indiscriminately, however. With an eye toward truth in advertising, they only select victims whose names boast nutritional value, such as "Miss Lamb" whose "leg" proves ideal for the restaurant's bill of fare. Cheap and terrible with unconvincing special effects. The bizarre humor does occasionally compensate, though.

The Unholy

Vestron Pictures, 1988; Color; 105 minutes
Director: Camilo Vila
Producer: Mathew Hayden
Writers: Philip Yordan, Fernando Fonseca
With: Ben Cross, Ned Beatty, William Russ, Jill Carroll, Hal Holbrook, Nicole Fortier, Trevor Howard

Priest Cross survives a demon-induced fall from the seventeenth floor of a New Orleans skyscraper without a scratch. Archbishops Holbrook and Howard therefore deem him sturdy enough to take on the malevolent spirit of a sensuous supernatural creature (dubbed "The Unholy") who materializes at Easter to claim pure

souls for the devil by making priests and other virgins have sex with her. Russ is the good guy/bad guy owner of a satanic night club who catches onto all the hocus-pocus long before Cross, and is crucified for his meddling. In the laughable finale (which has to be seen to be believed), Cross confronts The Unholy (Fortier), which transforms into what looks like a round-headed alligator. Aided by dwarfs that explode like blocks of granite, the creature makes the put-upon priest eat its/her slime. But Cross saves the day by uttering the immortal words: "Get thee behind me, Satan." An absolute stinkeroo!

The Unnamable

Yankee Classic Pictures, 1988; Color; 87 minutes
Director: Jean-Paul Oulette
Producers: Dean Ramser, Jean-Paul Oulette
Writer: Jean-Paul Oulette
With: Charles King, Mark Kinsey Stephenson, Alexandra Durrell, Laura Albert

Advances in ghoulish screen FX, plus the success of Stuart Gordon's *The Re-Animator* and *From Beyond,* have finally turned H. P. Lovecraft into a hot commercial property. This is a Canadian-made elaboration of a very short tale by Lovecraft of the same name. A vicious primordial creature born of man and woman (it killed mom during childbirth and later ripped dad's heart out) is kept imprisoned in a deserted New England house for two centuries. Several Miskatonic University students venture inside to see what's up and wind up getting their throats torn out and their heads bashed in. The film's bookish hero (Stephenson) finally entraps the creature by conjuring up tree spirits with the help of the *Necronomi-*

con. The film follows Lovecraft's flip 3,000-word story closely, but also pads it out interminably. The it/she creature (Katrin Alexandre) is suitably ghastly but has feet reminiscent of the Morlocks in George Pal's *Time Machine.* Not up to Gordon's Lovecraft films by far.

The Unseen

World Northal, 1981; Color; 88 minutes
Director: Peter Foleg
Producer: Anthony B. Unger
Writer: Micael L. Grace
With: Barbara Bach, Sydney Lassick, Karen Lamm, Doug Barr, Lois Young, Leila Goldoni

News reporter Bach and her assistants, camerawoman Lamm and gofer Young, are covering a "Danish Festival" in the midwest heartland. Circumstances force them to seek accommodations in a rooming house run by the grotesque Lassick and his sister (Goldoni), who harbor a secret—a badly deformed and subhuman son, the product of their incestuous union, hiding in the cellar. Sonny boy escapes, of course, and . . . well, you no doubt can guess what happens next. Not bad, but by no means good—and relatively restrained in the gore department, which, in light of the drab script, was probably not a wise decision.

The Upstate Murders

See Savage Weekend

Vampire Circus

Twentieth Century-Fox, 1971; Color; 87 minutes
Director: Robert Young
Producer: Wilbur Stark

Writer: Jud Kinberg
With: Laurence Payne, Adrienne Corri, Thorley Walters, Robert Tayman, John Moulder Brown

Desperately in need of some diverting entertainment, a plague-infested Serbian village (circa 1800) is visited by a mysterious circus whose performers have the ability to transform themselves into beasts and bats. They're vampires, you see. And they've come to get revenge on the villagers for having skewered one of their own in the film's bloody prologue. In keeping with most post-1970 Hammer Horrors, there's a lot more nudity and gore (and a lot less characterization) than in the studio's classic Gothics of the late fifties and early sixties. It also seems to end rather abruptly—due, perhaps, to budget constraints. Still, it's one of Hammer's more stylish and inventive latter-day vampire tales and is recommended despite its obvious imperfections.

Vault of Horror

Cinerama Releasing, 1973; Color; 86 minutes
Director: Roy Ward Baker
Producers: Max J. Rosenberg, Milton Subotsky
Writer: Milton Subotsky
With: Daniel Massey, Terry-Thomas, Glynis Johns, Anna Massey, Michael Craig, Tom Baker, Richard Todd

An anthology of five gruesome horror tales culled from the pages of William M. Gaines's well-known series of EC horror comics from the fifties. The wraparound story tells of five men trapped in an elevator, each of whom recounts a strange and gory tale of revenge and retribution in typical EC style. When the elevator opens, they find themselves in a cemetery and realize they're all dead. The stories include: "Midnight Mass"; "The Neat Job"—in which Todd's mutilated body parts come alive to terrorize the wife who killed him; "This Trick'll Kill You"; "Bargain in Death"; and "Drawn and Quartered." Perhaps not as good as its predecessor, *Tales from the Crypt* (1972)—though it *is* gorier, but on a par with *Creepshow* (1982).

Vice Squad

Avco Embassy, 1982; Color; 97 minutes
Director: Gary Sherman
Producer: Brian Frankish
Writers: Sandy Howard, Kenneth Peters, Robert Vincent O'Neill
With: Gary Swanson, Season Hubley, Wings Hauser

L. A. cop Swanson enlists the aid of prostitute Hubley to bring a psychotic pimp (Hauser), who enjoys beating up and mutilating his girls, to justice. Superviolent police drama. Wings Hauser really takes flight as the battering, knife-wielding pimp.

The Video Dead

Manson International, 1987; Color; 90 minutes
Director: Robert Scott
Producer: Robert Scott
Writer: Robert Scott
With: Roxanna Augesen, Rocky Duvall, Vickie Bastel, Sam David McClelland, Michael St. Michaels, Jennifer Miro

This film stinks, and it's not from the smell of rotting flesh. The script is riddled with clichés and implausible situations, the acting is consistently amateurish and the limp direction never manages to generate any real tension or suspense. Author

Henry Jordan mistakenly receives a cursed TV, and is soon murdered by the zombies who enter his home through its screen. Siblings Jeff and Zoe Blair (Duvall and Augesen), whose parents are abroad, move in next. Jeff falls for neighbor girl April (Bastel) but is almost seduced by a strange blond woman (Miro) through the TV before her throat is slit by a character called "The Garbage Man." We never see or hear from these two interesting characters again. Then April's father and the family maid, plus an elderly couple we've never seen before, are slaughtered by the zombies. April takes refuge with Jeff and Zoe, who have been joined by Texas zombie hunter Joshua Daniels (McClelland), but is soon carried off and killed nevertheless. Jeff and Joshua attack the zombies but are also killed, leaving Zoe to face the undead alone. She survives in a traumatized state, but then the video dead return. Two mediocre gore effects—live mice crawling in a zombie's guts and a chain-sawed zombie whose top half moves on its hands à la *Freaks*—are this films's only "good" points.—D. K.

Videodrome

Universal, 1983; Color; 90 minutes
Director: David Cronenberg
Producer: Claude Heroux
Writer: David Cronenberg
With: James Woods, Deborah Harry, Sonja Smits

Cable-TV pirate Woods discovers an unlawful but popular channel featuring scenes of torture and murder and he sets out to track its source. Instead, he becomes the ultimate couch potato—a grotesque blend of the medium and the message. Unlike in *The Brood* and *The Fly*, Cronenberg's splattery effects (orchestrated by Rick Baker) tend not to support this film's compelling theme, but ultimately drown it out.

Visiting Hours

Universal, 1982; Color; 103 minutes
Director: Jean Claude Lord
Producer: Claude Heroux
Writer: Brian Taggert
With: Michael Ironside, Lee Grant, William Shatner, Lenore Zann

Canadian-made quasi-*Coma* (1978) clone about a maniac (Ironside) who rips his way through a crowded city hospital, slaughtering victims right and left—and all without the benefit of being a doctor himself. His motive: to find and kill recuperating assault victim Grant before she can identify him.

The Wall

MGM, 1982; Color; 99 minutes
Director: Alan Parker
Producer: Alan Marshall
Writer: Roger Waters
With: Bob Geldof, Eleanor David, Bob Hoskins, Kevin McKeon

Just what the world was crying for—The Splatter Movie Meets the Rock Musical. This hideous, shapeless mess of a film would be less irritating was it not for the fact that filmmaker Alan Parker is one of our most creative directors—as he occasionally is even here when he isn't trying (and failing dismally) to be Ken Russell, or when he isn't swamped with bad, oh-so-trendy animation effects (by Gerald Scarfe), or when he isn't mired in Roger Waters's self-pitying, egotistical wallow of a screenplay. Unfortunately, those debits make up most of the film. Heady stuff if you want to see a future Nobel Prize candidate ineptly play a disintegrating rock musician who is given to flailing about in pools of blood and shaving off his nipples. To paraphrase Oscar Wilde, it must take a brain totally benumbed by narcotics to watch Bob Geldof in his underwear menaced by a giant animated flower-woman-vagina-monster and not burst out laughing.—K. H.

The War Game

BBC Films, 1965; B&W; 50 minutes
Director: Peter Watkins
Producer: Pater Watkins
Writer: Peter Watkins
With: Credits unavailable

A splatter movie with a message, this harrowing fictional documentary (*splattermentary?*) cautions against the proliferation of nuclear arms by portraying the ghastly aftereffects of nuclear war on the population of Great Britain. A grim, disturbing, and very realistic film that has lost little of its power over the years. Originally made for and by the BBC, it was never aired because of its graphic presentation.

The Werewolf vs. the Vampire Woman

Ellman Films, 1970; Color; 86 minutes
Director: Leon Klimovsky
Producer: Salvadore Romero
Writers: Jacinto Molina (Paul Naschy), Hans Munkel
With: Paul Naschy, Patty Shepard, Gaby Fuchs, Andres Resino, Julio Pena, Barbara Cappell

Another entry in Naschy's *El Hombre Lobo* series inspired by Universal's *The Wolf Man* (1941) in which he plays the Larry Talbotish Count Waldemar Daninsky, who turns into a vicious wolf whenever the moon is full. In this episode, the Count teams up with a pair of students to destroy an evil vampire countess (Shepard) patterned after Elizabeth Bathory. Followed by *The Fury of the Wolfman* (1971).

Werewolves on Wheels

The Fanfare Corporation, 1971; Color; 85 minutes
Director: Michael Levesque
Producer: Paul Lewis
Writers: Michael Levesque, David M. Kaufman
With: Stephen Oliver, Severn Darden, Billy Gray, D. J. Anderson, Barry McGuire

Sleazy riders get into a row with equally sleazy satanists, who get even by turning the bikers into werewolves—thus the title. Occasionally quite funny—though I'm not sure it's supposed to be—with lots of slow-motion violence that seems to have been influenced by Sam Peckinpah's *The Wild Bunch*, released two years earlier.

When a Stranger Calls

Columbia Pictures, 1979; Color; 97 minutes
Director: Fred Walton
Producers: Doug Chapin, Steve Feke
Writers: Fred Walton, Steve Feke
With: Charles Durning, Carol Kane, Colleen Dewhurst, Tony Beckley

The first twenty minutes of this film are scary as hell. A baby-sitter (Kane) starts getting threatening phone calls from psycho Beckley; when she has the police trace them, she finds they're coming from inside the house. The police arrive in time to save her, but not the children. The film then skips forward some years. Beckley is released from prison and is bent on taking his revenge on Kane by going after her own kids. Director Walton expanded the film from his college-made short. What he kept from the short—the film's first twenty minutes—remains the best part of the feature version.

Witchboard

Paragon Arts International, 1986;
    Color; 98 minutes
Director: Kevin S. Tenney
Producer: Gerald Geoffray
Writer: Kevin S. Tenney
With: Todd Allen, Tawny Kitaen,
    Stephen Nichols, Kathleen
    Wilhoite

At a party, Kitaen is introduced to the wonders of the Ouija board and makes the acquaintance of a dead ten-year-old boy named David who was killed in a boating accident. Hooked, she persists in making contact on her own, but she soon finds David to be more malevolent than friendly. A medium is called in to perform an exorcism but gets impaled on a sundial for her meddling efforts. Another friend who tries to help out gets an axe between the eyes. Turns out that David isn't the one behind all this mayhem—rather, Kitaen has unwittingly unleashed the vengeful spirit of a mass murderer killed by police many years before. Despite some obvious plot holes, this is an absorbing little thriller, directed by newcomer Tenney with style, wit, and something else you don't often see in splatter movies— well-drawn and believable characters for whom you genuinely care. The acting is uniformly excellent. Wilhoite is especially delightful as the punked-out medium with spiked hair ("Where did you find her?" hero Allen asks. "The circus?"). A real sleeper.

The Witches of Eastwick

Warner Brothers, 1987; Color; 118
    minutes
Director: George Miller
Producers: Neil Canton, Peter Guber,
    Jon Peters
Writer: Michael Cristofer
With: Jack Nicholson, Cher, Susan
    Sarandon, Michelle Pfeiffer,
    Veronica Cartwright

What do you get when you call upon the director of the *Mad Max* movies to adapt the work of one of America's premier serious novelists? You get an odd pairing, to be sure—but you also get a splatter movie full of blatant references to *The Exorcist* and *The Shining,* plus one scene virtually duplicated from *The Omen!* (Miller's directorial style at times even mimics the films of Ken Russell, particularly *Lisztomania.*) Three bored, frustrated New England women call upon the powers of darkness to grant them the man of their fantasies—and he turns up in the form of Jack Nicholson, a wealthy playboy who moves in and proceeds to seduce the women. Repressed violinist Sarandon undergoes the most startling character change due to his attentions, turning into a high-flying floozy. Cartwright catches on to the fact that he's the devil, but she is neutralized by a spell that causes her to vomit up cherry pits. In the end, the girls tire of Jack (be careful what you wish for, etc.) and subject him to some pit and feather puking as well, plus other astonishing ordeals. I have no idea what this film is about, but's it's as hilarious as it is disgusting, and vice versa. Nicholson is top-notch, as are the FX by Rob Bottin.

Without Warning

Filmways, 1981; Color; 89 minutes
Director: Greydon Clark
Producer: Greydon Clark
Writers: Lyn Freeman, Daniel
    Grodnik, Ben Nett, Steve Mathis
With: Jack Palance, Martin Landau,
    Tarah Nutter, Christopher S.
    Nelson, Cameron Mitchell,
    Neville Brand

What starts out as a teens-in-peril movie turns quickly into an everybody's-in-peril movie. What they're in peril from is an outer-space big-game hunter that kills by hurling some kind of alien leech creature at people; it attaches itself to their faces and sucks them dry. Don't know why it took so many writers to flesh out this simple tale of alien invasion, but for some strange reason, the movie actually works. There may not be enough splatter to satisfy all fans, but there are some good scares and a whole lot of laughs, most of the latter provided by Palance, Landau, and company, who chew up the scenery with delightful gusto. Grade Z to be sure, but fun.

The Wizard of Gore

A Mayflower Pictures Release, Inc., 1970; Color; 96 minutes
Director: Herschell Gordon Lewis
Producer: Herschell Gordon Lewis
Writer: Allen Kahn
With: Ray Sager, Judy Cler, Wayne Ratay, Phil Laurenson

Mad magician Montag the Magnificent (how's *that* for alliteration!) performs mutilation tricks onstage—fake disembowelings with a punch press, knives thrust through heads, swords poked down gullets, you know, *typical* stuff. After the show's over, his willing "victims," culled from the audience, get mutilated for real, their deaths patterned after Montag's onstage tricks. Though many of the gore effects aren't terribly convincing—particularly the knife-through-the-head trick (the mannequin that's getting skewered doesn't even look real), they are definitely sickening and guaranteed to make your gorge rise. Horrendously acted—even for a Lewis film.

Wolfen

Warner Brothers, 1981; Color; 115 minutes
Director: Michael Wadleigh
Producer: Rupert Hitzig
Writers: David Eyre, Michael Wadleigh
With: Albert Finney, Edward James Olmos, Diane Verona, Gregory Hines

A race of supernatural creatures evolved from wolves preys on derelicts and others who trespass on its bombed-out South Bronx turf. Finney is the police detective who discovers their existence and, in the end, pacifies them—despite the fact that they have eaten a number of his friends. Some mumbo jumbo about the white man's mistreatment of the American Indian is thrown in to give the effects-laden film a measure of social significance, but it's all rather fuzzy and slows the plot to a crawl. The wolves are scary, though, and there is some bright repartee between Finney and Hines. Based on a virtually unreadable novel by Whitley Streiber, who later claimed, in a work of *nonfiction,* to have been abducted by an alien spaceship.

The Wolfman

EO Studios, 1979; Color; 101 minutes
Director: Worth Keeter III
Producer: Earl Owensby
Writer: Darrell Cathcart
With: Earl Owensby, Kristina Reynolds, Maggie Lauterer, Ed L. Grady

With the advent of the videocassette, movie mogul Earl Owensby may finally succeed in reaching a wider audience for the thirty-three or so movies he's made since 1974 at his 200-acre studio in his hometown of Shelby, North Carolina. Most of those movies have never been screened theatrically outside of North and South Carolina, Owensby's main marketplace. Nevertheless, not a single one has ever lost money. In fact, they've made Owensby a millionaire—*seventy times over!*

All of them are genre pieces with lots of action and gore. *The Wolfman* marked Owensby's debut in the horror arena. Owensby, who doesn't claim to be an actor but often takes the lead roles in his films to keep costs down, plays a southern gent named Colin Glasgow who discovers his old man was a werewolf. When papa dies, Colin inherits the family curse, as well as the old man's hair suit, and starts clawing up the neighboring townsfolk. Shot in Georgia, this period gore film boasts some nice atmosphere and well-executed effects. Keeter is Owensby's "house director."

Wolfwoman

See Legend of the Wolfwoman

X-Ray

Cannon Films, 1982; Color; 88 minutes
Director: Boaz Davidson
Producers: Menahem Golan, Yoram Globus
Writers: Boaz Davidson, Marc Behm
With: Barbi Benton, Jon Van Ness, Chip Lucia, Den Surles

Made-in-Israel slasher movie with overtones of *My Bloody Valentine, Prom Night,* and their ilk. Former *Playboy* Playmate-of-the-Year Benton is the slasher's victim. Seems, as children, she and her brother rebuffed the overtures of another little boy to become friends. Out of rage, the boy killed her brother. Now an adult psycho, he goes after the grown-up Benton. He works in a hospital, where, conveniently, she turns up for an examination. She proves an elusive victim, however, and many others have to die in her stead before the psycho is finally brought down. Ample displays of Benton's uncovered anatomy turn this film into one long centerfold. Next to the one in *Coma,* the hospital in this film is one of the most deserted I've ever seen. It is aka *Hospital Massacre.*

Xtro

New Line Cinema, 1982; Color; 86 minutes
Director: Harry Bromley Davenport
Producer: Mark Forstater
Writers: Iain Cassie, Robert Smith
With: Bernice Stegers, Philip Sayer, Simon Nash, Danny Brainin

The unworldly progeny of a woman raped by a space creature grows up and settles down to a life of domestic bliss, but his "past" catches up with him. He turns his son into an alien; people in the neighborhood start getting splattered—well, you know the rest. Made in England.

The Zodiac Killer

Adventure Productions, 1985; Color; 87 minutes
Director: Tom Hanson
Producer: Tom Hanson
Writers: Ray Cantrell, Manny Mendoza
With: Hal Reed, Bob Jones, Ray Lynch, Tom Pittman

Bargain basement "docudrama" about the celebrated California sniper case of the late sixties. The killer randomly shot people, then wrote to the newspapers about his exploits, signing himself "Zodiac." The real killer was never caught. The film Zodiac isn't either, but we know who he is —a loner postman named Tom whose only friends are rabbits. Unlike the real Zodiac, Tom doesn't just shoot and stab people (though he does plenty of both). He also waylays them and crushes their heads under the hoods of their cars. Though ineptly acted—and a bit pretentious with its voice-overs warning society about the danger of serial killers like Zodiac—there is some diverting lowbrow humor, such as when the cops visit a flaky psychic hoping to learn the killer's identity and get a litany of nonsense instead. As they leave in frustration, they encounter a cabby, who says, "Hey, fellas, need a hack?" To which one of the cops replies, "No thanks, just had one."

Zombie

The Jerry Gross Organization, 1980; Color; 93 minutes
Director: Lucio Fulci
Producers: Ugo Tucci, Fabrizio de Angelis
Writer: Elisa Briganti
With: Ian McCulloch, Tisa Farrow, Richard Johnson, Auretta Gay

McCulloch and Farrow find themselves on a remote island called Matool, where mad doctor Johnson experiments with raising the dead. He succeeds and there are zombies, zombies everywhere, chowing down on the living—and even each other. Ultra-gore-filled rip-off of George A. Romero's *Dawn of the Dead* (1979) by Italy's reigning king of spaghetti splatter. In fact, in some parts of Europe, its title was changed to *Zombie 2* in order to make people think it was a legitimate sequel to Romero's film, known there as *Zombie*. As a filmmaker, the ceaselessly imitative Fulci has his detractors to be sure, but say what you will about him, he really knows what the genre is all about and can always be relied upon to dish out the gore with eye-popping virtuosity.

Zombie High

Cinema Group, 1987; Color; 91 minutes
Director: Ron Link
Producers: Aziz Ghazal, Marc Toberoff
Writers: Tim Doyle, Aziz Ghazal, Elizabeth Passarelli
With: Virginia Madsen, Richard Cox, James Wilder, Sherilyn Fenn

Madsen gets a scholarship to prestigious Ettinger Academy, a trendy prep school that's finally gone coed. Most of the students act like zombies; after visiting the infirmary, her rebellious friends become zombies, too. Seems the folks who run the place are making their students immortal by implanting crystals in their skulls, an operation that helps them get good grades but also turns them into cold emotionless pods. With the aid of a horny 102-year-old professor (who looks 30), Madsen switches the elevator-music cassette that controls the students' brain waves with a heavy-metal tape, prompting the dead heads to go up in smoke. She also destroys the serum that keeps the aging faculty alive, causing them to rot. Dull pastiche of everything from *Coma* to *The Stepford Wives*, with uninspired FX. Made in association with the U.S.C. film school.

Zombie Island Massacre

A Troma Team Release, 1983; Color; 89 minutes
Director: John N. Carter
Producer: David Broadnax
Writers: Logan O'Neill, William Stoddard
With: David Broadnax, Rita Jenrette, Tom Cantrell, Diane Clayre-Holub

With a better script, decent dialogue, and competent acting, this might not have been half bad. Unfortunately, it doesn't have them, so it's all bad. Still, you don't find too many splatter movies around that borrow from *The Maltese Falcon* (at the conclusion, the hero says to his duplicitous lover, "I'm not playing the sap for you anymore, Angel"). The plot is Agatha

Christie's *Ten Little Indians* (so that we'll
know, a character even makes reference
to it), this time set on a Caribbean island
populated by a murderous zombie tree
creature. A busload of vacationers gets
stranded and variously beheaded, impaled, and so on by the tree before the
truth comes out—the killer isn't a zombie tree creature at all, but rather a bunch
of vengeful Colombian drug runners! The
somnambulistic cast performs with less
energy than most zombies. Jenrette, who
gained prominence when her husband was
convicted during Washington's ABSCAM
scandal, removes her clothes several times,
but even that's not worth the price of
admission.

Zombie Nightmare

New World Pictures, 1986; Color; 89
    minutes
Director: Jack Bravman

Producer: Pierre Grise
Writer: David Wellington
With: Adam West, Jon Mikl Thor, Tim
    Carrere, Manuska. Frank Dietz

Teenage victim of a hit-and-run accident
is revivified by a family friend, a Haitian
witch who was saved from an assault years
ago by the boy's father. Armed with a
baseball bat, the zombie teen goes after
the punkers who flattened him. Ex-*Bat-
man* West plays the tight-lipped cop in
charge of the case. Mercifully for him, his
scenes in this dreadfully amateurish Canadian-made mess are brief. The splatter
effects are strictly poverty row. Each scene
seems to go on forever—as if the editor
had fallen asleep at his Moviola. The un-
forgettable heavy-metal score is provided
by those immortal groups Motorhead, Girl
School, Thor, Deathmask, and Fist.

ABOUT THE AUTHOR

John McCarty is the author of numerous film books, including the cult classic, *Splatter Movies: Breaking the Last Taboo of the Screen* (St. Martin's Press, 1984), which *Fangoria* magazine has called: "The definitive history of the gore film, and likely to remain as such." He is currently at work on a novel entitled *Deadly Resurrection*.

Copies of John McCarty's previous books are available from your local bookstore, or you can order them directly from St. Martin's Press by returning this coupon with check or money order to:

St. Martin's Press
175 Fifth Avenue
New York, N.Y. 10010
ATTN: Cash Sales Dept.

For credit card orders or bulk orders (25 copies or more) for resale, fund-raising, etc., please call the St. Martin's Press Special Sales Department toll-free at (800) 221-7945 for information about special discounts. In New York State, call (212) 674-5151.

Please send me _____ copy(ies) of *Splatter Movies: Breaking the Last Taboo of the Screen* @ $12.95 each $_____

Please send me _____ copy(ies) of *Psychos: Eighty Years of Mad Movies, Maniacs, and Murderous Deeds* @ $12.95 each $_____

Please send me _____ copy(ies) of *Alfred Hitchcock Presents* (coauthored by Brian Kelleher) @ $12.95 each $_____

Please send me _____ copy(ies) of *The Little Shop of Horrors Book* (coauthored by Mark Thomas McGee) @ $12.95 $_____

Postage & handling ($1.50 for first copy + $.75 for each additional) $_____

Sales tax (New York State residents only) $_____
Total enclosed $_____

Name _____

Address _____

City _____ State _____ Zip _____